getty images

Trains

The Early Years
Die Anfänge der Eisenbahn
Les Débuts du Chemin de Fer

Text by Beverley Cole

Picture research by
Alex Linghorn

h.f.ullmann

The departure of the royal train carrying the Prince of Wales (later Edward VIII) from Portsmouth Harbour, Hampshire, 11 October 1920. The locomotive is the London, Brighton & South Coast Railway 4-4-0 No. 46, *Prince of Wales.*

Der königliche Zug, an Bord der Prince of Wales (der spätere Edward VIII.), verlässt den Hafen von Portsmouth, Hampshire, 11. Oktober 1920. Die 2-B-Lokomotive ist die Nr. 46 der London, Brighton & South Coast Railway, die *Prince of Wales.*

Le train royal part du port de Portsmouth (Hampshire), le 11 octobre 1920, avec le prince de Galles (futur Édouard VIII) à son bord. La locomotive, de type 220, est la *Prince of Wales* n° 46 du London, Brighton & South Coast Railway.

© 2005 h.f.ullmann publishing GmbH

Photographs © 2001 Getty Images

Original title: *Trains*
Original ISBN: 978-3-8331-1355-0

For the publisher:
Managing editor: Sally Bald
Project editors: Lucile Bas, Meike Hilbring
Translation into German: Manfred Allié
Translation into French: Arnaud Dupin de Beyssat

For Getty Images:
Art Direction: Alex Linghorn
Editor: Richard Collins
Scanning: Getty Images scanning department
Proof reader: Liz Ihre

© 2011 for this edition: h.f.ullmann publishing GmbH

Special edition

Cover design: Simone Sticker

Overall responsibility for production: h.f.ullmann publishing GmbH, Potsdam, Germany

ISBN 978-3-8480-0519-2

Printed in China, 2013

10 9 8 7 6 5 4 3 2 1
X IX VIII VII V IV III II I

www.ullmann-publishing.com
newsletter@ullmann-publishing.com

Contents

Inhalt

Sommaire

Prologue

Entering the 21st century we live in a world that takes travelling across vast distances in style and comfort for granted. We enjoy personal freedom and expect infinite horizons and effortless mobility, but this was not always the case. Before the advent of the railways, no one could travel any further or faster on land than the horse would allow. In 1758 the Middleton Railway in Leeds became the first line to be authorised by an Act of Parliament, although the term 'railway' was not universally used. The new technology was also referred to as 'railroad', 'wagonway', 'tramway' and 'plateway'. These early railways linked mines and quarries and carried minerals to furnaces and waterways as part of the Industrial Revolution that began in Britain and was gradually to spread across Europe. 1804 saw another great step forward with the invention of the first steam railway locomotive. This was designed and built by Richard Trevithick and used at Penydarren in South Wales. Trevithick was also responsible for the first railway attraction in 1808 when he set up a circular track in Bloomsbury, London, which took passengers on a trip of sorts. A fashionable event, it did much to publicise the new railways. Trevithick's locomotive was called *Catch Me Who Can* but was nicknamed 'Captain Trevithick's Dragon'.

In 1812 Matthew Murray and John Blenkinsop introduced rudimentary rack and pinion railway to and from coal mines and in 1813, in the Tyne Valley, William Hedley's *Puffing Billy* and *Wylam Dilly* set the standard for the embryonic steam locomotive. George Stephenson appeared on the scene in 1814 with his first locomotive, *Blücher*, at Killingworth. Stephenson was the first proponent of wrought iron rather than cast iron railways, wrought iron being less likely to crack under pressure. In 1821 the Stockton and Darlington Act of Parliament was passed. The line – built by George Stephenson and his son Robert, with the financial backing of the Darlington entrepreneur Edward Pease – linked the two major industrial towns and was to carry passengers as well as goods and mineral. It opened on 27 September 1825 and was hauled by the 'Locomotive No. 1'. This railway was significant because it attracted the attention of other engineers and industrialists and, most importantly, made a profit for its shareholders.

Following the success of the Stockton & Darlington Railway, George Stephenson was contracted to build the Liverpool & Manchester Railway. The directors were reluctant to use the current steam locomotives which were slow, used too much coal and were incredibly unreliable. Realising that a more efficient locomotive was needed, the directors of the newly constructed Liverpool and Manchester Railway threw out a challenge to all locomotive builders at the time to design and build a locomotive that could pull three times its own weight along a mile and two-thirds of track forty times, the actual length of the Liverpool to Manchester Railway and back. The directors wanted a reliable steam locomotive to operate Britain's first passenger railway line. To ensure that this would happen they offered the princely sum of £500 as a reward to the winners. The prospect of winning such a prize excited every locomotive builder in the country, not least the Stephensons.

In 1829 George Stephenson won this competition, known as the Rainhill Trials, with the locomotive *Rocket;* this was to strike a spark that would start a revolution. The *Rocket* completed the course of seventy miles at an average speed of 13mph and an industry was born. Following the success of the Liverpool & Manchester Railway, railways spread all over Britain with engineers such as the Stephensons, Locke, Vignoles and Brunel collaborating with entrepreneurs like George Hudson, who was nicknamed 'the Railway King'. The term 'railway mania' came into existence in this period: by 1850 there were 6,000 miles of track in Britain.

During the next thirty years the railways expanded all over Europe and in America. Born in a time of great technological innovation, the railways opened up new horizons and began to change the world. They did so because they touched the lives of so many people, thanks in large part to visionaries such as George and Robert Stephenson and Isambard Kingdom Brunel. Brunel was a pioneer in the development of engineering technology. He was responsible for designing the Clifton Suspension Bridge in Bristol, the Great Western Railway and the SS *Great Britain* and many of his structures survive today. Both Stephenson and Brunel influenced the growth of a new way of travelling and seeing the world. When they started out, Britain was a rural country with a population of around 14 million; by the death of Queen Victoria in 1901 it had become an industrial nation with a population of over 30 million. A correspondent for the *Illustrated London News* predicted that there would be railways on the moon in his lifetime. From its beginnings as a rudimentary method of transport, the railway grew into the fastest, most efficient and popular means of travel.

During the 19th century, thanks largely to the British, the railways were spreading across the world. At first, British ideas

Previous page: Workers pause as a passenger express crosses the Forth Bridge at Queensferry in Scotland. The bridge consists of two double cantilevers and two connecting central girders. The bridge was opened in 1890.

Vorherige Seite: Streckenarbeiter warten, bis ein Personenexpress die Forth Bridge im schottischen Queensferry passiert hat. Die Brücke, aus zwei doppelten Auslegern und zwei verbindenden Gitterteilen konstruiert, wurde 1890 eingeweiht.

Page précédente : des cheminots travaillant sur le pont de Forth, à Queensferry (Écosse), interrompent leur travail au passage de l'express. Le pont, construit en 1890, se composait de deux travées supportées par deux arches en cantilever.

and equipment were exported but soon other countries were modifying technology to suit their own requirements. The Baltimore & Ohio Railroad, the first American passenger railway, opened in 1827, and by the mid-1830s the USA was exporting locomotives to Europe. The first German railway opened in 1835 between Nuremburg and Fürth with the English-built locomotive, *Der Adler*. The American locomotive designed by William Morris of Philadelphia and especially effective on steep inclines and sharp curves was exported to Austria in 1843. The first public railway in France opened in Le Pecq in 1837; in Japan the first steam-worked railway opened in 1872.

The influence of railway development on the history of the United States was phenomenal, the railroads creating centres of population in what had been a relatively empty continent. The *Tom Thumb*, a small experimental locomotive, made its first run on the Baltimore & Ohio in 1830; in 1869 the driving in of the 'Golden Spike' at Promontory Point, Utah, linked east with west once and for all. As time passed, the railways became a part of everyday life and attracted an ardent band of supporters and enthusiasts. By the 1920s it seemed as if it was the ambition of every young boy to be an engine driver. In the 1930s the *New York Herald Tribune* wrote: 'somewhere in the breast of every normal *Homo sapiens* there stretches a chord which vibrates only to the sight of a fine locomotive. Even now, with aeroplanes and motor cars to bid against it in its own field of romantic interest, the steam locomotive retains its fascination.'

In the 1930s the railways came to be associated with speed and style. On 3 July 1938 *Mallard* set the world speed record for a steam locomotive, reaching 126mph between London and Edinburgh. The world record for the fastest ever run between two stations on a scheduled power service with steam was set in America by the *Hiawatha* service covering the 412 miles between Chicago and Minneapolis. The railways of Europe and America were the first to introduce dining cars and luxury named trains. The *Golden Arrow (Flèche d'Or)* service opened between London and Paris in 1926 and a new boat train was built for *Golden Arrow* passengers. The *Coronation Scot* was the first Anglo-Scottish express to run between England and Scotland in 1937; in America, the *Super Chief* service, the American equivalent of the *Orient Express,* between Chicago and Los Angeles, came to be associated with gourmet food and Hollywood stars.

For the railway enthusiast the photograph was an ideal means of recording and collecting information and the camera and railway have been closely connected since the earliest days of photography. The first railway photograph – a daguerreotype of Linlithgow Station on the Edinburgh & Glasgow Railway – was taken in 1845 by David Octavius Hill and Robert Adamson. Since then, photographers worldwide have left a unique legacy of railway history, ranging from what some might consider the mundane and practical technical records to spectacular and breathtaking works of art. Of particular note in the latter category is the work of William England. England began as a portrait photographer but went on to become involved in travel photography in Switzerland and the USA. Although not specifically a railway photographer, he developed the stereoscopic technique and produced, among other things, outstanding views of New York City and the Niagara Falls, some of which incorporated railway imagery. Another British photographer, A.H. Robinson, although never a professional (but he did sell a number of his photographs to several British railway companies for display in the first class carriages), established himself among an elite band of photographers specialising in panoramic photography, of which the *Flying Scotsman* (cf. pp. 114–115) crossing the Royal Border Bridge at Berwick-upon-Tweed is a particularly fine example.

Trains: The Early Years offers an original view of the first century or so of railways and trains, reflecting the early influence of Stephenson's *Rocket* in England, through two world wars, prosperity, depression, resistance and acceptance to the middle of the 20th century. Included are spectacular line side images focusing on the power, action and motion of locomotives in some of the most desolate yet beautiful landscapes as well as in crowded stations, bustling cities and locomotive works. Much of the progress of the railways has been uniquely chronicled by the Hulton|Archive collection which documents the historical and technological growth of the railways and their impact on the world today.

In 1937 railway coaches were hired out to loyal subjects for £10 a night as sleeping accommodation before King George VI's Coronation. Here one over-nighter decorates her temporary home with flags and streamers.

Treue Untertanen, die 1937 zur Krönung Georgs VI. nach London kamen, konnten für £ 10 pro Nacht in Schlafwagen unterkommen. Hier schmückt eine Besucherin ihr Notquartier mit Fahnen und Girlanden.

Des voitures de chemin de fer furent louées 10 livres la nuit aux loyaux sujets de Sa Majesté à l'occasion du couronnement du roi George VI, en 1937. On voit ici une des passagères décorer de drapeaux et de banderoles la fenêtre de son compartiment.

Heute zu Beginn des 21. Jahrhunderts leben wir in einer Welt, die elegantes und komfortables Reisen über große Distanzen für eine Selbstverständlichkeit hält. Die Freiheit scheint grenzenlos, kein Horizont ist zu fern – aber das war nicht immer so. Bevor es Eisenbahnen gab, bestimmten Kraft und Tempo eines Pferdes, wie weit und wie schnell man reiste. Das britische Parlament genehmigte im Jahr 1758 die erste Eisenbahnlinie der Middleton Railway in Leeds. Der Ausdruck *railway* hatte sich damals noch kaum durchgesetzt; im Englischen hieß das neue Verkehrsmittel auch *railroad, wagonway, tramway* oder *plateway*. Diese ersten Bahnen waren Kinder der Industriellen Revolution, die sich von Großbritannien aus über ganz Europa verbreitete – sie transportierten Güter in Bergwerke und Steinbrüche und brachten Erze zu den Flusskähnen und Schmelzöfen. Das Jahr 1804 sah eine entscheidende Neuerung: die erste Dampflokomotive. Richard Trevithick entwarf und baute sie und setzte sie im südwalisischen Penydarren ein. Trevithick war es auch, der aus der Eisenbahn erstmals eine Publikumsattraktion machte: 1808 richtete er im Londoner Stadtteil Bloomsbury einen Rundkurs ein, auf dem zahlende Gäste mitfahren konnten. Das sorgte für Aufsehen und machte die Idee bekannt. Trevithick taufte seine Lokomotive auf den Namen *Catch Me Who Can* (»Fangt mich, wenn ihr könnt«), aber im Volksmund hieß sie »Captain Trevithicks Drache«.

1812 bauten Matthew Murray und John Blenkinsop für den Bergwerksbetrieb schon eine Art Zahnradbahn, und 1813 fuhren im Tal des Tyne William Hedleys *Puffing Billy* und *Wylam Dilly*, die unmittelbaren Vorläufer von Stephensons Lokomotive. George Stephenson betrat 1814 in Killingworth die Bühne mit seiner ersten Konstruktion *Blücher*. Stephenson verwendete für die Schienen statt Gusseisen erstmals Schmiedeeisen, das dem Gewicht der Maschinen besser standhielt. 1821 erteilte das Parlament die Genehmigung für den Bau der Bahn von Stockton nach Darlington. Die Strecke – gebaut von George Stephenson zusammen mit seinem Sohn Robert, finanziert vom Darlingtoner Unternehmer Edward Pease – verband die beiden wichtigen Industriestädte und sollte neben Waren und Erzen auch Fahrgäste befördern. »Locomotive No. 1« zog die Wagen, die am 27. September 1825 zur Eröffnung fuhren. Diese Strecke war von entscheidender Bedeutung für die weitere Entwicklung, denn sie lenkte die Aufmerksamkeit anderer Ingenieure und Industrieller auf das neue Transportmittel – und sie bescherte ihren Aktionären Profite.

Nach dem Erfolg der Stockton & Darlington Railway erhielt George Stephenson den Auftrag zum Bau der Strecke Liverpool–Manchester. Die Direktoren wollten dafür neue Lokomotiven, denn die verfügbaren waren langsam, sie verbrauchten viel Kohle und waren äußerst unzuverlässig. Die Betreiber wollten für die erste britische Personeneisenbahn eine Zugmaschine, auf die sie sich verlassen konnten, und schrieben einen Wettbewerb aus, offen für alle Konstrukteure: Ein Preis von £ 500 winkte demjenigen, der eine Lokomotive entwarf und baute, die das Dreifache ihres eigenen Gewichts 40 Mal über eine Strecke von 2,7 km ziehen konnte – was der Strecke Liverpool–Manchester und zurück entsprach. Die Aussicht auf eine so fürstliche Entlohnung feuerte jeden Ingenieur des Landes an, nicht zuletzt die Stephensons.

1829 ging George Stephenson mit seiner *Rocket* als Sieger aus diesem Wettbewerb, den so genannten Rainhill Trials, hervor, und das war der eigentliche Anfang des Eisenbahnzeitalters. Die *Rocket* legte die 113 km mit einer Durchschnittsgeschwindigkeit von ca. 21 km/h zurück – und eine neue Industrie war geboren. Nach dem Erfolg der Liverpool & Manchester Railway entstanden Bahnstrecken überall in Großbritannien, und Konstrukteure wie die Stephensons, Locke, Vignoles und Brunel arbeiteten Hand in Hand mit Unternehmern wie George Hudson, dem »Eisenbahnkönig«. Es kam zur *railway mania*, dem Eisenbahnfieber, und 1850 überzogen bereits 6000 Meilen (fast 10 000 Kilometer) Bahnstrecke die Insel.

In den folgenden drei Jahrzehnten eroberten Eisenbahnen Europa und Amerika. Gerade in dieser Zeit großer technischer Neuerungen eröffnete die Bahn neue Horizonte. Das Leben unzähliger Menschen veränderte sich durch die Leistungen von Visionären wie George und Robert Stephenson und Isambard Kingdom Brunel. Brunel setzte zahlreiche technische Neuerungen durch; er baute die Clifton-Hängebrücke in Bristol, die Great Western Railway und das Dampfschiff *Great Britain*, viele seiner Arbeiten sind bis heute erhalten. Mit den Erfindungen Stephensons und Brunels kam eine gänzlich neue Form des Reisens auf, Menschen sahen die Welt mit anderen Augen. Zu Beginn des Eisenbahnzeitalters war Großbritannien ein Agrarland mit einer Bevölkerung von etwa 14 Millionen; als Königin Victoria im Jahr 1901 starb, war daraus eine Industrienation mit über 30 Millionen Einwohnern geworden. Ein Korrespondent der *Illustrated London News* prophezeite, dass es noch zu seinen Lebzeiten Eisenbahnen auf dem Mond geben werde. Seit ihren Anfängen als notdürftiges Transportmittel hatte die Eisenbahn sich zur schnellsten, praktischsten und populärsten Art zu reisen entwickelt.

Hauptsächlich den Briten ist es zu verdanken, dass sich im Laufe des 19. Jahrhunderts ein weltumspannendes Eisenbahnnetz entwickelte. Zuerst wurden Maschinen und Ingenieurswissen noch aus Großbritannien importiert, aber bald gingen die Länder eigene Wege und passten die neue Technik ihren eigenen Bedürfnissen an. Die erste amerikanische Personenbahn, die Baltimore & Ohio Railroad, eröffnete 1827, und Mitte der 1830er Jahre verkaufte die USA bereits Lokomotiven nach Europa. Die erste deutsche Bahn fuhr 1835 zwischen Nürnberg und Fürth – die Lokomotive *Adler* kam aus England. Die Österreicher entschieden sich 1843 für die Maschine von William Morris aus Philadelphia, die sich besonders gut an starken Steigungen und in engen Kurven bewährt hatte. Die erste französische öffentliche Bahn verkehrte seit 1837 in Le Pecq, die erste japanische Dampfeisenbahn nahm 1872 ihren Betrieb auf.

Der Einfluss, den der Eisenbahnbau in den Vereinigten Staaten auf die Entwicklung des Landes hatte, war phänomenal; an den Bahnknotenpunkten entstanden selbst im Inneren des zuvor eher unbewohnten Landes ganze Städte. *Tom Thumb* (»Däumling«), der Prototyp einer leichten Lokomotive, unternahm seine erste Fahrt auf der Baltimore & Ohio im Jahr 1830; 1869 wurde am Promontory Point in Utah der »goldene Schienennagel« eingeschlagen, und die endgültige Verbindung zwischen Ost- und Westküste war geschaffen. Im Laufe der Zeit fanden die Eisenbahnen ihren Platz im Alltagsleben und hatten bald ihre begeisterte Anhängerschar. In den zwanziger Jahren war Lokomotivführer der Traumberuf jedes Jungen. In den Dreißigern schrieb der *New York Herald Tribune:* »Irgendwo in der Brust jedes normalen *Homo sapiens* gibt es eine Saite, die nur erklingt, wenn er eine prachtvolle Lokomotive erblickt. Selbst jetzt, wo ihr auf diesem romantischen Felde mit Flugzeug und Motorwagen zwei Konkurrenten erwachsen sind, bleibt die Dampflok doch faszinierender als alles andere.«

In den Dreißigern waren die Eisenbahnen der Inbegriff von Eleganz und Geschwindigkeit. Am 3. Juli 1938 stellte die *Mallard* auf der Strecke London–Edinburgh mit 203 km/h den Geschwindigkeitsweltrekord für Dampflokomotiven auf. Die schnellste fahrplanmäßige Fahrt bot der amerikanische *Hiawatha* auf den 663 Kilometern zwischen Chicago und Minneapolis. Auf den europäischen und amerikanischen Strecken gab es die ersten Speisewagen, und Luxuszüge bekamen einen Namen. Der *Golden Arrow (Flèche d'Or)* verkehrte seit 1926 zwischen London und Paris, auf der englischen Seite mit einem komplett neuen Zug. Der *Coronation Scot,* 1937 eingesetzt, war der erste Expresszug zwischen England und Schottland; der *Super Chief,* das amerikanische Gegenstück zum *Orient-Express* und berühmt für seine Gourmetküche, war der Zug der Hollywoodstars, der zwischen Chicago und Los Angeles verkehrte.

Für den Bahnliebhaber waren Fotos das ideale Mittel, die Entwicklung festzuhalten und Informationen zu sammeln. Seit den Anfängen der Fotografie gehören Eisenbahn und Kamera zusammen. Das erste Eisenbahnbild nahmen David Octavius Hill und Robert Adamson 1845 auf – eine Daguerreotypie des Bahnhofs Linlithgow auf der Edinburgh & Glasgow Railway. Seither haben Fotografen weltweit einen Fundus von Aufnahmen geschaffen, eine einmalige Geschichte der Eisenbahn in Bildern, von – für manche Augen vielleicht trockenen – Dokumentationen technischer Details bis hin zu spektakulären, atemberaubenden künstlerischen Aufnahmen. In dieser Kategorie bemerkenswert sind die Arbeiten von William England. Er begann seine Laufbahn als Porträtfotograf, widmete sich dann aber in der Schweiz und den USA der Reisefotografie, teils in stereoskopischen Aufnahmen, und schuf prachtvolle Ansichten von New York und den Niagarafällen. Er war nie ein ausgesprochener Eisenbahnfotograf, etliche seiner Bilder befassen sich aber mit dem Thema. Ein anderer britischer Fotograf, A. H. Robinson – der diesen Beruf nicht professionell ausübte, auch wenn er mehreren Bahngesellschaften Bilder für die Abteile erster Klasse verkaufte –, machte sich einen Namen mit Panoramabildern, von denen seine Aufnahme des *Flying Scotsman* auf der Royal Border Bridge in Berwick-upon-Tweed (Seite 114–115) ein besonders schönes Beispiel ist.

Die Anfänge der Eisenbahn präsentiert das erste Jahrhundert der Bahngeschichte aus einem originellen Blickwinkel; der Band verfolgt die Entwicklung, die Stephensons *Rocket* in England in Gang brachte, durch zwei Weltkriege, durch Wohlstand und Wirtschaftskrise, vom Spielzeug zur Selbstverständlichkeit bis in die Mitte des 20. Jahrhunderts hinein. Wundervolle Aufnahmen von Lokomotiven in voller Fahrt in entlegenen, doch malerischen Landschaften wechseln mit Bildern von den Menschen auf den Bahnhöfen, von blühenden Städten und dem geschäftigen Treiben in den Betriebswerken. All das ist im unerschöpflichen Hulton|Archive in Fotos festgehalten, die uns an der historischen und technischen Entwicklung der Eisenbahn teilhaben lassen und uns vor Augen führen, woher die Welt kommt, die wir heute kennen.

The NER's rulebook stated: 'Each man shall devote such time as may be required to the company's service.' A signalman goes about his all-important duties in 1907.

Im Regelbuch der NER hieß es: »Jeder Mann soll so viel von seiner Zeit einsetzen, wie die Erfordernisse des Betriebs verlangen.« In dieser Aufnahme von 1907 geht ein Weichensteller in einem Stellwerk seiner verantwortungsvollen Aufgabe nach.

Le règlement du NER stipulait que « chaque homme doit consacrer autant de temps qu'il est nécessaire au service de la compagnie ». En 1907, cet aiguilleur s'apprête à accomplir sa tâche, l'une des plus importantes dans la circulation des chemins de fer.

Prologue

En ce début de XXIᵉ siècle, nous connaissons un monde qui tient pour acquis de voyager sur de grandes distances dans le confort et l'élégance. Puisque nous vivons dans une société de liberté individuelle, nous voulons profiter des horizons infinis du monde et d'une mobilité sans entraves. Mais ce ne fut pas toujours le cas. Avant l'avènement des chemins de fer, nul ne pouvait se déplacer plus loin et plus vite que ne le permettait le cheval, seul mode de traction terrestre dont on disposait alors. Ce n'est qu'en 1758 qu'un acte du Parlement britannique autorise l'exploitation à Leeds du Middleton Railway, qui devient ainsi la première ligne ferroviaire, dans l'arrière-plan historique des débuts de la révolution industrielle en Grande-Bretagne. Le terme de « chemin de fer » (traduction française de « railway » utilisée à partir de 1823) n'est d'ailleurs pas employé par tout le monde, ce nouveau type de transport s'appelant également « railroad », « wagonway », « tramway » ou « plateway ». Ces premiers chemins de fer, qui desservaient mines et carrières et assuraient le transport du minerai vers les hauts-fourneaux et à proximité des voies navigables, se répandirent progressivement dans toute l'Europe. L'année 1804 marque un autre grand pas en avant dans l'histoire des chemins de fer avec l'invention de la première locomotive à vapeur, conçue et construite par Richard Trevithick et mise en service à Penydarren, en Galles du Sud. En 1808, ce même Trevithick crée la première attraction ferroviaire en installant à Bloomsbury (Londres) une voie circulaire acceptant des passagers pour une sorte de tour de manège, un spectacle à la mode qui fit beaucoup pour promouvoir les nouveaux chemins de fer. La locomotive de Trevithick, baptisée *Catch Me Who Can* (c'est-à-dire « M'attrape qui peut ») fut surnommée le « Dragon du capitaine Trevithick ».

En 1812, Matthew Murray et John Blenkinsop mettent en service un chemin de fer rudimentaire, à crémaillère et roue dentée, pour la desserte des houillères ; l'année suivante, dans la vallée de la Tyne, William Hedley définit la norme, embryonnaire, de la locomotive à vapeur avec les *Puffing Billy* et *Wylam Dilly*. George Stephenson apparaît en 1814 avec sa première locomotive, la *Blücher*, construite à Killingsworth. Il fut le premier à adopter des rails en fer laminé plutôt qu'en fonte, cette dernière ayant tendance à se fissurer sous le poids des machines. En 1821, le Parlement britannique promulgue l'Acte dit Stockton and Darlington. Construite par George Stephenson et son fils Robert avec le soutien financier de Edward Pease, un entrepreneur de Darlington, et ouverte le 27 septembre 1825

par la « Locomotive n°1 », cette ligne de chemin de fer reliait les deux grandes villes industrielles et assurait un service régulier de transport voyageurs, marchandises et minerai. Elle eut un impact significatif car elle attira l'attention d'autres ingénieurs et industriels et, plus important, fit réaliser un bénéfice aux actionnaires de sa compagnie propriétaire.

Après le succès du Stockton & Darlington Railway, George Stephenson est engagé pour construire le Liverpool & Manchester Railway. Désirant disposer d'une robuste locomotive à vapeur pour desservir la première ligne de voyageurs de Grande-Bretagne, et peu disposés à utiliser les locomotives à vapeur existantes, qu'ils jugent trop lentes, consommant trop de charbon et étant peu fiables, les administrateurs de la compagnie lancent un défi à tous les ingénieurs de l'époque : construire une machine capable de remorquer quarante fois le triple de son propre poids sur 2,7 km, c'est-à-dire la longueur de la ligne du Liverpool and Manchester Railway et retour. Pour encourager les concurrents, ils offrent au vainqueur la somme fabuleuse de 500 £. La perspective de remporter le prix stimule tous les constructeurs de locomotives du pays, notamment les Stephenson.

George Stephenson remporte ce concours de Rainhill avec sa *Rocket (Fusée)* en 1829 ; ce succès va produire l'étincelle qui va déclencher une révolution. La *Rocket* parcourut les 113 km à la vitesse moyenne de 21 km/h. Une industrie est née tandis qu'apparaît le terme de « railway mania ». Les chemins de fer se répandent alors rapidement au Royaume-Uni après ce succès du Liverpool & Manchester Railway et grâce à des ingénieurs comme les Stephenson, Locke, Vignoles et Brunel, soutenus par des entrepreneurs comme George Hudson, surnommé « le Roi du chemin de fer ». En 1850, la Grande-Bretagne compte déjà 9 650 km de voies ferrées.

Le chemin de fer va s'étendre en Europe et aux États-Unis au cours des trente prochaines années. Nés à une grande époque d'innovations technologiques, les chemins de fer ouvrent de nouveaux horizons et commencent à transformer le monde. Cette révolution des transports, qui touche la vie d'énormément de gens, s'est effectuée en grande partie grâce à des visionnaires comme George et Robert Stephenson et Isambard Kingdom Brunel, un pionnier de l'ingénierie, auteur du Clifton Suspension Bridge de Bristol, du Great Western Railway et du vapeur *Great Britain*, dont nombre des réalisations subsistent de nos jours. Au début de leurs travaux, la Grande-Bretagne était un pays rural de 14 millions d'habitants environ ; à la mort de la

A guard on the Swedish railways. All ranks took pride in their work and medals and certificates were often given to long-serving employees, some of whom might start working as young as fourteen.

Ein Schaffner der schwedischen Eisenbahnen. Alle Dienstränge waren stolz auf ihre Arbeit, und langjährige Angestellte wurden oft mit Medaillen oder Urkunden ausgezeichnet; manche fingen schon mit 14 Jahren an.

Un chef de train des chemins de fer suédois. Tous les cheminots, quel que soit leur rang, étaient fiers de leur travail. Pour les honorer, les compagnies distribuaient fréquemment des certificats aux plus anciens, dont certains étaient entrés dans les chemins de fer dès l'âge de 14 ans.

reine Victoria, en 1901, c'était une nation industrielle comptant une population de plus de 30 millions d'individus. Un correspondant de l'*Illustrated London News* prédisait même qu'il verrait des chemins de fer sur la lune. De moyen de transport rudimentaire, le chemin de fer devenait le mode de déplacement le plus rapide, le plus efficace et le plus populaire.

Après l'ouverture en 1827 du Baltimore & Ohio Railroad, première ligne de voyageurs américaine, les États-Unis commencent déjà à expédier leurs locomotives en Europe à partir du milieu des années 1830. C'est ainsi que la locomotive conçue par William Morris, de Philadelphie, particulièrement adaptée aux fortes rampes et aux courbes prononcées, est exportée en Autriche en 1843. Auparavant, c'est une locomotive d'origine anglaise, *Der Adler,* qui inaugurait la première voie ferrée allemande, créée en 1835 entre Nuremberg et Fürth. En France, la première ligne publique de voyageurs est ouverte entre Paris et Le Pecq en 1837, tandis qu'au Japon le premier chemin de fer à vapeur est mis en service en 1872. L'influence des chemins de fer sur l'histoire des États-Unis est phénoménale en ce qu'ils ont permis de créer de nouveaux foyers de peuplement dans un continent autrement relativement vide. Après que le *Tom Thumb,* une petite locomotive expérimentale, a effectué son premier trajet en 1830 sur le Baltimore & Ohio, la pose du dernier crampon, dit le Clou en Or, à Promontory Point (Utah) en 1869 permet de relier définitivement l'Est et l'Ouest des États-Unis.

Les chemins de fer participent chaque jour davantage à la vie quotidienne et s'attirent l'engouement de partisans et de passionnés toujours plus nombreux à tel point que, dans les années 1920, on peut croire que presque tous les enfants rêvent de devenir mécanicien de locomotive. Vers 1930, on peut aussi lire dans le *New York Herald Tribune :* « Il y a, quelque part dans la poitrine de chaque *homo sapiens* normal, une corde sensible qui ne sait vibrer qu'en voyant une belle locomotive. Aujourd'hui, et malgré la concurrence romantique des aéroplanes et des voitures, la locomotive à vapeur conserve toute sa fascination. »

C'est également au cours des années 1930 que l'image du chemin de fer est associée à vitesse et élégance. Le 3 juillet 1938, la *Mallard* s'arroge le record du monde de vitesse pour une locomotive à vapeur, ayant atteint 203 km/h entre Londres et Édimbourg. En revanche, le record de vitesse en service normal entre deux gares est établi entre Chicago et Minneapolis (663 km) aux États-Unis par le rapide *Hiawatha.* Les chemins de fer européens et américains sont les premiers à mettre en service des trains de luxe et des voitures-restaurants. Le service du *Golden Arrow* – le train anglais, dont l'équivalent en France était la *Flèche d'Or* – est inauguré en 1926 entre Londres et Paris, et conduira à la construction d'un ferry spécial. En Grande-Bretagne, le *Coronation Scot* est, en 1937, le premier express à assurer la relation Angleterre-Écosse. Aux États-Unis, la réputation du *Super Chief,* équivalent américain de l'*Orient Express* et mis en service entre Chicago et Los Angeles, doit beaucoup à la gastronomie et aux stars de Hollywood qui l'empruntent.

La photographie et le chemin de fer ont toujours été étroitement liés. Pour le ferrovipathe, la photographie reste le moyen idéal d'enregistrer et de rassembler des informations. La première photographie d'un chemin de fer – un daguerréotype de la gare de Linlithgow, sur le Edinburgh & Glasgow Railway – fut prise en 1845 par David Octavius Hill et Robert Adamson. Depuis, des photographes du monde entier nous ont légué un héritage unique sur l'histoire des chemins de fer, qui va du cliché ordinaire et technique à l'œuvre d'art spectaculaire, dont les photos de William England sont un exemple. England, qui commença sa carrière comme portraitiste, se lança dans l'illustration de voyage, réalisant ses clichés en Suisse et aux États-Unis ; ayant développé la technique de la stéréoscopie, il prit des vues extraordinaires de la ville de New York et des chutes du Niagara, certaines mettant accessoirement en scène des chemins de fer. Un autre photographe britannique, A. H. Robinson, sans être un professionnel, vendit un grand nombre de ses œuvres à des compagnies ferroviaires britanniques pour orner les voitures de première classe. On peut le placer également parmi l'élite des photographes ferroviaires, son *Flying Scotsman* franchissant le Royal Border Bridge à Berwick-upon-Tweed (voir pp. 114–115) étant un exemple particulièrement réussi de son art.

Les Débuts du Chemin de Fer propose une vision originale du premier siècle de l'histoire des trains, depuis la *Rocket* de Stephenson en Angleterre jusqu'au milieu du XXe siècle. Il offre une série d'images spectaculaires où sont mis en relief la puissance, la mécanique et le mouvement des locomotives dans certains des paysages les plus désolés et les plus beaux de la terre, mais aussi dans des ateliers ferroviaires, des gares ou des villes. Cette chronique du chemin de fer, rendue possible grâce aux documents uniques de la collection Hulton|Archive, nous permet ainsi de mieux saisir l'évolution du chemin de fer et son impact sur le monde actuel.

—1—
Raising Steam

Following the success of the Liverpool & Manchester Railway, the railway network spread rapidly, first through Britain and then to Europe and America. With the invention of photography coming so soon after the steam locomotive, it is hardly surprising that the two often complimented each other. Since the 1840s locomotives and their surroundings have been a major point of focus for railway photographers. While the commercial base of the railway system was goods traffic and two-thirds of revenue came from goods, it was the passenger train that caught the eye – and the camera. In Britain, photographers such as Richard Keene of Derby recorded the changing scene brought about by the growth of the railway industry. R.H. Bleasdale of Warwick began photographing locomotives in 1857. He received much cooperation from the railway companies and special access to railway works and sheds. By the time he retired in the early 1890s he had produced more than 3,000 railway photographs. By the 1880s all the major railway companies in Britain employed official photographers, the first being the London & North Western at Crewe works. Photographers were employed to record accidents as an investigation aid and to record newly completed or refurbished locomotives and rolling stock. The locomotives themselves would be photographed before they were painted because they reproduced better on glass plate negatives in this state, which was called 'works grey'. Often they were photographed against a specially constructed background of white sheeting.

In the beginning, railway stations were modest points of departure. The first were rudimentary wooden shacks next to the tracks where passengers could buy tickets and wait for trains. They were also one of the few public places where all classes of society could be seen mixing freely and going about their business. They thus became popular with artists and photographers at the time and resulted in such masterpieces in oil as William Powell Frith's *The Railway Station* (1852) in which he represents many classes of society, from the criminal to the aristocratic young bride. To accommodate all strata of society, stations had to provide three classes of service for its travellers. The best – first class – promised luxury compartments very similar to the stage-coach. These compartments were also the furthest removed from the bumps and jolts of the wheels and therefore offered the smoothest ride. Second class was similar but offered less leg room (it was abolished in 1875 because of the connotations of the word 'second'). Third class travellers had a rough ride: their compartments had basic, cramped conditions and were located over the wheels. In the very early days these carriages were open-topped and passengers were known to freeze to death in winter. Tickets, waiting rooms and station entrances were also dictated by class.

The advent of the railways also changed attitudes to home and work. Commuters – the word 'commuter' derives from the American term for the holder of second class, or 'commutation' tickets – were those who travelled between home and work. Before this, workers walked and their managers rode in horse-drawn vehicles. All this resulted in cramped slums for the poor in industrial cities and towns and suburbs for the wealthier but, when the railways introduced cheap fares for workmen and reduced rate 'season tickets', it became possible for people to move away from city centres.

In Britain the railways were built by the navvy, a shortened version of the word 'navigator'. Navvies were a travelling workforce brought together from all over the country who lived along the line they were constructing. They had a reputation for being tough and were often lawless. By 1873 the railways were the largest employers in Britain, putting to work some 274,000 men. Railway towns developed, most notably Swindon for the GWR and York for the NER. In those days, the company would provide from the cradle to the grave and it expected undivided loyalty in return. This resulted in strong discipline and pride which was reflected in the company's image. In the USA the railroads were built by crews living on site in the railway locomotives and carriages, the train moving along the line as it was completed. The locomotive would provide steam heating and hot water. As the earth and rocks were removed from the track they were used to build the embankments and foundations for the trestle bridges. The first steam train in New York State was hauled by the *De Witt Clinton* locomotive on 9 August 1831. It was a procession of stagecoaches on tracks with passengers on the top of vehicles as well as inside. Next came the *John Bull*, a four-wheeled British locomotive which had a tendency to derail. This was the first locomotive to be fitted with a cowcatcher. The lack of defences along the tracks of the early American railroads made this a necessity so as to reduce the possibility of derailment by the locomotives hitting buffalo or steers.

Some of the construction problems which arose in the early days – due to the physical geography of a place – were ingeniously overcome. Today we take bridges, racks and pinions and ferries for granted, forgetting that, more often than not they were invented by early railway pioneers. Mount Rigi, near Lucerne in Switzerland, was the first railway to use a rack and pinion system, inaugurated in 1871. Here a toothed rack was laid between the rails and a powered cog on the locomotive drove the train up the mountain. In reverse, it restrained the train's descent. The same system was used on the Snowdon Mountain Railway in Wales in 1896. The greatest cantilever bridge was opened in 1890 across the Firth of Forth in Scotland and the first mountain rack railway opened in the USA in New Hampshire in 1869 with a maximum gradient of one in three.

Inevitably there were accidents and in the early days this usually involved trains colliding. As average speed increased and breaks and signalling equipment improved, however, the number of accidents decreased. When accidents did occur, the results could be catastrophic, as was the case when the Tay Bridge over the Firth of Tay collapsed in December 1879 in atrocious weather, killing seventy-five people.

Excursion trains were at first regarded as frivolous and an interference with the proper running of the railway, but before long they came to be seen as an important source of revenue. By the mid-1840s the excursion was an established event. The working classes from Britain's industrial towns and cities would escape for a day to seaside towns such as Scarborough, Skegness and Morecambe. As early as 1841 Thomas Cook chartered a special train from Leicester to Loughborough to take 570 passengers to a Temperance meeting. At first the seaside locals disapproved of 'trippers', as they became known, because of their drunkenness and the popular entertainments they favoured, but eventually the potential profit to be realised from such visitors overcame most reservations and trippers were both accepted and encouraged. Other popular excursions included naval events, sporting fixtures, agricultural shows and even public hangings. In fact, the railway companies were most disappointed in 1868 when public executions were abolished, with subsequent loss of revenue to the railways.

Royalty quickly adapted to rail travel. Queen Victoria made the first railway journey in 1842 and was said to be 'quite charmed' by it. She became an inveterate traveller and her favourite saloon was built by the LNWR (London & North Western Railway) in 1869. The wood used in the carriage was

bird's eye maple and the upholstery and ceiling covers were of silk. Initially it was lit with oil lamps but these were replaced with the newly developed electric lights in 1895. Some stations, such as Gosport in Hampshire, were built especially for royal use for when the Queen was travelling to Osborne House, her residence on the Isle of Wight.

And so the steam railways developed and expanded, thus becoming the most important form of land transport. They had the advantage of speed, capacity and economy and were to go on to become one of the largest and most complex examples of a transport system the world had known.

Nach dem Erfolg der Strecke Liverpool–Manchester entwickelte sich das Eisenbahnnetz rasch, zuerst in Großbritannien, dann auch auf dem Kontinent und in Amerika. Schon bald nach den ersten Lokomotiven kam die Fotografie auf, und so wundert es nicht, dass die beiden sich gegenseitig ergänzten. Seit den 1840er Jahren hielten Eisenbahnfotografen vor allem die Lokomotiven in ihrem Umfeld in Bildern fest. Die kommerzielle Basis des Bahnsystems war der Güterverkehr, der zwei Drittel des Gewinns erwirtschaftete, doch die Blicke der Betrachter – und auch der Kamera – zogen eher die Personenzüge auf sich. In Großbritannien dokumentierten Fotografen wie der aus Derby stammende Richard Keene den Siegeszug der Eisenbahn. R. H. Bleasdale aus Warwick fotografierte seit 1857 Lokomotiven. Die Bahngesellschaften waren gern zur Zusammenarbeit bereit und gewährten ihm Zugang zu Betriebswerken und Lokschuppen. Als er sich Anfang der 1890er Jahre zur Ruhe setzte, konnte er auf ein Werk von über 3000 Eisenbahnfotos zurückblicken. In den 1880ern hatten die großen britischen Gesellschaften bereits ihre offiziellen Fotografen – den ersten stellte die London & North Western für ihr Betriebswerk in Crewe an. Bei Unfällen wurden Aufnahmen gemacht, die zur Aufklärung beitragen sollten; vor allem aber lieferten die Fotografen Bilder von den neu gebauten oder aufgearbeiteten Lokomotiven und Waggons. Lokomotiven nahm man vor dem Lackieren auf, weil sie sich in »Originalgrau« besser auf die Platte bannen ließen als in späteren Farben. Oft wurde eigens für die Aufnahme ein Hintergrund aus weißen Tüchern gespannt.

Bahnhöfe waren anfangs nur bescheidene Haltestellen. Hölzerne Schuppen standen unmittelbar entlang der Strecke und boten Fahrkartenschalter sowie einen Unterstand für die Fahrgäste. Sie zählten auch zu den wenigen öffentlichen Orten, an denen alle Schichten der Bevölkerung zusammenkamen und miteinander umgingen – was ihre Beliebtheit bei Künstlern und Fotografen der Zeit erklärt und uns Meisterwerke wie William Powell Friths Ölbild *The Railway Station* (1852) bescherte, auf dem das gesamte soziale Spektrum vom Gauner bis zur jungen aristokratischen Braut porträtiert ist. Allerdings bestand unter dem gemeinsamen Dach doch ein Dreiklassensystem. Die beste davon – die erste Klasse – versprach Luxusabteile, die einer Postkutsche sehr ähnlich waren, und diese Abteile lagen in der Mitte der Wagen, wo man die Stöße der Räder am wenigsten spürte. Die zweite Klasse war ähnlich ausgestattet, doch ein wenig enger (sie wurde 1875 aufgegeben, weil niemand »zweitklassig« sein wollte). In der dritten Klasse ging es spartanisch zu, und die engen, schlecht ausgestatteten Abteile lagen über den Rädern. Anfangs waren die Wagen der dritten Klasse offen, und so kam es, dass Reisende im Winter auf der Fahrt erfroren. Jede Klasse hatte eigene Schalter, Warteräume und Eingänge im Bahnhof.

Eisenbahnen veränderten die Einstellung zu Wohnort und Arbeitsplatz. Pendler – das Wort *commuter* kommt von *commutation ticket*, dem amerikanischen Wort für einen Zweiter-Klasse-Fahrschein – waren nicht mehr auf eine Wohnung am Arbeitsort angewiesen. Zuvor waren Arbeiter zu Fuß gegangen, ihre Arbeitgeber fuhren in Pferdewagen. In den Industriestädten waren enge Slums für die Unterschicht entstanden, die Wohlhabenderen wohnten in den Vororten – doch als die Bahnen mit niedrigen Fahrpreisen und verbilligten Zeitkarten lockten, zogen viele aus der Innenstadt fort.

Der Bau der Bahnen gab zahlreichen Männern Arbeit. Die *navvies*, wie sie in England hießen (kurz für *navigator*) – verrufene, gesetzlose Männer –, kamen aus allen Teilen des Landes und wohnten an der Strecke, die sie bauten. 1873 waren die Eisenbahnen mit etwa 274 000 Beschäftigten bereits der größte Arbeitgeber in Großbritannien. Städte wurden zu »Eisenbahnstädten«, allen voran Swindon für die GWR und York für die NER. Die Bahngesellschaften jener Tage sorgten für ihre Angestellten und deren Familien von der Wiege bis zum Grabe, erwarteten dafür aber auch bedingungslose Loyalität. Entsprechend groß war die Disziplin. Der Stolz auf die Firma schlug sich wiederum in deren Bild in der Öffentlichkeit nieder. In den USA wurden die Bahnen von Trupps gebaut, die in den Waggons und Lokomotiven lebten. Der Zug fuhr mit der Strecke immer weiter voran. Die Lokomotive sorgte für Dampfheizung und heißes Wasser. Erdboden und Stein, die beim Bau der Trasse geräumt wurden, dienten wiederum zum Aufschütten des Bahndamms und als Fundament der Bockbrücken. Der erste amerikanische Dampfzug fuhr am 9. August 1831, gezogen von der Lokomotive *De Witt Clinton*. Es war eine Prozession von Postkutschen auf Schienen. Die Fahrgäste saßen nicht nur in den Wagen, sondern auch oben auf dem Dach. Als nächste Zugmaschine kam die vierrädrige britische *John Bull*, die einen Hang zum Entgleisen hatte. Dies war auch die erste Lokomotive, die mit einem Gleisräumer (»Kuhfänger«)

ausgestattet war – eine notwendige Vorsichtsmaßnahme, da die frühen amerikanischen Strecken nicht eingezäunt waren und eine Kollision mit einem Büffel oder Ochsen einen Zug aus den Schienen werfen konnte.

Die ersten Bahnstrecken stellten mit ihren geographischen Gegebenheiten die Ingenieure oft vor schwierige Aufgaben, die sie mit viel Phantasie meisterten. Brücken, Zahnradbahnen und Fähren sind für uns heute eine Selbstverständlichkeit, und wir vergessen, dass vieles davon Erfindungen der Eisenbahnpioniere sind. Die 1871 eröffnete Bahn auf den Rigi, nicht weit vom schweizerischen Luzern, war die erste europäische Zahnradbahn. Zwischen den beiden Schienen verlief eine Zahnstange. Ein angetriebenes Zahnrad der Lokomotive griff hinein und hievte den Zug den Berg hinauf. Bei Bergabfahrten verhinderte es, dass der Zug zu viel Fahrt gewann. Nach demselben Prinzip wurde 1896 in Wales die Bahn auf den Snowdon gebaut. Die größte Auslegerbrücke der Welt entstand 1890 in Schottland über den Firth of Forth, und die erste Zahnradbahn der USA, 1869 in New Hampshire in Betrieb genommen, bewältigte selbst Steigungen von 33 %.

Unfälle kamen in diesen frühen Tagen häufig vor, meist Zusammenstöße zwischen zwei Zügen. Doch als mit höherer Geschwindigkeit auch die Bremsen und Signalanlagen besser wurden, nahm die Zahl der Unfälle ab. Wenn Eisenbahnunglücke geschahen, waren es allerdings wirkliche Katastrophen, etwa im Dezember 1879, als in einem Unwetter die Brücke über den Firth of Tay einstürzte und 75 Menschen in den Tod riss.

Sonderzüge galten zunächst als abwegige Idee, die nur den geregelten Bahnverkehr störten, aber schon bald entwickelten sie sich zur wichtigen Einnahmequelle. Mitte der 1840er Jahre waren Bahnausflüge bereits weit verbreitet. Die Werktätigen flohen für einen Tag aus der Enge der britischen Industriestädte in Badeorte wie Scarborough, Skegness oder Morecambe. Schon 1841 hatte Thomas Cook einen Zug gemietet, mit dem er 570 Abstinenzler aus Leicester zu einer Versammlung nach Loughborough brachte. Die Einheimischen der Badeorte sahen die Ausflügler anfangs nicht gern, weil sie zum Trunk neigten und in zwielichtigen Lokalen verkehrten, doch der Profit, der sich mit ihnen machen ließ, half alle Skrupel zu überwinden, und bald warb man sogar schon um Besuche. Populär waren auch Bootsausflüge, Fahrten zu Sportereignissen, Landwirtschaftsausstellungen und sogar zu öffentlichen Hinrichtungen. Tatsächlich nahm das

Passagieraufkommen spürbar ab, als das Parlament 1868 beschloss, die Urteile in Zukunft in den Gefängnissen zu vollstrecken.

Die Königsfamilie fand rasch Gefallen an der Eisenbahn. Königin Victoria unternahm ihre erste Fahrt 1842, und es heißt, sie sei »bezaubert« gewesen. Bald war sie ein häufiger Gast auf den Bahnstrecken, am liebsten in dem Salonwagen, den die LNWR (London & North Western Railway) 1869 für sie baute. Er war mit Vogelaugenahorn getäfelt, und Polster und Deckenbespannung waren aus Seide. Das Licht lieferten Öllampen, von 1895 an die neuartigen elektrischen Lampen. Manche Bahnhöfe entstanden speziell für die Queen, etwa Gosport in Hampshire, wo sie Station machte, wenn sie nach Osborne House, ihrer Residenz auf der Isle of Wight, fuhr.

Und so wuchsen und gediehen die Dampfeisenbahnen und waren bald zur wichtigsten Form des Landverkehrs geworden. Sie waren schneller, billiger und leistungsfähiger als ihre Konkurrenten und sollten sich zum größten und komplexesten Transportsystem entwickeln, das die Welt je gesehen hatte.

Horse- and locomotive-drawn trains on the Baltimore & Ohio Railroad, c. 1830. A race between the locomotive *Tom Thumb* and a horse-drawn train resulted in the latter winning.

Pferde- kontra Dampfbetrieb auf der Baltimore & Ohio Railroad, ca. 1830. Beim Wettrennen zwischen einem Pferdezug und der Lokomotive *Tom Thumb* blieb das Pferd Sieger.

Deux trains, l'un tiré par un cheval et l'autre remorqué par une locomotive, circulent sur le Baltimore & Ohio Railroad, vers 1830. La compétition organisée entre la locomotive *Tom Thumb* et un train hippomobile fut remportée par ce dernier.

A worker taking tools and equipment to a new Canadian Pacific Railway line near Moose Jaw Amulet, Saskatchewan. Later, these railroads were to help the grain farmers by taking men from the East to the West to help bring in the crops.

Ein Arbeiter mit Werkzeug und Materialien für eine neue Strecke der Canadian Pacific Railway bei Moose Jaw Amulet, Saskatchewan. Später brachten solche Bahnen Erntehelfer aus dem Osten zu den Getreidefeldern im Westen des Landes.

Un cheminot avec ses outils et son matériel circule sur une nouvelle ligne du Canadian Pacific Railway, près de Moose Jaw Amulet, dans le Saskatchewan. Ces chemins de fer permirent aux céréaliers de l'Ouest de bénéficier plus facilement d'une main-d'œuvre venue de l'Est au moment des récoltes.

Après le succès du Liverpool & Manchester Railway, le réseau ferroviaire s'agrandit rapidement, en Grande-Bretagne puis en Europe et aux États-Unis. L'invention de la photographie suivant de peu celle de la locomotive à vapeur, il n'est pas surprenant qu'elles soient fréquemment associées. Les locomotives et leur environnement sont devenus le centre d'intérêt principal des photographes ferroviaires depuis les années 1840. Et si le trafic des marchandises représente l'essentiel du commerce des chemins de fer, en assurant aux compagnies les deux tiers de leurs revenus, ce sont toutefois les trains de voyageurs qui attirent l'œil du public – et l'objectif des appareils photo. En Grande-Bretagne, des photographes comme Richard Keene, de Derby, décrivent par l'image les changements de décor provoqués par la croissance de l'industrie ferroviaire. R. H. Bleasdale, de Warwick, commence à photographier des locomotives dès 1857 et, bénéficiant de la coopération des compagnies de chemin de fer, peut accéder librement aux ateliers et aux dépôts du réseau ferré. Lorsqu'il prend sa retraite, au début des années 1890, il a réalisé plus de 3 000 photographies ayant pour sujet les chemins de fer. Dans les années 1880, toutes les grandes compagnies ferroviaires de Grande-Bretagne engagent officiellement des photographes, la première étant le London & North Western dans ses ateliers de Crewe. Ils sont alors employés à photographier les lieux des accidents – leur travail servant de complément d'enquête – de même que les locomotives et le matériel roulant neufs ou rénovés. Les machines étaient d'ailleurs photographiées en « gris atelier » – c'est-à-dire avant leur mise en peinture – car leur image était ainsi mieux reproduite sur les plaques de verre et souvent sur un fond blanc monté spécialement pour l'occasion.

Les premières gares n'étaient que de modestes points de départ, sortes de cabanes rudimentaires en bois où les voyageurs pouvaient acheter leur billet et attendre leur train. Mais, à l'époque, c'était aussi l'un des rares lieux publics où pouvaient se confondre et se brasser librement toutes les classes de la société. L'ambiance particulière qu'elles offraient alors les firent apprécier des photographes et des artistes. Certains peintres produisirent des chefs-d'œuvre comme *The Railway Station* (1852) de William Powell Frith, où sont représentées presque toutes les classes de la société britannique, du criminel à la jeune fiancée aristocratique. Les chemins de fer britanniques offraient trois classes aux voyageurs : la première classe – la meilleure – proposait des compartiments luxueux, rappelant les diligences, situés au centre des voitures et loin des roues pour offrir les conditions de voyage les plus agréables ; la seconde classe était similaire mais accordait moins de place pour les jambes (elle fut abolie en Grande-Bretagne en 1875 en raison des connotations du mot « seconde ») ; en troisième classe, d'un inconfort certain, les compartiments étaient étroits et d'aménagement simple, souvent placés au-dessus des roues. Les voitures étant découvertes, il arrivait que des voyageurs y meurent de froid en hiver pendant le trajet ! Les guichets, les salles d'attente et les entrées des gares étaient également distincts selon ces mêmes classes.

Le chemin de fer modifia également les habitudes des travailleurs et la physionomie des villes. Jusqu'alors, les ouvriers se rendaient à pied à leur travail tandis que leurs patrons se déplaçaient à cheval. Les uns vivaient dans les taudis exigus des cités industrielles, les autres en périphérie des villes. Grâce au chemin de fer, et à la création de billets à tarif réduit et des cartes d'abonnement, les ouvriers purent enfin s'éloigner des centres urbains et coloniser les banlieues – d'où le terme anglais *commuter* (navetteur en français), emprunté à l'américain *commutation* (trajet journalier), qui désigne les détenteurs d'un abonnement et s'applique plus généralement à tous les banlieusards.

En 1873, les compagnies de chemins de fer britanniques étaient les plus grosses entreprises de Grande-Bretagne, employant près de 274 000 personnes. Le réseau ferroviaire du pays était construit essentiellement par des terrassiers itinérants (ou *navvy*), venus de tous les coins du pays, qui vivaient le long des voies qu'ils installaient et avaient la réputation d'être rudes et souvent sans foi ni loi. C'est à cette époque aussi que se créent des cités ferroviaires comme Swindon pour le GWR ou York pour le NER, compagnies qui fournissaient tout le nécessaire à ses ouvriers, « du berceau au tombeau », en espérant bénéficier en retour d'une loyauté à toute épreuve. La discipline et la fierté des cheminots ainsi traités valorisaient l'image de la compagnie. Aux États-Unis, les équipes d'ouvriers du chemin de fer vivaient à bord du train de chantier, qui se déplaçait le long de la voie à mesure de son avancement, la vapeur de la locomotive fournissant chaleur et eau chaude. La terre et les pierres enlevées servaient au ballast ou de fondation aux ponts sur chevalets. Le premier train à vapeur de l'État de New York – une procession d'espèces de diligences sur rail où les voyageurs s'entassaient sur le toit comme à l'intérieur des voitures – fut remorqué par la locomotive *De Witt Clinton* le 9 août 1831. Vint ensuite la *John Bull,* une locomotive d'origine britannique à deux essieux – la première équipée d'un chasse-bœufs – qui avait une nette propension à dérailler. L'absence de protection le long des voies des chemins de fer américains obligeait à installer ce type de pare-chocs pour éviter le déraillement des trains ayant heurté des bisons en liberté.

Les problèmes de construction qui surgirent dans les premiers temps – en raison de la géographie physique des lieux – furent ingénieusement réglés. Aujourd'hui, nous considérons comme évidents les tunnels, les ponts cantilever (le plus grand fut longtemps celui du Firth of Forth, en Écosse, construit en 1890), les systèmes à crémaillère et pignons ou les ferries, en oubliant qu'ils furent bien souvent inventés par les pionniers du rail. Si le premier chemin de fer à crémaillère fut mis en service en 1869 dans le New Hampshire (États-Unis) pour franchir une rampe maximum de 33 %, ce sont les Suisses qui perfectionnèrent cette technique. En 1871, le chemin de fer du mont Rigi, près de Lucerne (Suisse), fut ainsi le premier à utiliser un système à pignons et crémaillère, par lequel les pignons d'une roue, actionnée par la locomotive, accrochaient les dents d'une crémaillère placée entre les rails permettant au convoi de gravir les fortes pentes en montée et de le ralentir en descente. Ce système fut également utilisé pour le Snowdon Mountain Railway (Pays de Galles) en 1896.

Les accidents de chemin de fer étaient inévitables. Dans les premiers temps, il s'agissait essentiellement de collisions entre trains. Cependant, et malgré l'augmentation de la vitesse moyenne des convois, les améliorations apportées aux freins et à la signalisation ferroviaire permirent de diminuer fortement le nombre des accidents. Il n'en demeure pas moins que leurs conséquences se révélaient souvent catastrophiques, comme lors de la tempête de décembre 1879 qui fit s'effondrer le pont franchissant le Firth of Tay au passage d'un train, provoquant la mort de 75 voyageurs.

Si les trains d'excursion furent d'abord considérés comme assez futiles et perturbant le fonctionnement normal des chemins de fer, ils devinrent vite une source importante de revenus pour les compagnies ferroviaires. Vers le milieu des années 1840, les excursions étaient un phénomène entré dans les mœurs et les ouvriers des cités industrielles britanniques avaient pris l'habitude de s'échapper une journée dans des villes balnéaires telles que Scarborough, Skegness et Morecambe. Et c'est en 1841 que Thomas Cook se lance dans les voyages organisés en affrétant un train spécial entre Leicester et Loughborough où 570 personnes doivent assister à une réunion de tempérance. Certes, les habitants des stations balnéaires n'apprécièrent pas tout de suite les « excursionnistes » en raison de leur trop fréquent état d'ébriété et des spectacles trop populaires qu'ils appréciaient, mais devinrent vite plus aimables en voyant les bénéfices qu'il y avait à tirer de ces nouveaux clients. Les raisons de voyager étaient alors multiples, depuis les régates aux rencontres sportives en passant par les foires agricoles ou les pendaisons de criminels. Les compagnies de chemin de fer firent d'ailleurs grise mine en voyant diminuer une part importante de leurs revenus lorsque les exécutions publiques furent abolies en 1868 en Grande-Bretagne.

La royauté britannique s'adapta également rapidement aux transport ferroviaire. La reine Victoria fit son premier voyage en train en 1842 et on dit qu'elle en fut « charmée ». Devenue une voyageuse invétérée, elle disposait d'une voiture-salon particulière, construite en 1869 par le LNWR (London & North Western Railway), dont l'intérieur en loupe d'érable était entièrement tapissé de soie des murs au plafond. Les lampes à huile de l'éclairage d'origine furent remplacées en 1895 par des ampoules électriques d'invention récente. Certaines gares, notamment celle de Gosport (Hampshire), furent également spécialement construites pour accueillir la reine lorsqu'elle se rendait à Osborne House, sa résidence de l'île de Wight.

Offrant l'avantage de la vitesse, de la capacité et de l'économie, et bénéficiant d'un réseau chaque jour plus étendu, les chemins de fer à vapeur sont déjà, en cette fin de XIXe siècle, le principal mode de transport terrestre. En peu de temps, ils vont devenir l'un des systèmes de transport les plus répandus et les plus complexes que le monde ait jamais connu.

This photograph could be the symbol of urban development, a microcosm of industrial society: the river, the horse, the railway, the aeroplane and Alexandre Gustave Eiffel's tower, Paris, 18 October 1909.

Diese Aufnahme vom 18. Oktober 1909 verdeutlicht geradezu die Entwicklung der Städte – ein Mikrokosmos der Industriegesellschaft: Fluss, Pferd, Eisenbahn, Flugzeug und im Hintergrund der Eiffelturm von Alexandre Gustave Eiffel.

Cette photographie symbolise le développement des villes au début du XXe siècle, sorte de microcosme de la société industrielle : le fleuve, le cheval, le chemin de fer et l'avion, avec la tour d'Alexandre Gustave Eiffel se détachant à l'arrière-plan, le 18 octobre 1909.

'1827'

A staged re-enactment of events on the Baltimore & Ohio Railroad in Maryland, USA, to celebrate 100 years of American railways. The centenary pageant was held between 27 September and 15 October 1927 and was attended by more than 1¼ million people.

»1827«

Ein Bild der Baltimore & Ohio Railroad in Maryland, USA, nachgestellt zur Hundertjahrfeier der amerikanischen Eisenbahn. Das Jubiläum, das zwischen dem 27. September und dem 15. Oktober 1927 begangen wurde, zog 1¼ Millionen Menschen an.

« 1827 »

Le centenaire de la naissance des chemins de fer américains fut célébré entre le 27 septembre et le 15 octobre 1927 au cours d'une reconstitution sur le Baltimore & Ohio Railroad, dans le Maryland (États-Unis). Ce spectacle fut suivi par près de 1 250 000 spectateurs.

The early steam engine

The steam locomotive is unlike any other machine in one remarkable respect: its various parts all interact. The performance of the engine affects the boiler via the action of the blast so that the same boiler will react differently when mounted on a different chassis. The position of the engine directly affects the behaviour of the locomotive on the track and the track affects the boiler by its disturbance of the fire. (Above) The metropolitan Northern Outfall sewer works were opened in London in 1863. They would have used their own locomotives within the works. (Below) The newly built locomotive named after the Polish astronomer Kopernicus, 1858.

Frühe Dampflokomotiven

Eines gilt für die Dampflok mehr als für jede andere Maschine: Ihre Teile beeinflussen einander. Je nach Dampfmaschine wird der Druck im Kessel unterschiedlich sein, und derselbe Kessel wird sich bei jedem Fahrgestell anders verhalten. Die Position der Dampfmaschine beeinflusst unmittelbar das Fahrverhalten auf der Trasse, und die Trasse beeinflusst mit ihrer Wirkung auf die Feuerung wiederum den Kessel. (Oben) Die Nordlondoner Kläranlage nahm ihren Betrieb 1863 mit eigenen Lokomotiven auf. (Unten) Die nach dem polnischen Astronomen benannte *Kopernicus*, aufgenommen 1858.

La première machine à vapeur

La locomotive à vapeur se distingue de toutes les autres machines par un point particulier : l'interaction entre ses différents éléments. Les caractéristiques du moteur modifient l'action de la vapeur, et donc le rendement de la chaudière, à tel point qu'elle peut fonctionner différemment suivant le châssis sur lequel elle est montée. De même, l'architecture du moteur affecte directement le comportement de la locomotive sur la voie tandis que la voie agit sur l'efficacité de la chaudière en perturbant le foyer. (En haut) Le constructeur de l'égout urbain de la Northern Outfall, dont les travaux furent entamés à Londres en 1863, disposait de ses propres locomotives. (En bas) La nouvelle locomotive *Kopernicus*, photographiée en 1858, tient son nom de l'astronome polonais.

Home and away

(Above) A Kitson Meyer 0–8–6–0 T
locomotive built by Kitson & Co. in
Leeds for export to the Chilean
Transandine Railway, c. 1909.
(Right) A South Eastern Railway
2–4–0 locomotive, second half of the
19th century.

Nah und Fern

(Oben) Eine Kitson Meyer DC
T-Lokomotive, um 1909 bei Kitson
& Co. in Leeds für die chilenische
Andenbahn gebaut. (Rechts) Die
1B der britischen South Eastern
Railway fuhr in der zweiten Hälfte
des 19. Jahrhunderts.

À l'étranger et à domicile

(Ci-dessus) Cette locomotive Kitson
Meyer 0430T, construite vers 1909
par Kitson & Co. à Leeds, est
destinée au Chilean Transandine
Railway. (À droite) Une locomotive
120 du South Eastern Railway, dans
la seconde moitié du XIXe siècle.

Building the railroads

From South Africa to North America, railway construction was being undertaken at a furious pace. Thousands of labourers or navvies worked on the construction of the railways organised by contractors appointed by the railway companies. The work was brutally hard and dangerous: if accidents did not kill them, disease often did. (Above) Railway engineers at a camp at the summit of the Selkirk Mountains in the Rockies, British Columbia, during the construction of the Canadian Pacific Railway, c. 1880. (Middle) A steam shovel working in Fish Cut, Green River, Wyoming, 1900. (Below) Laing's Nek Tunnel, Natal, South Africa, 1889.

Die Eisenbahnen entstehen

Von Südafrika bis Nordamerika baute man Bahnlinien in rasendem Tempo. Tausende von Arbeitern waren auf den Baustellen beschäftigt, die Bauunternehmer im Auftrag der Bahngesellschaften betrieben. Die Arbeit war hart und gefährlich: Wer nicht Unfällen zum Opfer fiel, kam oft durch Krankheit um. (Oben) Ein Lager der Bahningenieure auf dem Gipfel der Selkirk Mountains in den Rockies, British Columbia, beim Bau der Canadian Pacific Railway, ca. 1880. (Mitte) Ein Dampfbagger bei der Arbeit am Fish Cut, Green River, Wyoming, 1900. (Unten) Laing's Nek Tunnel, Natal, Südafrika, 1889.

La construction des voies

La construction des voies ferrées a été menée à vive allure de l'Afrique du Sud à l'Amérique du Nord grâce aux milliers d'ouvriers et de terrassiers engagés sur les chantiers pour le compte des compagnies de chemin de fer. Ce travail était particulièrement difficile et dangereux et, s'ils ne trouvaient pas la mort dans un accident, la maladie s'en chargeait. (En haut) Le camp des ingénieurs du chemin de fer, établi à proximité du sommet des Selkirk Mountains, dans les Rocheuses (Colombie britannique), pendant la construction du Canadian Pacific Railway, vers 1880. (Au centre) Une grue à vapeur à Fish Cut, Green River (Wyoming), en 1900. (En bas) La construction du tunnel de Laing's Nek, au Natal (Afrique du Sud), en 1889.

The Golden Spike

On 10 May 1869, the race between the Union Pacific and the Central Pacific railroads ended with the two chief engineers, Dodge and Montague, laying the golden spike – the last tie – at Promontory Point, Utah. This represented the unification of the continent, the formal meeting of east and west. Dodge (UP, on the left) and Montague (CP) can be seen shaking hands in the centre.

Der goldene Nagel

Am 10. Mai 1869 war der Wettlauf zwischen Union Pacific und Central Pacific zu Ende, und in Promontory Point, Utah, schlugen die beiden Chefingenieure Dodge und Montague einen goldenen Nagel in die letzte Schwelle – die symbolische Verbindung von Ost und West, die Vollendung der Eisenbahnverbindung quer durch den amerikanischen Kontinent. In der Bildmitte reichen sich Dodge (UP, links) und Montague (CP) die Hände.

Le « Golden Spike »

La course entre l'Union Pacific et la Central Pacific s'achève le 10 mai 1869 à Promontory Point (Utah) par la pose du Golden Spike – le dernier crampon, dit le Clou en Or – par les deux ingénieurs en chef, Dodge (UP) et Montague (CP), au centre. Cet acte symbolisait l'unification du continent américain et le rapprochement formel des côtes Est et Ouest.

Uncivil war

It was a fact that the Northern states partly owed their
victory in the American Civil War to their industrial
and technical superiority. With such might behind him,
in 1864 General Sherman had encircled Atlanta, Georgia.
On taking the city he put it to the torch, destroying the
lines and the railway depot. (Above) The remains of the
roundhouse, with the locomotive the *O.A. Bull* on the
turntable, the *Telegraph* in the foreground. (Below left
and right) Railroads also meant that both troops and
arms could be transported quickly and efficiently to war
zones. (Opposite) The locomotive *Firefly* on the Orange
& Alexandria Railroad, Virginia, c. 1870. The wooden
trestle bridge was erected to replace the original one
destroyed in the war. The photographer is the celebrated
chronicler of the Civil War, Matthew Brady.

Die Bürger und ihr Krieg

Dass die Nordstaaten ihren Sieg im amerikanischen
Bürgerkrieg nicht zuletzt ihrer technischen Überlegenheit
verdanken, ist unbestritten. Gestärkt von der Macht der
Industrie kreiste General Sherman im Jahr 1864 Atlanta,
Georgia, ein, setzte die Stadt in Brand und zerstörte auch
Zuglinien und Einrichtungen. (Oben) Die Überreste des
Lokomotivschuppens, mit dem *O. A. Bull* auf der Dreh-
scheibe und der *Telegraph* im Vordergrund. (Unten links
und rechts) Eisenbahnen sorgten dafür, dass Truppen
und Material rasch und effektiv an die Front kamen.
(Gegenüberliegende Seite) Die Lokomotive *Firefly* der
Orange & Alexandria Railroad, Virginia, um 1870. Eine
hölzerne Gitterbrücke ersetzt notdürftig die originale, die
im Krieg zerstört worden war. Die Aufnahme stammt von
Matthew Brady, dem großen Chronisten des Bürgerkriegs.

Une guerre peu civile

Il est avéré que les Nordistes ont dû en grande partie leur
victoire pendant la guerre de Sécession à la puissance de
leur industrie et à la supériorité de leur technique. Grâce à
cela, le général Sherman a pu assiéger Atlanta (Georgie)
en 1864 puis mettre le feu à la ville une fois prise, détrui-
sant les voies et la gare du chemin de fer. (En haut) Les
ruines de la rotonde, avec la locomotive *O. A. Bull* sur la
plaque tournante et la *Telegraph* au premier plan. (En bas,
à gauche et à droite) Les chemins de fer permettaient
également de transporter rapidement et efficacement les
troupes et le matériel de guerre dans la zone de conflit.
(Ci-contre) La *Firefly* sur le Orange & Alexandria Railroad
(Virginie) vers 1870. Ce pont à chevalets de bois fut construit en remplacement du premier ouvrage, détruit pendant la guerre. Cette photographie fut prise par Matthew
Brady, célèbre chroniqueur de la guerre de Sécession.

Railway stations east and west

The railway station was a shrine to technology and a symbol
of the confidence and power of the company that built it.
St Pancras in north London was built between 1863 and 1867 by
Barlow and Ordish for the Midland Railway. The station itself
can be seen stretching out behind the more dominant Midland
Grand Hotel (opposite), designed by Sir Giles Gilbert Scott.
The exuberant neo-Gothic style of the entire building contrasts
with the more subdued design of the station at Hyderabad,
India (above).

Bahnhöfe auf zwei Kontinenten

Ein Bahnhof war eine Huldigung an den Fortschritt und
symbolisierte Vertrauenswürdigkeit und Stellung einer Bahngesellschaft. St. Pancras im Norden Londons erbauten Barlow
und Ordish 1863–67 für die Midland Railway. Auf dem Bild
(gegenüberliegende Seite) erstreckt sich der Bahnhof hinter
dem dominanten Midland Grand Hotel von Sir Giles Gilbert
Scott. Ein schöner Kontrast zur üppigen Neogotik dieses
Komplexes ist die zurückhaltendere Bahnstation im indischen
Haiderabad (oben).

Gares d'Orient et d'Occident

La gare était un haut lieu de la technologie et un symbole de
la confiance et de la puissance de la compagnie qui l'avait
construite. La gare de Saint-Pancras, au nord de Londres,
fut construite entre 1863 et 1867 par Barlow et Ordish pour le
Midland Railway. Elle s'étend derrière le Midland Grand Hotel,
qui la domine, conçu par sir Giles Gilbert Scott (ci-contre).
Le style néogothique exubérant de l'ensemble du bâtiment
contraste avec l'architecture plus discrète de la gare
d'Hyderabad, en Inde (ci-dessus).

A long and winding road

Trestles or viaducts were common in American railroad building. Most long crossings over deep gorges were built from timber up until the 1860s. However, after this engineers experimented with cross-braced wrought iron and cast-iron bends as well as masonry and timber walls. In 1869, the Baltimore Bridge Company was the first American firm to win a contract in Peru for a trestle bridge in direct competition with British engineers. (Above) A trestle on the California Western Railroad and Navigation Company line. (Below) A section of the New York Elevated Railroad, 1884.

Auf verschlungenen Pfaden

Gitterbrücken und Viadukte waren im amerikanischen Eisenbahnbau weit verbreitet. Bis in die 1860er Jahre überbrückte man tiefe Schluchten meist mit Holz, danach experimentierten die Ingenieure mit Konstruktionen aus Schmiede- oder Gusseisen, aber auch mit massiven steinernen oder hölzernen Wänden. 1869 setzte sich die Baltimore Bridge Company bei einem Brückenprojekt in Peru erstmals gegen die britische Konkurrenz durch. (Oben) Eine Gitterbrücke auf einer Linie der California Western Railroad and Navigation Company. (Unten) Ein Blick auf die New Yorker Elevated Railroad, 1884.

Une voie longue et sinueuse

Les ponts sur chevalets et les viaducs étaient fréquents sur le réseau des chemins de fer américains. La plupart des ouvrages de franchissement furent construits en bois jusque dans les années 1860, où les ingénieurs employèrent des chevalets en fer ou en fonte soutenus par des piles en maçonnerie et bois. En 1869, la Baltimore Bridge Company, alors en concurrence directe avec les ingénieurs anglais, fut la première entreprise américaine à remporter un contrat au Pérou pour la construction d'un pont sur chevalets. (En haut) Un pont sur la ligne de la California Western Railroad and Navigation Company. (En bas) Une section du New York Elevated Railroad, en 1884.

EL R.R. COENTIES SLIP N.Y.

The New York Elevated Railroad, 1867–1956
The 'El' brought great changes to living patterns in New York. It eased the journey from home to work for millions. By 1880 it was possible to live in Upper Manhattan and travel by 'El' to jobs downtown. However, it also brought darkness, noise and slum conditions to those who lived along its route. Here a train rounds the 'S' curve at Coenties Slip on the Lower East Side.

Die New York Elevated Railroad, 1867–1956
Die »El« veränderte das Leben in New York. Millionen kamen damit leichter von ihrer Wohnung zum Arbeitsplatz – schon 1880 konnte man von Upper Manhattan mit der »El« zur Arbeit in die Innenstadt fahren. Den Anwohnern bescherte sie allerdings Dunkelheit, Lärm und Verslumung. Hier nimmt ein Zug die S-Kurve Coenties Slip, Lower East Side.

Le New York Elevated Railroad, 1867–1956
Le « El » a apporté de grands changements à New York en facilitant les déplacements de millions de New-Yorkais entre leur domicile et leur lieu de travail. En 1880, il devenait possible de résider dans Upper Manhattan et de se rendre dans le centre en « El ». Cependant, ce nouveau mode de transport a rendu les rues plus sombres et plus bruyantes et appauvri les quartiers dans lesquels il passait. On voit ici un train prendre la courbe en S de Coenties Slip, dans le Lower East Side.

Railways and shipping

And so to sea... The railway companies did
not confine their activities only to the rails
but operated a range of services to support
their main business and shipping companies. They saw the benefits of mutual
cooperation. Australia's first railway line
was built by the Hobson's Bay Company
between Melbourne and Sandridge in 1854.
The gold-rush stimulated population growth
away from the major coastal cities.
(Right) Sandridge Pier, by Charles Nettleton.
(Above) The port at Colombo, Sri Lanka, in
the 1870s.

Bahn und Schiff

Die Eisenbahngesellschaften waren nicht
nur im Schienenverkehr aktiv, sondern
sorgten auch für den Weitertransport der
Waren. Sie verstanden früh, wie wichtig die
Zusammenarbeit mit anderen Transport-
unternehmen war. Die erste australische
Bahnstrecke richtete die Hobson's Bay
Company 1854 zwischen Melbourne und
Sandridge ein. Der Goldrausch sorgte dafür,
dass auch Städte abseits der besiedelten
Küstenzone entstanden. (Rechts) Sandridge
Pier, eine Aufnahme von Charles Nettleton.
(Oben) Der Hafen von Colombo, Sri Lanka,
in den 1870er Jahren.

Chemins de fer et navires

Également vers la mer ... Les compagnies
de chemin de fer ne limitaient pas leurs
activités au rail mais développaient aussi
une gamme de services divers venant en
complément de leur activité principale et en
s'assurant le concours des compagnies de
navigation. Cette coopération mutuelle était
tout à leur avantage. La première ligne de
chemin de fer d'Australie, construite par la
Hobson's Bay Company entre Melbourne et
Sanbridge en 1854, joua ainsi un rôle dans
l'accroissement de population vers l'intérieur du pays au moment de la ruée vers
l'or. (À droite) Le quai de Sanbridge, par
Charles Nettleton. (Ci-dessous) Le port de
Colombo, Sri Lanka, dans les années 1870.

Continental travel

The railways made continental travel more accessible. In Britain, it was possible to travel from Victoria Station (above) in London to Paris, Brussels and Cologne via the London, Chatham & Dover Railway. The Isle of Wight was a select resort favoured by Queen Victoria and her family. She had, before mass railway travel became available, favoured Brighton but had to move offshore when the railways made Brighton accessible to the masses. (Below) The pier at Ryde, Isle of Wight, in the 1890s.

Auf den Kontinent

Die Briten kamen mit der Eisenbahn leichter auf den Kontinent. Die London, Chatham & Dover Railway brachte Reisende von der Victoria Station (oben) nach Paris, Brüssel und Köln. Königin Victoria und ihre Familie fuhren in den Ferien gern auf die Isle of Wight. Bevor die Bahn das Zeitalter des Massentourismus einläutete, hatte sie die Sommer oft in Brighton verbracht, doch als mit den Zügen die Urlauberscharen kamen, zog sie sich auf die Insel vor der Küste zurück. (Unten) Der Fähranleger von Ryde, Isle of Wight, in den 1890er Jahren.

Voyages continentaux

Le chemin de fer a facilité les voyages sur le Continent. Ainsi était-il possible de se rendre à Paris, Bruxelles et Cologne depuis la gare londonienne de Victoria (en haut) par le London, Chatham & Dover Railway. L'île de Wight était un lieu de villégiature chic apprécié par la reine Victoria et sa famille. Avant que les voyages en train ne deviennent accessibles au commun des mortels, elle préférait Brighton mais dut s'éloigner des côtes lorsque le peuple envahit cette station. (En bas) Les quais de Ryde (île de Wight) dans les années 1890.

Snow and sand

The advent of railway travel made adventurous holidays and travel generally easier and affordable for more people. (Above) Intrepid English mountaineering on the Mer de Glace, Chamonix, in the Alps, c. 1865. (Below) Within easier reach, perhaps, for Americans vacationing, New Jersey's Atlantic City was an ever-popular resort, access to which was made simpler by regular trains to the coast, c. 1886.

Schnee und Sand

Die Bahn war der Weg zum großen Abenteuer und ermöglichte immer mehr Menschen bequemere und erschwinglichere Reisen. (Oben) Eine wagemutige britische Bergexpedition, Mer de Glace in den Alpen von Chamonix, um 1865. (Unten) Für die Amerikaner lag ein Besuch in Atlantic City, New Jersey, näher. Mit regelmäßigen Zügen an die Küste war der Badeort, hier etwa 1886, beliebter denn je.

Neige et plage

Les voyages en train facilitèrent les voyages et les vacances aventureuses en les mettant à portée de bourse d'un plus grand monde. (En haut) D'intrépides Anglais se promènent sur la mer de Glace, à Chamonix (Alpes françaises), vers 1865. (En bas) Vers 1886, Atlantic City (New Jersey), plus proche sans doute pour les vacanciers américains, devint une station balnéaire d'autant plus populaire qu'elle bénéficiait d'une desserte régulière en train.

Building bridges in North America
The photographer William England chose an unconventional but eyecatching way of photographing these North American railroad bridges. (Above) The High Bridge over the Genesee River, near Rochester, New York, 1859. (Opposite) The Victoria Bridge over the St Lawrence River in Montreal during its construction the same year.

Brückenbau in Nordamerika
Zwei Aufnahmen des Fotografen William England, der die beiden amerikanischen Bahnbrücken mit unkonventionellen Perspektiven effektvoll in Szene setzte. (Oben) Die High Bridge über den Genesee River bei Rochester, New York, 1859. (Gegen-überliegende Seite) Die im Bau befindliche Victoria Bridge über den Sankt-Lorenz-Strom in Montreal, aufgenommen im selben Jahr.

La construction des ponts en Amérique du Nord …
Le photographe William England a choisi un angle insolite mais intéressant pour photographier ces ponts de chemin de fer américains. (Ci-dessus) Le High Bridge franchit la Genesee, près de Rochester (New York), 1859. (Ci-contre) Le pont Victoria, jeté sur le Saint-Laurent à Montréal, pendant sa construction, la même année.

And building bridges in Britain

The Forth Bridge crosses the Forth estuary in Scotland to connect the east coast railway line between London and Aberdeen. The bridge was designed by Sir John Fowler and Sir Benjamin Baker and was opened by the Prince of Wales in 1890. (Left) The north cantilever and Garvie Main Pier under construction at Queensferry in 1889.

Und in Großbritannien

Die Forth Bridge überspannt für die Ostküstenstrecke London–Aberdeen die schottische Forth-Mündung. Der Prince of Wales eröffnete die von Sir John Fowler und Sir Benjamin Baker entworfene Brücke im Jahr 1890. (Links) Der nördliche Ausleger und der Tragmast von Garvie beim Bau in Queensferry, 1889.

... et en Grande-Bretagne

Le pont qui franchit l'estuaire du Forth, en Écosse, assure la continuité de la ligne de chemin de fer de la côte Est entre Londres et Aberdeen. Cet ouvrage d'art fut dessiné par sir John Fowler et sir Benjamin Baker et inauguré par le prince de Galles en 1890. (À gauche) Le cantilever nord et le quai principal de Garvie en cours de construction à Queensferry, en 1889.

The Tay and Royal Albert bridges

In 1879 the original Tay Bridge, on the North British
Railway, designed by Sir Thomas Bouch, collapsed during
a violent storm while a train was crossing it, resulting in
the deaths of seventy-five people. The locomotive survived,
was retrieved from the river bed and used for years after
the disaster. It was known thereafter as 'the Diver'. In 1859,
Isambard Kingdom Brunel built the Royal Albert Bridge at
Saltash (right) to link Devon and Cornwall for the GWR.

Tay Bridge und Royal Albert Bridge

Die von Sir Thomas Bouch konstruierte erste Tay Bridge
stürzte 1879 bei einem Orkan ein, als gerade ein Zug darüber fuhr; 75 Menschen fanden den Tod. Die Lokomotive
wurde aus dem Fluss geborgen und fuhr noch Jahre nach
dem Unglück – von da an trug sie den Spitznamen »der
Taucher«. 1859 baute Isambard Kingdom Brunel für
die Great Western Railway die Royal Albert Bridge in
Saltash (rechts) und verband damit Devon und Cornwall.

Les ponts de Tay et Royal Albert

En 1879, le premier pont de Tay, situé sur la ligne du North
British Railway et conçu par sir Thomas Bouch, s'effondre
brusquement pendant qu'un train le franchit lors d'une
violente tempête, provoquant la mort de 75 voyageurs. La
locomotive, retrouvée dans le lit du fleuve et dès lors surnommée « la Plongeuse », continua d'être utilisée plusieurs
années après la catastrophe.
En 1859, Isambard Kingdom Brunel construit le Royal
Albert Bridge à Saltash (à droite), permettant ainsi de
relier le Devon et la Cornouailles pour le GWR.

Wooden structures

A wooden trestle bridge in Dale Creek, Wyoming Territory, c. 1865. It was built for the Union Pacific Railroad and was later replaced with a steel structure before the route was abandoned altogether for a more direct one. The photograph is by A.J. Russell.

Holzbau

Diese hölzerne Bockbrücke, ca. 1865, führte die Union Pacific Railroad über den Dale Creek, Wyoming Territory, bis eine stählerne sie ersetzte. Später wurde die Strecke zugunsten einer direkteren aufgegeben. Die Fotografie stammt von A. J. Russell.

Ouvrages en bois

Un pont sur chevalets de bois à Dale Creek (Territoires du Wyoming), vers 1865. Il fut construit pour l'Union Pacific Railroad et remplacé ensuite par une structure en fer avant l'abandon de la ligne au bénéfice d'un tracé plus direct. La photographie est de A.J. Russell.

Iron structures

English-speaking North America claims to have one bridge for
approximately every mile of track. Bridges were cheaper than
tunnels in this part of the world. The earliest bridges, trestles
and culverts were made of timber. Wooden piles or log cribs
supported them over marshy areas. Later they would be constructed from iron and steel. The influence obviously spread
further south: this is an early iron bridge in Mexico, 1879.

Eisenbau

In Nordamerika, heißt es, kommt auf jede Meile Bahntrasse
eine Brücke. In diesem Teil der Welt waren Brücken billiger zu
bauen als Tunnel. Die frühen Kasten- oder Bockbrücken waren
aus Holz; behauene oder auch rohe Baumstämme stützen sie
auf sumpfigem Gelände. Später ging man zu Eisen- und Stahl-
konstruktionen über, eine Technik, die sich offensichtlich auch
nach Süden ausbreitete: Hier eine frühe mexikanische Eisen-
brücke, 1879.

Ouvrages en fer

L'Amérique du Nord revendique de disposer d'un pont par mile
de voie ferrée environ. En effet, dans cette partie du monde, il
revenait moins cher de construire des ponts que des tunnels.
Les premiers ponts sur chevalets ou aqueducs étaient construits
en bois, soutenus également par des piles en bois ou en rondins
dans les régions marécageuses. Ils furent par la suite édifiés en
fer et en acier. Ce système se répandit ensuite plus au sud,
comme ici au Mexique, en 1879.

Indian railway construction

Nineteenth-century construction in India (above and below) was hard for skilled and unskilled workers alike: it was a tough, physically demanding job and inherently dangerous. The possibility of accidental death or injury was ever present. Bridge superstructures took men to heights where mishaps could send an individual plunging to certain death. Embankments frequently collapsed and careless construction of locomotives took life and limb. (Above) A freight train derailment on the East India Railway. The locomotive is an 0–6–0. Note the external blinds on the carriage still standing, to combat the intense heat in the days before air conditioning.

Die indische Eisenbahn

Der Bau des indischen Bahnnetzes im 19. Jahrhundert (oben und unten) war Schwerarbeit, für die gelernten wie die ungelernten Arbeiter: hart, anstrengend und sehr gefährlich. Jeder musste ständig damit rechnen, dass er bei einem Unfall verletzt wurde oder umkam. Brückenbauer mussten in einer Höhe arbeiten, bei der jeder Sturz den sicheren Tod bedeutete. Böschungen rutschten ab, und leichtsinnig konstruierte Lokomotiven kosteten Leben oder Gliedmaßen. (Oben) Ein entgleister Güterzug der East India Railway. Die Lokomotive ist eine C. Auffällig sind die außen angebrachten Jalousien an dem Personenwagen, in Zeiten, als es noch keine Klimaanlagen gab, ein Schutz vor der Hitze des Tages.

La construction des voies ferrées en Inde

Au XIXᵉ siècle, la construction des voies ferrées en Inde (en haut et en bas) était une tâche difficile pour tous les ouvriers. Le travail était dur, physiquement éprouvant et souvent dangereux. Certains ponts présentaient une telle hauteur de tablier que tout faux pas entraînait inévitablement la mort de ceux qui y travaillaient. De plus, il n'était pas rare que les remblais s'effondrent et que la mauvaise qualité de construction des locomotives provoque des accidents également mortels. (En haut) Le déraillement d'un train de marchandises, tracté par une locomotive de type 030, sur l'East India Railway. Remarquez la présence, sur la voiture de queue, de stores extérieurs permettant de lutter contre la chaleur à une époque où l'air conditionné n'existait pas encore.

Indian derailment, c. 1880

Onlookers pose on top of derailed 0–6–0 steam locomotive
No. 666, surrounded by workers apparently more interested in
the photographer than in the accident, which may well have
been caused by flooding. There were no trains in India in 1850,
but by 1875 a huge railway network existed.

Zugunglück in Indien, ca. 1880

Zuschauer posieren auf der entgleisten C Dampflok Nr. 666,
umgeben von Arbeitern, die sich offenbar mehr für den Fotografen als für das Unglück interessieren, das gut Folge einer
Überschwemmung gewesen sein kann. 1850 gab es noch keine
Eisenbahn in Indien, 1875 hatte das Land schon ein ausgedehn-
tes Streckennetz.

Déraillement en Inde, vers 1880

Les spectateurs de ce déraillement posent sur une locomotive
à vapeur de type 030 immatriculée 666. Les ouvriers semblent
apparemment plus intéressés par le photographe que par
l'accident, qui pourrait bien avoir été provoqué par les crues
de la proche rivière. L'Inde disposa d'un vaste réseau ferroviaire dès 1875 alors qu'il n'y avait aucun train jusqu'en 1850.

Mountain railways in India

The Bhore Ghat section of the Great Indian Peninsula Railway near Bombay opened in 1865 and closed in 1928. The Poona line climbed onto the Deccan Plateau and boasted a reversing station. Poona is about 500 metres above sea level. Sadly, little of the Bhore Ghat's original alignment survives.

Bergbahnen in Indien

Die Bhore-Ghat-Strecke der Great Indian Peninsula Railway bei Bombay war von 1865 bis 1928 in Betrieb. Die Puna-Linie arbeitete sich mit Hilfe von Reversbahnhöfen hinauf in das Hochland von Dekkan; Puna liegt etwa 500 Meter über dem Meeresspiegel. Leider ist von der ursprünglichen Trasse der Bhore-Ghat-Bahn kaum noch etwas erhalten.

Chemins de fer de montagne en Inde

La section du Ghât de Bhore, près de Bombay, sur la ligne du Great Indian Peninsula Railway, fut ouverte en 1865 et fermée en 1928. Cette gare de tête (ou zigzag) de Poona, à près de 500 mètres au-dessus du niveau de la mer, permettait d'inverser le convoi pour escalader plus facilement le plateau du Deccan. Malheureusement, il ne subsiste plus guère de ces alignements.

And in Ceylon

The Ceylon Government Railway (now Sri Lanka Railways) ran from Colombo to Kandy. It was Built by the British to encourage economic reform on the island and was the first railway in Ceylon. It opened on 2 October 1896.

... und in Ceylon

Die Ceylon Government Railway (heute Sri Lanka Railways) führte von Colombo nach Kandy. Die Engländer bauten diese Bahn zur Förderung des wirtschaftlichen Aufschwungs der Insel. Sie eröffnete am 2. Oktober 1896 und war die erste Eisenbahn in Ceylon.

Et à Ceylan

Première voie ferrée de Ceylan, la ligne du Ceylon Government Railway (aujourd'hui les Sri Lanka Railways), qui reliait Colombo à Kandy, fut construite par les Britanniques pour favoriser le développement économique de l'île. Elle fut inaugurée le 2 octobre 1896.

Railways in a landscape 1

Opening his offices in Colombo, Thomas Cook had called Ceylon 'a land of exquisite beauty and romance'. Sensation Rock, near Colombo, photographed in the 1870s, which afforded an extraordinary view, no doubt lived up both its name and to Cook's claim.

Bahn und Landschaft

Thomas Cook hatte Ceylon bei der Eröffnung seines Büros in Colombo »ein Land voller Romantik, von traumhafter Schönheit« genannt. Sensation Rock bei Colombo, hier in einer Aufnahme aus den 1870er Jahren, bot spektakuläre Ausblicke und hielt nicht nur, was sein Name, sondern auch, was Cook versprach.

Chemin de fer dans le paysage 1

En ouvrant ses bureaux à Colombo, Thomas Cook a qualifié Ceylan de « pays d'une beauté et d'un romantisme exquis ». Sensation Rock, près de Colombo, photographié ici dans les années 1870, par la vue extraordinaire qu'il offrait, méritait sans aucun doute et son nom et l'éloge de Cook.

Railways in a landscape 2
Halfway to Heaven… The Darjeeling Himalayan Mountain Railway. This shows where the radius of the curve tightened from 70 feet to 43 feet. Perhaps not surprisingly, it became known as 'Agony Point'.

Landschaft und Bahn
Schon fast auf dem Dach der Welt – auf der Himalajabahn (Darjeeling Himalayan Mountain Railway). An dieser Stelle verengt sich der Kurvenradius von 21 auf 13 Meter, und so wundert es nicht, dass sie als »Agony Point« (»Spitze der Qualen«) bekannt war.

Chemins de fer dans le paysage 2
À mi-chemin entre ciel et terre … sur le Darjeeling Himalayan Mountain Railway. On voit bien comme le rayon de courbure de la voie se raccourcit, passant de 21 à 13 mètres. Ce n'est donc pas sans raison que cet endroit fut surnommé « Agony Point ».

Mountain railways

The Ffestiniog (below) was the first narrow gauge railway in Britain. It opened as a single line in 1866 and offered a cheap single line service for quarrymen. In 1869 the line was doubled. Its unique feature was its use of double bogie engines to get round sharp curves and steep gradients. The Rigi railway (above) in Switzerland was Europe's first mountain railway, opened in 1871. Both the Ffestiniog and the Rigi railways still operate and attract tourists today.

Bergbahnen

Die Ffestiniog Railway (unten) war die erste britische Schmalspurbahn. Sie eröffnete einspurig im Jahr 1866 als billiges Transportmittel, das Bergarbeiter zu ihren Minen brachte. 1869 wurde sie zweispurig ausgebaut. Die große Neuerung waren die Lokomotiven mit zwei beweglichen Fahrgestellen, die auch enge Kurven und große Steigungen bewältigen konnten. Als erste Bergbahn auf dem Kontinent nahm die schweizerische Rigibahn (oben) 1871 ihren Betrieb auf. Ffestiniog- und Rigibahn fahren zur Freude der Touristen beide noch heute.

Chemins de fer de montagne

La ligne du Ffestiniog (en bas) fut la première à voie étroite de Grande-Bretagne. Une première liaison à voie unique fut ouverte en 1866 pour les carriers avant d'être dédoublée en 1869. Elle se distinguait par l'emploi de machines à double bogie acceptant des virages à fort rayon de courbure et permettant de grimper des pentes à pourcentage élevé. (En haut) Ouverte en 1871, la ligne du Rigi, en Suisse, fut le premier chemin de fer de montagne. Ces deux lignes – Ffestiniog et Rigi – fonctionnent toujours et attirent de nombreux touristes.

Early tourist railways

(Above) The lower station of the Vesuvius funicular railway, c. 1870. A funicular railway is a hybrid elevator. Two cars of equal size and weight are attached by a cable that loops over pulleys and a drivewheel at the upper station. As the drivewheels move the cable, one car goes up and the other down. The two cars pass at mid-point. Funiculars have long been used on slopes that are too steep for conventional railways. (Below) A narrow gauge salt mine tourist train in Obersalzberg, Berchtesgaden.

Frühe Touristenbahnen

(Oben) Die Talstation der Standseilbahn auf den Vesuv, um 1870. Eine Standseilbahn ist ein Mittelding zwischen Eisenbahn und Aufzug. Zwei Wagen von gleicher Größe und gleichem Gewicht sind über ein Seil miteinander verbunden, das über Rollen und ein Triebrad in der Bergstation in einer Endlosschleife läuft. Das Seil zieht jeweils den einen Wagen nach oben, den anderen nach unten; in der Mitte begegnen sie sich. Solche Bahnen haben sich auf Steigungen bewährt, die zu steil für konventionelle Eisenbahnen sind. (Unten) Eine Schmalspurbahn zur Besichtigung des Salzbergwerks im Obersalzberg, Berchtesgaden.

Premières lignes touristiques

(En haut) La gare inférieure du funiculaire du Vésuve, vers 1870. Un funiculaire est une sorte d'ascenseur double, où deux voitures de dimension et de poids identiques sont accrochées à un même câble, enroulé sur un tambour à la gare supérieure. Lorsque cette poulie est mise en mouvement, une des voitures monte et l'autre descend, les deux véhicules se croisant à mi-chemin. Les funiculaires ont longtemps été employés pour franchir des pentes trop fortes pour les chemins de fer conventionnels.
(En bas) Le train touristique à voie étroite d'une mine de sel à Obersalzberg, près de Berchtesgaden.

The first excursion train

Thomas Cook, a staunch Baptist, spent his spare time campaigning against the evils of alcohol. In 1841 he had an idea that led him to opening his eponymous travel business: he organised a short train excursion from Leicester to a Temperance Society meeting in Loughborough on the newly extended Midland Railway. The venue was a success and he decided to start his own business. (Above) A gentle (and scenic) ride in the Swiss Alps, perhaps also courtesy of Mr Cook.

Die erste Gruppenreise

Thomas Cook, ein überzeugter Baptist, verbrachte seine Freizeit mit Kampagnen gegen den Dämon Alkohol. 1841 kam ihm eine Eingebung, die das Unternehmen begründete, das seinen Namen trägt: Er organisierte einen Bahnausflug auf der kürzlich ausgebauten Midland Railway von Leicester zu einer Anti-Alkohol-Versammlung in Loughborough. Die Fahrt war ein Erfolg, und daraufhin eröffnete er sein Reisebüro. (Oben) Ausflug in die idyllischen Schweizer Alpen, vielleicht auch von Cook organisiert.

Le premier train touristique

Thomas Cook, un baptiste bon teint, passait ses heures de loisirs à faire campagne contre les méfaits de l'alcool. Ayant organisé en 1841, un bref voyage en train sur la ligne du Midland Railway, entre Leicester et Loughborough, où devait se tenir la réunion d'une société de tempérance, il eut l'idée qui le conduisit à ouvrir son agence de voyages éponyme. (Ci-dessus) Image d'une excursion paisible – et touristique – dans les Alpes suisses, peut-être également préparée par Mr Cook.

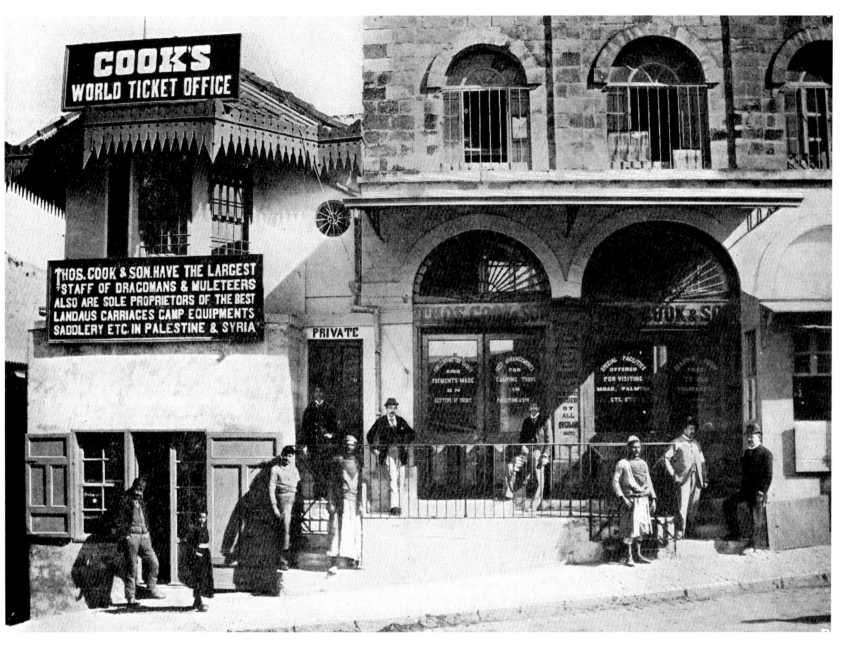

Thomas Cook's expansion

In 1849 Thomas Cook took 500 people from Leicester on a tour of Scotland and arranged for 165,000 people to attend the Great Exhibition in Hyde Park, London. In 1865 he moved his business to London where he arranged tours to Europe. By 1872 he was offering a 212-day tour for 200 guineas. The journey included a steamship across the Atlantic and a paddle ship to Japan. The rest is history. This is his Jerusalem office, c. 1880.

Thomas Cook in aller Welt

1849 unternahm Thomas Cook von Leicester aus eine Schottlandreise mit 500 Teilnehmern und organisierte für 165 000 Besucher die Fahrt zur Weltausstellung im Londoner Hyde Park. 1865 verlegte er sein Geschäft nach London und bot Europareisen an. 1872 hatte er schon eine 212-tägige Weltreise für 200 Guineen im Programm, die per Dampfschiff über den Atlantik und mit dem Raddampfer nach Japan führte. Der Rest ist Geschichte. Hier das Büro in Jerusalem, um 1880.

L'expansion de Thomas Cook

En 1849, Thomas Cook organisait un tour d'Écosse pour 500 habitants de Leicester et proposait la visite de la Grande Exposition de Londres, à Hyde Park, à 165 000 personnes. En 1865, il installait ses bureaux à Londres, d'où il préparait des voyages en Europe. En 1872, il offrait un circuit de 212 jours pour 200 guinées, comprenant la traversée de l'Atlantique à bord d'un vapeur et celle du Pacifique jusqu'au Japon dans un navire à aubes. La suite appartient à l'histoire. Ici, son agence de Jérusalem vers 1880.

Giants of steam

Smoke-belching locomotives that helped open up continents to settlement. (Opposite, clockwise from top left) An Australian locomotive in the desert between Murphys and Highfield, Queensland; a Canadian transcontinental train; *Pioneer*, the first locomotive used in California, 1852. (Above) The Manchester-built locomotive *Spitfire*, 1859, used by the Great Western Railway of Canada.

Giganten des Dampfzeitalters

Solche dampfwolkenspeienden Ungeheuer halfen ganze Kontinente zu erschließen. (Gegenüberliegende Seite, im Uhrzeigersinn von oben links) Eine australische Lok im Ödland zwischen Murphys und Highfield, Queensland; ein Transkontinentalzug in Kanada; *Pioneer*, die erste kalifornische Lokomotive, 1852. (Oben) Die in Manchester gebaute *Spitfire*, 1859, im Einsatz bei der Great Western Railway of Canada.

Les géantes de la vapeur

Ce sont des locomotives comme celles-ci qui permirent d'ouvrir des continents entiers à la colonisation. (En haut à gauche) Une locomotive australienne dans le désert du Queensland, entre Murphys et Highfield ; (en haut à droite) un train intercontinental canadien ; (en bas) la *Pioneer* en 1852, première locomotive utilisée en Californie. (Ci-dessus) La *Spitfire*, locomotive construite à Manchester en 1859, utilisée par le Great Western Railway of Canada.

Enticing the ladies to travel
This photograph was most probably produced by a British railway company to allay the fears that female travellers, and no doubt their male relations, had about travelling alone. Ladies never went anywhere without a chaperone at this time. However, the railways solved this problem by not only segregating the classes but also by opening women-only compartments. This lady seems to be enjoying a comfortable journey, c. 1850.

Damen auf Reisen
Dieses Bild dürfte von einer britischen Bahngesellschaft stammen, die damit Befürchtungen der Frauen und gewiss auch ihrer männlichen Angehörigen ausräumen wollte. Eine Dame ging damals nie ohne Begleitung aus, doch die Eisenbahn bot ihr nun die Möglichkeit, allein zu reisen – nicht nur durch die Trennung der Klassen, sondern auch durch eigene, Frauen vorbehaltene Abteile. Die Dame auf dem Foto, etwa 1850, scheint ihre Fahrt zu genießen.

Inciter les femmes au voyage
Cette photographie a probablement été prise vers 1850 pour le compte d'une compagnie de chemin de fer britannique afin d'apaiser les craintes que les voyageuses – tout comme leurs compagnons sans doute – avaient à se déplacer seules en train ; à cette époque en effet, aucune femme ne sortait encore nulle part sans chaperon. Les compagnies de chemin de fer résolurent toutefois ce problème non seulement en séparant les classes mais en ouvrant aussi des compartiments uniquement réservés aux femmes.

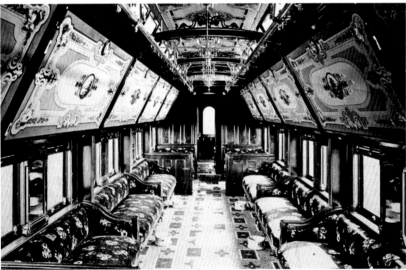

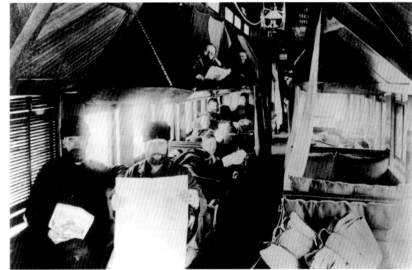

Travelling in luxury
The Pullman car (named after George Mortimer Pullman, 1831–97) was the best and most comfortable way to travel. It would have offered a restaurant car and the highest standards of luxury, usually for the payment of a supplementary fare. (Top) An express passenger train on the Great Central Railway, c. 1870; (above left) a luxurious smoking lounge on a Pullman train; (above right) a third class sleeping-car on the CPR, 1870s.

Reisen im Luxus
Die beste und bequemste Art zu reisen war der Pullmanwagen (benannt nach George Mortimer Pullman, 1831–97). Diese Züge boten, meist gegen höhere Fahrpreise, einen Speisewagen und allen erdenklichen Luxus. (Oben) Ein Express der Great Central Railway, um 1870; (unten links) ein üppiger Pullman-Salon; (unten rechts) ein Schlafwagen dritter Klasse bei der CPR, 1870er Jahre.

Voyager dans le luxe
La voiture Pullman (du nom de George Mortimer Pullman, 1831–1897) permettait de voyager le mieux et le plus confortablement possible. Ces trains disposaient d'une voiture-restaurant et d'un niveau d'excellence luxueux, généralement accessibles sur supplément. (En haut) Un train de voyageurs express du Great Central Railway, vers 1870 ; (en bas à gauche) un luxueux salon fumoir d'un train Pullman ; (en bas à droite) une voiture de troisième classe du CPR dans les années 1870.

Early station architecture

Numerous photographers captured the splendour of railway station architecture in the second half of the 19th century. (Opposite, clockwise from top) Brindisi, Italy, 1866, by Otto Herschorn; Malmö, Sweden (the land route on the southern main line opened in 1864), by Otto Ohm; Frankfurt, Germany, c. 1880. (Right) The Gare de l'Est, Paris (formerly the Gare de Strasbourg), c. 1860, by William England, built between 1847 and 1850.

Frühe Bahnhöfe

Die Pracht der Bahnhöfe in der zweiten Hälfte des 19. Jahrhunderts hielten zahlreiche Fotografen im Bild fest. (Gegenüberliegende Seite, im Uhrzeigersinn von oben) Brindisi, Italien, 1866, von Otto Herschorn; Malmö, Schweden (die südliche Landroute war 1864 fertig gestellt), von Otto Ohm; Frankfurt, ca. 1880. (Rechts) Gare de l'Est, Paris (ursprünglich Gare de Strasbourg, erbaut 1847–50), von William England, aufgenommen ca. 1860.

L'architecture des premières gares

Nombre de photographes immortalisèrent la splendeur architecturale des gares de chemin de fer de la seconde moitié du XIXᵉ siècle. (Ci-contre, en haut) La gare de Brindisi (Italie) en 1866, par Otto Herschorn ; (en bas à droite) la gare de Malmö (Suède), par Otto Ohm – la ligne intérieure sur la ligne principale du sud ouvrit en 1864 ; (en bas à gauche) la gare de Francfort (Allemagne), vers 1880. (À droite) La gare de l'Est (anciennement gare de Strasbourg), construite entre 1847 et 1850 à Paris par William England, vers 1860.

York carriage sidings

This shows York city's first station sidings, c. 1860, built just outside the city walls for the York & North Midland Railway. The first station opened in 1841 and an archway was made in the city walls to reach the station. A new station, outside the walls, to serve an ever expanding rail network, was built in 1877. York was the headquarters of the North Eastern Railway and the London & North Eastern Railway (LNER).

Rangiergleise in York

Die ersten Rangiergleise der Stadt York, um 1860, vor der Stadtmauer für die York & North Midland Railway erbaut. Der erste Bahnhof entstand 1841, und die Züge liefen durch einen Torbogen in der Mauer ein. Die neue Station, durch das immer weiter expandierende Bahnnetz notwendig geworden, baute man 1877 außerhalb. York war der Sitz der North Eastern Railway und London & North Eastern Railway (LNER).

Les voies de garage de York

On voit ici, vers 1860, les premières voies de garage de la gare de York, construites juste à l'extérieur de la ville pour le York & North Midland Railway. Il avait fallu percer une porte voûtée dans le mur d'enceinte de la cité pour permettre d'atteindre la première gare, créée en 1841. Une nouvelle gare fut ensuite construite en 1877 à l'extérieur pour répondre à l'extension du réseau ferré. York était en effet le siège du North Eastern Railway et du London & North Eastern Railway (LNER).

Railways in Sri Lanka

Labourers building the permanent way at Breakwater Point in Colombo, 1874. Built by British colonialists, the importance of the unification of the shipping and railway systems was recognised and Sri Lanka's first railway began from the port of Colombo.

Eisenbahnbau in Sri Lanka

Arbeiter legen die Trasse am Breakwater Point in Colombo an, 1874. Die britische Kolonialverwaltung wusste, wie wichtig die Zusammenarbeit von Eisenbahn und Schifffahrt war, und so begann die erste Bahnlinie Sri Lankas am Hafen von Colombo.

Des voies ferrées pour le Sri Lanka

Des ouvriers aménagent la voie ferrée à Breakwater Point, près de Colombo, en 1874. Les colons britanniques ayant compris l'intérêt de connecter les systèmes de transport par bateau et par rail, la première voie ferrée du Sri Lanka partait du port de Colombo.

Trading in Malta – Valetta, c. 1895

Valetta railway station opened on 28 February 1883. The line ran from Valetta to the ancient capital Mdina. It was single track and the journey began from an underground station at Valetta. It could carry forty-four passengers (twenty-six in third class, eighteen in first) and the carriages were wooden with steel chassis.

Handel in Malta – Valetta um 1895

Der Bahnhof in Valetta wurde am 28. Februar 1883 eröffnet. Von der unterirdischen Station führte die einspurige Linie zur alten Hauptstadt Mdina; der Zug fasste 44 Passagiere, 26 in der dritten Klasse, 18 in der ersten, und die hölzernen Waggons fuhren auf einem Stahlchassis.

Commerce à La Valette – Malte, vers 1895

La gare souterraine du chemin de fer de La Valette fut inaugurée le 28 février 1883. Cette ligne à voie unique reliait La Valette à Mdina, l'ancienne capitale maltaise. Le train pouvait transporter 44 passagers (26 en première classe, 18 en seconde) dans des voitures en bois sur châssis en acier.

'The Midland' – travelling to Buxton

A Midland Railway train running through Ashwood in Derbyshire's Peak District, c. 1900. The Midland Railway was by this time notoriously unpunctual. Competition had led the company to make promises it could not keep. It did offer its own particular benefits: it claimed to be 'the best way', to run 'a proper working railway' and to have the most scenic routes, the most comfortable carriages and the best-served food.

»Die Midland« auf dem Weg nach Buxton

Ein Zug der Midland Railway in Ashwood, Peak District, Derbyshire, um 1900. Die Midland Railway war damals für ihre Unpünktlichkeit bekannt. Durch den scharfen Wettbewerb ließ sie sich zu Versprechen hinreißen, die sie nicht halten konnte. Aber die Gesellschaft sah die Sonnenseite: Sie pries den Midland-Stil als »beste Art, eine anständige Eisenbahn zu führen« und warb mit den landschaftlich schönsten Strecken, den bequemsten Wagen und dem besten Essen.

« The Midland » en route vers Buxton

Un train du Midland Railway passe à Ashwood, dans le Peak District, vers 1900. Le Midland Railway était alors réputé pour ses retards car la concurrence avait poussé la compagnie à faire des promesses qu'elle ne pouvait pas tenir. Elle mettait cependant l'accent sur les avantages qu'elle proposait, se targuant d'être « la meilleure ligne », de disposer « d'un chemin de fer en bon fonctionnement » et d'offrir les lignes les plus pittoresques, les voitures les plus confortables et la nourriture de la meilleure qualité.

Goods traffic

In North America, freight traffic was of more importance than passenger travel. Both the grain and cotton industries and the economic prosperity they brought were dependent on mass transportation over thousands of miles that only the railroads could provide. (Above) A Canadian Pacific worker in Winnipeg taking grain samples from each wagon for inspection. (Left) Bales of raw cotton in a marshalling yard ready for delivery, Atlanta, Georgia, c. 1880.

Güterverkehr

In Nordamerika war der Güter- wichtiger als der Personenverkehr. Die Getreide- und Baumwollwirtschaft und der von ihnen gewährleistete Wohlstand waren auf Massentransport über Tausende von Meilen angewiesen, wie nur die Bahn ihn bieten konnte. (Oben) Ein Arbeiter der Canadian Pacific nimmt in Winnipeg zur Begutachtung aus jedem Getreidewaggon eine Probe. (Links) Ballen mit Rohbaumwolle, fertig zum Abtransport auf einem Rangierbahnhof in Atlanta, Georgia, ca. 1880.

Trafic de marchandises

En Amérique du Nord, le trafic de marchandises avait plus d'importance que celui de voyageurs. Les industries céréalières et cotonnières, et la prospérité économique qu'elles généraient, dépendaient de la capacité à transporter des quantités massives de produits sur des milliers de kilomètres que seuls les chemins de fer pouvaient offrir. (En haut) Un ouvrier du Canadian Pacific Railway à Winnipeg vérifie la qualité de la marchandise en prélevant un peu de céréales dans chaque wagon.
(À gauche) C'est en gare de triage que ces milliers de balles de coton brut attendent d'être livrées à Atlanta (Georgie), vers 1880.

Capturing railway history

The railways changed the way people lived and photography the way they saw the world. (Above) An early Canadian railway company distributing treaty money to the Indians. (Below) Northern Pacific Railroad crew posing for the photographer. (Opposite) A Northern Pacific railway excursion cab has been used for a successful hunting expedition to Crystal Springs, Mississippi, to produce the North American equivalent of a big game hunting photograph.

Bahngeschichte im Bild

Die Eisenbahn veränderte das Leben der Menschen und die Fotografie die Art, wie sie die Welt sahen. (Oben) Eine frühe kanadische Bahngesellschaft zahlt den Indianern Pachtgelder für ihr Land. (Unten) Eine Mannschaft der Northern Pacific Railroad posiert für den Fotografen. (Gegenüberliegende Seite) Nach erfolgreichem Jagdausflug mit der Northern Pacific nach Crystal Springs, Mississippi, entstand diese amerikanische Variante eines Großwildjagd-Fotos.

Des moments dans l'histoire du chemin de fer

Si les chemins de fer ont modifié le mode de vie des gens, la photographie a transformé la manière dont ils voyaient le monde. (En haut) Les responsables d'une des premières compagnies de chemin de fer du Canada remettent de l'argent aux Indiens en contrepartie de la signature d'un accord. (En bas) Des cheminots du Northern Pacific Railroad posent pour le photographe. (Ci-contre) Une voiture du Northern Pacific sert de support au tableau de chasse après une expédition fructueuse à Crystal Springs (Mississippi).

Underground, overground…

Railways do not always follow the permanent way overground
from station to station. (Above) In 1862 William Gladstone, rode
on the world's first underground railway in London. (Opposite,
anti-clockwise from top) The first modern electric train was
demonstrated at the Berlin Trade Fair, 1879; the French sea-
faring electric railway ('Daddy Longlegs') which crossed the
tidal harbour at St Malo in Brittany, 1878; the first elevated
railway in America on its trial run, 1867.

Unter Tage, über Tage …

Eine Trasse muss nicht unbedingt ebenerdig von Bahnhof
zu Bahnhof verlaufen. (Oben) 1862 fuhr William Gladstone in
London mit der weltweit ersten Untergrundbahn. (Gegenüberliegende Seite, entgegen dem Uhrzeigersinn von oben) Der erste
moderne Elektrozug war 1879 in Berlin zu sehen; die elektrische
Hafenbahn von St.-Malo in der Bretagne steckte 1878 ihre langen
Beine ins flache Wasser; erste Versuche mit einer Hochbahn gab
es 1867 in den Vereinigten Staaten.

Sous terre et sur terre …

Les chemins de fer ne suivaient pas toujours des voies ferrées
de surface. (Ci-dessus) En 1862, à Londres, William Gladstone
emprunte le premier chemin de fer souterrain du monde.
(Ci-contre, en haut) Démonstration du premier train électrique
à la Foire de Berlin, en 1879 ; (en bas à gauche) en 1878, une
plate-forme sur rails mue par une machine à vapeur traverse
le port de Saint-Malo (France) ; (en bas à droite) le premier
chemin de fer surélevé d'Amérique lors de ses essais, en 1867.

The universal locomotive

Knowing how to operate a steam locomotive and being a part of a locomotive crew was, and still is, a universal language. There were, of course, practical differences, but the principals remained the same. A variety of locomotives (opposite, clockwise from top): a German-built locomotive, c. 1860; an American 2-6-0 Baldwin-built locomotive c. 1890, with cowcatcher; a French locomotive with footplate crew, 1872. (Right, top to bottom) The Canadian Union Pacific's first locomotive, known as *General Sherman*, c. 1865; an Austrian locomotive on the Bavarian Railway, 1852; a British GWR broad gauge locomotive (note the massive driving wheel).

Die Weltlokomotive

Wer eine Dampflok fahren kann oder als Heizer mitfährt, gehört bis heute zu einer weltweiten Gemeinschaft. Natürlich gab es in der Praxis Unterschiede, aber die Grundprinzipien waren stets dieselben. Hier ein buntes Sortiment an Lokomotiven: (Gegenüberliegende Seite, im Uhrzeigersinn von oben) Ein deutsches Baumuster, etwa 1860; eine amerikanische Baldwin 1 C, ca. 1890, mit Gleisräumer; eine französische Lokomotive mit Mannschaft, 1872. (Rechts, von oben nach unten) Die erste Lokomotive der Canadian Union Pacific, um 1865, bekannt als *General Sherman;* eine österreichische Lok auf der Bayrischen Eisenbahn, 1852; eine britische Lokomotive mit auffällig großem Antriebsrad für das Breitspurnetz der GWR.

La locomotive universelle

Les cheminots du monde entier parlaient un langage universel dès qu'il s'agissait du fonctionnement d'une locomotive à vapeur, malgré les inévitables différences pratiques entre les modèles de machines. (Ci-contre, en haut): locomotive de construction allemande, vers 1860 ; (en bas à droite) une Baldwin 130 américaine avec chasse-buffles, vers 1890 ; (en bas à gauche) locomotive française avec son équipe de conduite, en 1872. (À droite, de haut en bas) La première locomotive du Canadian Union Pacific Railway, appelée *General Sherman*, vers 1865 ; locomotive autrichienne du Bavarian Railway en 1852 ; locomotive à grand écartement du GWR britannique (remarquez l'énorme roue motrice).

Early Canadian locomotives (overleaf)

The Clifton Depot on the Great Western Railway, c. 1859, by William England. The GWR, later to become part of the Canadian Pacific Railway, was the first railway in southern Ontario and ran the 229 miles from Niagara to Windsor. The photograph shows the locomotive *Essex* and coaches at the depot in 1859, with passengers looking on.

Frühe kanadische Lokomotiven (folgende Doppelseite)

Der Bahnhof Clifton an der Great Western Railway, aufgenommen von William England, um 1859. Die GWR, die später in der Canadian Pacific Railway aufging, war die erste Bahnlinie im südlichen Ontario und verkehrte über 368 km von Niagara nach Windsor. Das Bild zeigt die Lokomotive *Essex* mit Personenwagen und wartenden Fahrgästen im Jahr 1859.

Premières locomotives canadiennes (pages suivantes)

Le Clifton Depot du Great Western Railway, vers 1859, par William England. Le GWR, qui allait constituer en partie le Canadian Pacific Railway, fut le premier chemin de fer du sud de l'Ontario dont la ligne de 368 kilomètres reliait Niagara à Windsor. On voit ici une locomotive *Essex* et ses voitures au dépôt, en 1859, observées par les voyageurs en attente.

3645.

2
Wheels in Motion

In the period leading up to the First World War the railway networks in Europe and America had become well established; the railways were now a part of everyday life and no longer merely a novelty. The teething problems had been overcome and, after a period of consolidation, improvements were made to the existing railway systems and the technology exported all over the world. In 1899 the Great Central Railway built the last line into London Marylebone from Sheffield and Manchester. In South Africa, the Boer War had started. In 1904 the GWR 4-4-0 No. 344 *City of Truro* locomotive reached a speed of over 100mph at Wellington Bank, Somerset, on an Ocean Mail special running from Plymouth to London. This was the first time a locomotive had travelled over 100mph.

By 1900 there were 25,000 miles of railways in India, funded by British investors and engineers and built by millions of Indian workers. The first Ugandan railway opened in 1901 between Mombasa and Kisumu on Lake Victoria. Another opened in 1910 from Jinja, on Lake Victoria, to Namasagahi which connected Lake Victoria and Kioga. The lure of gold was the catalyst for the development of Australia's railways. By 1901, when the British Commonwealth came into being, four state capitals – Brisbane, Sydney, Melbourne and Adelaide – were linked by rail and by 1917 the Trans Continental Railway opened to connect Perth with the other capitals. In South America in 1910 the Transandine Railway had been constructed, linking Chile and Argentina across the Andes. It was built at a height of 10,000 feet above sea level, with five summits of over 15,000 feet, the highest being the Galera Tunnel at 15,690 feet.

In North Africa railways were completed by the French after the 1914–18 war, developed from the military tracks built to assist the French Foreign Legion overcome the warring sheiks of the Riff. The Moroccan Railway Company opened in 1922, again taking over the old military railways, as did the Luxor Aswan Railway in Egypt following the first Sudan campaign. In 1907 the Japanese railways were nationalised and the system carried 101,115,793 passengers during this year. In America the Grand Trunk Pacific Railway Act was passed on 24 October 1903 and the line was completed in 1910. Washington Union Station opened in 1907 and Pennsylvania Station in 1910. The electrification of New York Central's passenger terminal lines began in 1906 to coincide with the construction of Grand Central Station in New York and the Pennsylvania Railroad was extended under the Hudson River to New York in 1910.

As more and more lines were built so the competition increased and railway companies realised that it was important to have a corporate identity that distinguished them from their competitors. Nowhere was this more important than in a small island like Britain. With this in mind, the companies put their insignias on all parts of their property: the cutlery, crockery, carpets, bedding, stationery, fire buckets, tickets, uniforms and the buildings they owned were stamped – even the chamber pots bore the companies' crest. Inspiration for such crests often came from the coats of arms of the main towns served by the lines and were universally recognised. Such identification was important because much of the workforce was illiterate. Locomotives were also distinguished by their colours and liveries. Sometimes the results could be a little unexpected. An anecdote of the time recalls that William Stroudley, the man responsible for the LB&SCR (London, Brighton & South Coast Railway), chose 'improved engine green' for the company livery but, because he was colour blind, all the locomotives emerged from the paint shop a light toffee colour. Another side of this competition and rivalry was reflected in luxurious passenger facilities. For the railway companies the equation was relatively simple: the more luxury they offered the more business they acquired. In the USA, where long-distance trains made arduous journeys inevitable, luxury sleeping carriages and first class dining facilities were promoted. Soon afterwards, the companies built hotels beside major stations, making travelling a stylish pastime for wealthier passengers. Despite their differences in appearance, the railway companies all had the same opinion about standards: only the best would do. In Britain, for example, crockery was supplied by the reputable Staffordshire firms, Minton and Spode, and the silverware by Mappin and Webb of Sheffield. Such standards were extended to every aspect of railway work.

So began an era of luxury – for those who could afford it. The Wagon Lits Company operated high quality sleeping cars across Europe. One of these was the *Orient Express* which acquired its notorious reputation for decadent travel before the outbreak of the First World War. Even today, nicknamed the 'Grand Old Lady' of Europe, it is still the most famous of trains. It ran from Gare de l'Est in Paris to Bucharest, passing through France, Germany, Austria, Czechoslovakia, Hungary and Romania. Passengers were served the finest food and wine in sumptuous surroundings.

Perhaps one of the most spectacular rail journeys of this period was Queen Victoria's funeral. She died on 22 January 1901, aged eighty-three, at Osborne House and left elaborate instructions for her funeral. Her coffin travelled to Portsmouth on the royal yacht *Alberta* and then on a funeral train to London Victoria and finally on to the Frogmore royal mausoleum at Windsor Castle, where she was laid to rest.

However, personal trains were not exclusive to royalty. Winston Churchill hired a special train for his 1910 election campaign and the Duke of Sutherland had his own locomotive and carriage which he kept in Scotland. Other named trains ran during this time, on which anyone could travel. The GWR *Cornish Riviera Express* was introduced as a non-stop service from Paddington to Plymouth for connection with transatlantic liners and then onto Cornwall. In 1914 the Pullman car *Topaz* was built for the South Eastern & Chatham Railway (SECR). It was the ultimate in passenger comfort: all the seats were armchairs; each had a glass-topped table, a brass table lamp and bell pushes to call the attendant. All meals were served at the passengers' seats.

While the basic principles of locomotive design, adopted all over the world because of the strength, simplicity and reliability they provided, were not to change over this period, there were constant improvements, alterations and adaptations. Locomotive cabs were now enclosed to protect the driver from the elements. A new type of articulated locomotive, known as the Beyer-Garratt, was built in Britain in 1909 for the Tasmanian Railways. Essentially, it was two steam power units pivoted at either end of the main frame which carried the boiler and cab. These were versatile for use on lines with sharp curves and inclines and were later used in Africa, India and Australia. The North Eastern Railway built the first electric locomotive in 1904 to replace steam locomotives on a freight line which had a badly ventilated tunnel which the steamer filled with fumes. The current ran through an overhead pantograph. Dr Rudolf Diesel built the first diesel locomotive in Germany in 1897. In diesel locomotives the engine powers a generator which produces an electric current. Instead of driving the wheels directly, the diesel engine fired electricity which then turned the wheels. Perhaps the biggest single aid to locomotive efficiency was the superheater devised by Wilhelm Schmidt in Germany, also in 1897. It

increased the temperature of the steam produced by the boiler, making better use of its expansive power within the cylinders. In Britain the GWR was a pioneer in introducing not only road services to feed its lines but also air services. The first GWR motor bus ran between Helston and the Lizard in Cornwall in 1903 to connect with the passenger train. By 1907 the GWR had ninety-five motor buses, four hundred other vehicles and an extensive fleet of delivery vans.

During this period, suspended overhead railways and monorails were also developed. They were cheaper to build and avoided conflict with traffic on the ground and on water. The funicular line in Monmartre in Paris was built in 1900 and the first commercial monorail opened in Wuppertal in north-west Germany with electric trains suspended beneath the rails in 1901. The first underground railway was the Paris Metropolitan railway, soon to be known simply as the Métro, which opened in 1900 initially operating between Porte de Vincennes and Porte Maillot.

London & South Western Railway porters admiring a new platform ticket machine at Waterloo Station in May 1913. Platform tickets permitted people who were not actually travelling by train to go onto the platform. The cost of a ticket was nominal.

Gepäckträger der London & South Western Railway bewundern einen neuen Bahnsteigkarten-Automaten auf dem Bahnhof Waterloo, Mai 1913. Bahnsteigkarten gestatteten Begleitern, die nicht mit dem Zug fuhren, gegen einen nominellen Preis Zugang zum Bahnsteig.

Des porteurs du London & South Western Railway admirent le nouveau distributeur de tickets de quai, installé en gare de Waterloo en mai 1913. Pour une somme modique, ceux qui ne prenaient pas le train pouvaient ainsi venir jusque sur le quai saluer les voyageurs en partance.

Bis zum Ersten Weltkrieg waren die Eisenbahnen in Europa und Amerika weit verbreitet; die Eisenbahn war kein Kuriosum mehr, sondern Teil des Alltagslebens. Die Kinderkrankheiten waren ausgestanden, und nach einer Zeit der Konsolidierung wurden bestehende Strecken auf den neuesten Stand gebracht und die Technik in die ganze Welt exportiert. 1899, als in Südafrika schon der Burenkrieg tobte, legte in England die Great Central Railway die letzte der Hauptstrecken an, von London Marylebone über Sheffield nach Manchester. 1904 fuhr die *City of Truro*, 2B Lokomotive Nr. 344 der GWR, in Wellington Bank, Somerset, mit einem Postzug von Plymouth nach London erstmals schneller als 100 Meilen die Stunde.

Das indische Streckennetz umfasste zur Jahrhundertwende 40 225 km, finanziert von britischen Investoren, gebaut unter britischer Leitung von Millionen indischer Arbeiter. Die Ugandabahn nahm 1901 zwischen Mombasa und Kisumu am Viktoriasee ihren Betrieb auf; eine zweite, 1910 entstandene von Jinja nach Namasagahi verband Viktoria- und Kiogasee. Die Hoffnung auf Gold brachte die ersten australischen Bahnen ins Rollen. 1901, im Gründungsjahr des British Commonwealth, gab es zwischen den vier Provinzhauptstädten Brisbane, Sydney, Melbourne und Adelaide eine Bahnverbindung, und 1917 war die Trans Continental Railway fertig, mit der auch Perth Anschluss fand. In Südamerika entstand bis 1910 die Andenbahn, die Argentinien und Chile verband. Sie verlief 3000 Meter über dem Meeresspiegel, mit fünf Strecken über 4500 Meter, die höchste davon der Galera-Tunnel auf 4782 Meter Höhe.

Nach dem Ersten Weltkrieg bauten die Franzosen in Nordafrika Bahnstrecken auf den Fundamenten der Militärbahnen, mit deren Hilfe die Fremdenlegion versucht hatte, sich gegen die kriegerischen Scheichs des Rif-Gebirges zu behaupten. Auch die Marokkobahn, die seit 1922 verkehrte, nutzte Militärtrassen, ebenso wie in Ägypten die Luxor-Assuan-Bahn auf den Schienen des ersten Sudanfeldzugs fuhr. 1907 wurden die japanischen Bahnen verstaatlicht und beförderten in jenem Jahr 101 115 793 Fahrgäste. Das amerikanische Parlament verabschiedete am 24. Oktober 1903 das Gesetz zum Bau der Grand Trunk Pacific Railway, und 1910 war die Strecke vollendet. Der Bahnhof Washington Union wurde 1907 eröffnet, Pennsylvania 1910. Die Elektrifizierung des Personenverkehrs der New York Central begann 1906 parallel zum Bau der Grand Central Station, und 1910 brachte ein Tunnel unter dem Hudson die Pennsylvania Railroad bis nach New York.

Je mehr Strecken hinzukamen, desto größer wurde die Konkurrenz, und die Bahngesellschaften erkannten, wie nützlich eine Corporate Identity war, die sie von den anderen unterschied. Nirgends war das wichtiger als auf einer kleinen Insel wie Großbritannien. Dort fanden sich überall die Firmenzeichen: auf Geschirr und Besteck, Teppichen, Bettzeug, Briefpapier, Feuereimern, Fahrkarten, Uniformen und den Gebäuden – selbst Nachttöpfe waren mit dem Signet der Firma geschmückt. Inspiration holte man sich oft von den Wappen der Großstädte, die von der Linie versorgt wurden. Zeichen waren wichtig, denn ein Großteil der Belegschaft konnte nicht lesen. Auch Lokomotiven erkannte man an Farben und Bemalung, auch wenn manche anders ausfielen als erwartet. Eine Anekdote der Zeit berichtet von William Stroudley, der als Verantwortlicher für die LB&SCR (London, Brighton & South Coast Railway) ein »eigenes Maschinengrün« als Farbe für die Gesellschaft wählte; er war jedoch farbenblind, und als die Lokomotiven aus der Lackiererei zurückkehrten, hatten sie allesamt ein helles Toffeebraun. Ein anderes Feld, auf dem sich die Rivalität zeigte, war die luxuriöse Ausstattung der Personenzüge. Für die Gesellschaften war die Formel einfach: Je mehr Luxus sie anboten, desto mehr Fahrgäste lockten sie an. In den USA, wo große Entfernungen zu überbrücken waren, wurde mit dem Komfort der Schlafwagen und Speisewagen erster Klasse geworben. Bald kamen von den Bahngesellschaften betriebene Hotels an den großen Bahnhöfen hinzu, und die Wohlhabenden reisten stilvoller denn je. So unterschiedlich sie sich in ihrem Auftreten auch gaben, waren die Bahngesellschaften sich doch in einem einig: Nur das Beste war gut genug. In Großbritannien stammte zum Beispiel das Porzellan von den angesehenen Manufakturen in Staffordshire, von Minton und Spode, und das Tafelsilber von Mappin and Webb in Sheffield. Und solche Standards herrschten bis in die kleinsten Details hinein.

So begann ein Zeitalter des Luxus – für jene, die ihn sich leisten konnten. Wagons-Lits bot überall in Europa seine hochwertigen Schlafwagenzüge an. Einer davon war der *Orient-Express*, der in der Zeit vor dem Ersten Weltkrieg zum Inbegriff des dekadenten Reisens wurde. Selbst heute gilt er noch als *grande dame* der europäischen Eisenbahn, der berühmteste Zug aller Zeiten. Er verkehrte vom Pariser Gare de l'Est nach Bukarest, durch Frankreich, Deutschland, Österreich, die Tschechoslowakei, Ungarn und Rumänien. Die Reisenden wurden mit feinster Küche und erlesenen Weinen in stilvollem Ambiente verwöhnt.

Wohl eine der spektakulärsten Bahnfahrten jener Zeit war Königin Victorias Trauerzug. Sie starb am 22. Januar 1901 mit 83 Jahren in Osborne House und hinterließ genaue Anweisungen für ihr Begräbnis. Die königliche Jacht *Alberta* brachte ihren Sarg nach Portsmouth, und von dort ging er per Eisenbahn zum Bahnhof London Victoria und weiter zum Frogmore-Mausoleum, Schloss Windsor, wo die Königin zur letzten Ruhe gebettet wurde.

Nicht nur gekrönte Häupter hatten ihre eigenen Züge. Winston Churchill mietete für seine Wahlkampagne von 1910 einen Sonderzug, und der Herzog von Sutherland hielt sich in Schottland einen eigenen Wagen mit zugehöriger Lokomotive. Kommerzielle Züge bekamen Namen. Die GWR setzte den *Cornish Riviera Express* ein, der nonstop von Paddington nach Plymouth fuhr, wo er Anschluss an die Transatlantikdampfer hatte, und von dort weiter nach Cornwall. 1914 stellte die South Eastern & Chatham Railway (SECR) den Pullmanwagen *Topaz* in Dienst, das Nonplusultra an Komfort: Jeder Fahrgast hatte seinen eigenen Polstersessel mit Glastisch, Messinglampe und einem Knopf, mit dem er den Kellner rufen konnte. Alle Mahlzeiten wurden am Platz serviert.

Die Grundkonstruktion der Lokomotiven, die sich weltweit durchgesetzt hatte, blieb in dieser Zeit unverändert, weil die Maschinen kräftig, einfach und verlässlich waren, aber im Einzelnen gab es natürlich ständige Verbesserungen. Die Führerstände waren nun geschlossen, sodass der Führer vor Wind und Wetter geschützt war. Die erste Beyer-Garratt-Lokomotive mit beweglichem Fahrgestell wurde 1909 in England für die tasmanische Eisenbahn gebaut. Sie bestand aus zwei Dampftriebwerken, die über Gelenke mit dem Hauptrahmen verbunden waren, der Kessel und Führerstand trug. Solche Maschinen waren wendiger in engen Kurven und konnten Steigungen besser bewältigen; später kamen sie auch in Afrika, Indien und Australien zum Einsatz. Die North Eastern Railway baute 1904 die erste Elektrolok für eine Güterzuglinie durch einen schlecht belüfteten Tunnel, in dem sich der Rauch der Dampflokomotiven staute. Der Strom wurde durch einen Scherenstromabnehmer auf der Oberseite zugeführt. 1897 stellte Rudolf Diesel in Deutschland die erste Diesellokomotive vor. Der Verbrennungsmotor treibt bei solchen Lokomotiven die Räder nicht direkt an, sondern einen Generator, der elektrische Energie erzeugt. Die vielleicht bedeutendste Errungenschaft zur Leistungssteigerung war der ebenfalls 1897 in Deutschland entwickelte Dampfüberhitzer

von Wilhelm Schmidt. Mit diesem Verfahren konnte der Kessel heißeren Dampf erzeugen, der sich in den Zylindern mehr ausdehnen und so größere Kraft entfalten konnte. In Großbritannien band die GWR als Erste nicht nur den Land-, sondern sogar den Luftverkehr in ihre Dienste ein. Der erste Omnibus der GWR wurde 1903 in Cornwall als Zubringer zum Zug zwischen Helston und der Landspitze Lizard eingesetzt. 1907 verfügte die GWR bereits über 95 Busse, 400 weitere Fahrzeuge und eine große Flotte von Lieferwagen.

In dieser Zeit entstanden auch die Konzepte für Schwebe- und Einschienenbahnen. Solche Bahnen waren einfacher zu bauen und kamen nicht mit dem Straßen- oder Schiffsverkehr in Konflikt. Die Montmartre-Standseilbahn in Paris stammt aus dem Jahr 1900, und im Jahr darauf nahm in Wuppertal die Schwebebahn mit an den Schienen hängenden Elektrozügen ihren Betrieb auf. Die erste Untergrundbahn war die Pariser *métropolitain*, die bald nur noch als Métro bekannt war; der Betrieb des ersten Teilstücks wurde 1900 zwischen Porte de Vincennes und Porte Maillot aufgenommen.

Striking French workers put a locomotive on the tracks to halt traffic in northern France. The French railway strike of 1910 was suppressed by the Premier Aristide Briand who sent in soldiers to do the work.

Streikende Arbeiter blockieren in Nordfrankreich mit einer Lokomotive den Schienenverkehr. Premierminister Aristide Briand schlug den Eisenbahnerstreik von 1910 mit Hilfe von Soldaten nieder, die den Betrieb übernahmen.

Des cheminots français en grève remettent sur la voie une locomotive afin d'interrompre le trafic dans le nord de la France. Aristide Briand, alors Premier ministre, envoya la troupe remplacer les cheminots et brisa ainsi la grève des chemins de fer français de 1910.

Pendant la décennie précédant la Première Guerre mondiale, les réseaux ferrés sont déjà bien développés, en Europe comme aux États-Unis, et le chemin de fer fait désormais partie de la vie quotidienne et n'a plus autant qu'autrefois l'attrait de la nouveauté. Une fois surmontées les difficultés initiales, les réseaux ferroviaires existants sont progressivement unifiés et améliorés. En 1899, le Great Central Railway construit la dernière ligne à pénétrer au centre de Londres et qui arrive à la gare de Marylebone en provenance de Sheffield et Manchester. En 1904, la *City of Truro*, une 220 n° 344 du GWR, remorquant dans la rampe de Wellington Bank (Somerset) le train postal maritime spécial Plymouth–Londres, devient la première locomotive à vapeur à dépasser les 100 miles (160 km/h).

La Grande-Bretagne exporte la technologie ferroviaire dans toutes les parties du monde qu'elle contrôle. En 1900, l'Inde possède déjà un réseau de 40 225 km de voies ferrées, créées à l'initiative d'investisseurs et d'ingénieurs britanniques et construites par des millions de travailleurs indiens. En 1901, dans leur Protectorat d'Afrique Orientale, les Britanniques achèvent la ligne de chemin de fer entre Mombasa et Kisumu, sur le lac Victoria, qu'ils prolongeront jusqu'à Jinja puis, en 1910, jusqu'à Namasagahi, sur le lac Kioga. En Australie, la ruée vers l'or fut le catalyseur du développement des chemins de fer. En 1901, époque de la création du Commonwealth britannique, les capitales de quatre États australiens – Brisbane, Sydney, Melbourne et Adelaide – sont reliées par voie ferrée ; il faut toutefois attendre 1917 pour que le Trans Continental Railway les relie à Perth. Achevée en 1910, la ligne du Transandin traverse les Andes entre le Chili et l'Argentine à 3 000 m d'altitude en moyenne, mais en franchissant cinq cols de plus de 4 500 m, le plus élevé étant au tunnel de Galera, à 4 782 m d'altitude. En Afrique du Nord, après la guerre de 1914–1918, les Français aménagent pour le trafic civil les voies ferrées créées par les unités de la Légion étrangère dans leur lutte contre les scheiks rebelles du Rif. C'est ainsi que la Compagnie des chemins de fer du Maroc peut se créer en 1922, tout comme le Luxor Aswan Railway en Égypte après la campagne du Soudan. Au Japon, 101 115 793 voyageurs ont pris le train en 1907, l'année même de la nationalisation des chemins de fer. Aux États-Unis, le vote du Grand Trunk Pacific Railway Act le 24 octobre 1903 permet de construire la ligne, qui sera achevée en 1910. L'électrification des lignes du terminal de voyageurs du New York Central commence en 1906 et accompagne la construction de la gare de Grand Central. Si la gare de l'Union, à Washington, ouvre en 1907, celle de Pennsylvania, à New York, ne sera inaugurée qu'en 1910, l'année où la ligne du Pennsylvania Railroad est prolongée en passant sous l'Hudson.

Plus il y a de lignes, plus la compétition augmente entre les compagnies. Elles comprennent rapidement qu'elles doivent avoir une identité propre qui les distingue de leurs concurrents auprès du public. Le phénomène est particulièrement évident en Grande-Bretagne, où le réseau ferroviaire est très développé mais excessivement morcelé. C'est ainsi que les compagnies de chemin de fer apposent partout leur sigle : couverts, vaisselle, tapis, lits, papeterie, seaux à incendie, billets, uniformes et bâtiments sont tous marqués – jusqu'aux pots de chambre qui portent l'écusson de la compagnie. Ces sigles, pour la plupart inspirés par les armoiries des principales villes desservies par la compagnie, sont facilement reconnaissables et permettent aux cheminots, souvent illettrés, de mieux identifier leurs trains. Les locomotives se distinguaient également par leur livrée, ce qui a pu parfois produire des résultats étonnants. On raconte ainsi que William Stroudley, responsable du LB&SCR (London, Brighton & South Coast Railway), avait choisi « un beau vert moteur » pour les machines de la compagnie ; mais, comme il était daltonien, toutes les locomotives sortirent des ateliers de couleur caramel clair ! La concurrence et la rivalité entre compagnies se traduisaient également dans l'aménagement du matériel roulant. L'équation était relativement simple : plus les compagnies pouvaient offrir de luxe, plus elles gagnaient de l'argent. Et, malgré leurs différences, elles étaient alors toutes d'accord pour dire que seule l'excellence est profitable. En Grande-Bretagne par exemple, la vaisselle était fournie par des entreprises réputées du Staffordshire, Minton et Spode, tandis que l'argenterie provenait de Mappin and Webb de Sheffield. Aux États-Unis, où les distances entre les villes rendaient inévitables les très longs trajets, elles mirent en service de luxueuses voitures-couchettes et des voitures-restaurants de première classe sur les trains de voyageurs. Elles financèrent également, dans de nombreux pays, la construction de grands hôtels à proximité des gares principales afin de rendre les voyages le plus agréable possible aux gens fortunés. Cette volonté d'excellence fut étendue à tous les aspects des chemins de fer.

Ce début du XXᵉ siècle fut sans doute un âge d'or des chemins de fer par le luxe qu'ils pouvaient offrir à ceux qui en avaient les moyens. La voiture Pullman *Topaz*, construite pour le SECR en 1914, était du dernier cri en matière de confort : pas de banquettes mais des fauteuils, chaque voyageur ayant à disposition une table à plateau de verre, une lampe en cuivre et un bouton de sonnette pour appeler le garçon ; tous les repas étaient servis à la place. Les voitures-lits de la Compagnie Internationale des Wagons-Lits circulaient alors dans toute l'Europe. Surnommé la « grande vieille dame » de l'Europe, l'Orient Express en était sans doute un des fleurons les plus prestigieux et demeure aujourd'hui le plus célèbre des trains de luxe de cette époque. Partant de la gare de l'Est à Paris, il traversait la France, l'Allemagne, l'Autriche, la Tchécoslovaquie, la Hongrie et la Roumanie pour arriver finalement à Bucarest après un voyage où l'on servait aux passagers la meilleure nourriture et les meilleurs vins dans un cadre somptueux. D'autres trains que l'*Orient Express* portaient un nom. Le GWR propose ainsi le Cornish Riviera Express entre la gare de Paddington et la Cornouailles, avec un arrêt à Plymouth pour assurer la correspondance avec les paquebots transatlantiques.

C'est à l'occasion de ses funérailles, qu'elle avait minutieusement réglées avant sa mort, survenue le 22 janvier 1901 à l'âge de 83 ans, que la reine Victoria offrit à ses sujets l'un des convois ferroviaires les plus spectaculaires de l'époque. La dépouille de la reine, décédée dans l'île de Wight à Osborne House, fut en effet transportée à bord du yacht royal *Alberta* jusqu'à Portsmouth, d'où elle traversa toute l'Angleterre en train spécial jusqu'à la gare londonienne de Victoria avant d'atteindre finalement le château de Windsor, où elle repose désormais au mausolée royal de Frogmore. Mais la royauté britannique ne fut pas la seule à disposer de trains personnels. Winston Churchill loua ainsi un train spécial complet pour sa campagne électorale de 1910, et le duc de Sutherland possédait en propre une locomotive et une voiture qu'il conservait en Écosse.

Si les locomotives à vapeur, désormais adoptées dans le monde entier en raison de la robustesse, de la fiabilité et de la simplicité de leurs principes de fonctionnement, ne feront pas l'objet de transformations radicales, elles vont cependant bénéficier de constantes améliorations ou adaptations. La cabine de la plupart des locomotives est désormais fermée afin de mieux protéger l'équipe de mécaniciens des intempéries. En 1909, un nouveau type de locomotive articulée, dite Beyer-Garratt, fut construit en Grande-Bretagne pour les lignes difficiles des Tasmanian Railways. Cette machine, qui se composait de deux groupes moteurs indépendants, réunis par un

berceau sur pivot à chaque extrémité du châssis principal supportant la chaudière et le poste de conduite, était particulièrement agile sur les lignes à fort rayon de courbure et présentant des rampes importantes. Ces locomotives furent fréquemment employées sur les réseaux d'Afrique, de l'Inde et de l'Australie.

Mais le succès de la vapeur n'exclut pas d'employer d'autres types de force motrice. En 1897, le Dr Rudolf Diesel, un Allemand, construit une locomotive dont le moteur à essence entraîne un générateur, lequel fournit alors le courant électrique nécessaire au moteur qui actionne les roues ; ainsi naît la première locomotive diesel. La même année, et également en Allemagne, Wilhelm Schmidt a l'idée d'adjoindre un surchauffeur à la chaudière des locomotives ; ce système, qui permet, en augmentant la température de la vapeur produite, de disposer d'une puissance d'expansion accrue à l'intérieur des cylindres et donc d'améliorer le rendement de la locomotive, fait faire un grand pas en avant aux chemins de fer. En 1904, le North Eastern Railway remplace ses machines à vapeur par une locomotive électrique à pantographe pour assurer le service d'une ligne de marchandises, dont un tunnel présente l'inconvénient de s'emplir de fumée au passage des convois traditionnels.

L'application du principe de la voie ferrée, au sens propre, suscite bien d'autres développements. Certains ingénieurs proposent la solution de voitures suspendues, de monorails ou de funiculaires, systèmes qui évitent les problèmes de tracé au sol d'une ligne de chemin de fer « normale » et dont le coût de construction est moindre. C'est à Paris que s'ouvre en 1900 la première ligne de métropolitain entre la porte de Vincennes et la porte Maillot, l'année même où est mis en service le funiculaire de Montmartre. L'année suivante, Wuppertal, au nord-ouest de l'Allemagne, dispose du premier monorail électrique aérien.

Mais l'avenir des chemins de fer passe également par les services de complément. En Grande-Bretagne, le GWR innove en mettant en place non seulement des services de bus mais également des services aériens. En 1903, le GWR met en place la première ligne d'autobus entre Helston et Lizard, pour assurer la connexion avec le train de voyageurs. En 1907, le GWR dispose de 95 bus à moteur, de 400 autres véhicules et d'une flotte importante de camions de livraison. En ce début du XXe siècle, le réseau des compagnies ferroviaires s'étend aux quatre coins du monde comme une véritable toile d'araignée.

The interior of the coach in which Marshal Foch, the Supreme Commander of the Allied Armed Forces, signed the Armistice on 11 November 1918 at Rethondes in France to end the First World War.

Das Innere des Wagens, in dem Marschall Foch, der Oberkommandierende der alliierten Streitkräfte, am 11. November 1918 im Wald von Compiègne den Waffenstillstand mit Deutschland unterzeichnete, mit dem der Erste Weltkrieg zu Ende ging.

L'intérieur de la voiture installée à Rethondes, en France, où le maréchal Foch, Commandant suprême des forces alliées, signa l'Armistice du 11 novembre 1918 marquant la fin de la Première Guerre mondiale.

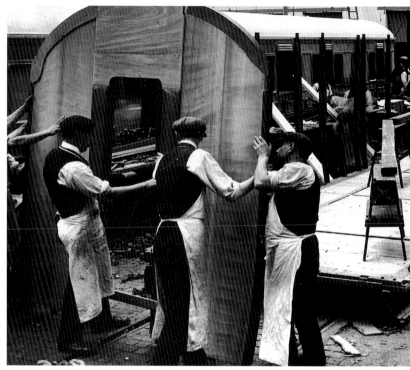

Building the rolling stock, Wolverton, 1910
Wolverton, Bucks, was a true railway town where the works run by the LNWR employed over 5,000 men. The LNWR had a reputation for high standards of craftsmanship. (Opposite, clockwise from top left) French polishing; bodybuilding; stuffing upholstery; framing carriage prints. (Above) Adding the finishing touches.

Waggons aus Wolverton, 1910
Wolverton im englischen Buckinghamshire war eine wahre Eisenbahnstadt, und das Waggonwerk der LNWR beschäftigte über 5000 Personen. Die LNWR war bekannt für ihre hohen Qualitätsstandards. (Gegenüberliegende Seite, im Uhrzeigersinn von oben links) Politur mit Schellack; Karosseriebau; Polsterung; Rahmung von Bildern. (Oben) Die letzte Lackschicht.

L'assemblage du matériel roulant, Wolverton, 1910
Wolverton (Buckinghamshire) était une véritable cité ferroviaire, où plus de 5 000 personnes étaient employées au LNWR, réputé pour la grande qualité de sa production. (Ci-contre, en haut à gauche) Vernissage ; (en haut à droite) carrossage ; (en bas à droite) rembourrage ; (en bas à gauche) encadrement de tableaux. (Ci-dessus) Des ouvriers font les finitions.

Building the locomotives, Crewe, 1910

Crewe was another LNWR town. In 1850 it was a small village but when the works opened in 1843 Crewe fast became the largest and most celebrated locomotive works in Britain. Each locomotive part had to be drawn, cast, moulded, gauged and riveted before the whole was completed. (Opposite) Welding, riveting and moulding engine parts. (Right, above and below) Inside the workshops. Today, only a handful of workshops survive, mostly owned by international engineering companies.

Lokomotiven aus Crewe, 1910

Eine weitere LNWR-Stadt war Crewe. 1850 noch ein Dorf, entwickelte Crewe sich, nachdem 1843 dort ein Betriebswerk eingerichtet wurde, rasch zur Metropole des britischen Lokomotivenbaus. Jedes Teil musste entworfen, gegossen, abgeformt und genietet werden, bis aus den Teilen eine Lokomotive entstand. (Gegenüberliegende Seite) Schweißen, Vernieten und Abformen von Bauteilen. (Rechts, oben und unten) Zwei Blicke in die Werkshallen. Heute können nur noch einige wenige Lokomotivfabriken bestehen, meist als Teil internationaler Großkonzerne.

Construction des locomotives, Crewe, 1910

Crewe était un autre fief du LNWR. Petit village en 1850, la ville devint rapidement le plus grand et le plus célèbre centre de construction de locomotives de Grande-Bretagne lorsque l'usine ouvrit en 1843. Chaque élément de la locomotive était dessiné, coulé, moulé, ajusté et assemblé par rivetage dans ces ateliers. (Ci-contre) Soudage, rivetage et moulage des parties du moteur. (À droite, en haut et en bas) L'intérieur des ateliers. Aujourd'hui, seules subsistent quelques chaînes de montage, la plupart appartenant désormais à des compagnies d'ingénierie internationales.

Queen Victoria's funeral train

The Queen died at Osborne House, the Isle of Wight, on 22 January 1901. Her coffin was taken to London Victoria via the London, Brighton & South Coast Railway in the Diamond Jubilee saloon (left), and then on a gun carriage to Paddington Station (above). The train was wreathed with purple and white decorations and pulled by an engine temporarily named the *Royal Sovereign*, which took her coffin on to St George's Chapel, Windsor.

Königin Victorias Trauerzug

Die Queen starb am 22. Januar 1901 in Osborne House auf der Isle of Wight. Der Leichnam wurde mit der London, Brighton & South Coast Railway im Salonwagen des diamantenen Jubiläums (links) zur Victoria Station und von da per Lafette zur Paddington Station überführt. Dort wartete ein in Purpur und Weiß geschmückter Zug (oben), dessen Lokomotive aus diesem Anlass in *Royal Sovereign* umbenannt wurde, und brachte den Sarg zur St. George's Chapel in Windsor.

Train mortuaire de la reine Victoria

La reine est décédée à Osborne House, dans l'île de Wight, le 22 janvier 1901. Son cercueil fut emmené à la gare Victoria de Londres dans la voiture-salon du Diamond Jubilee (à gauche) par la London, Brighton & South Coast Railway, puis transporté sur un affût de canon jusqu'à la gare de Paddington (ci-dessus). Le train, entièrement décoré en violet et blanc, fut tracté jusqu'à la chapelle St George à Windsor par une locomotive baptisée pour l'occasion *Royal Sovereign*.

Queen Victoria's coach

Victoria was 'charmed' by train travel, not least because she could travel long distances without the ordeal of noisy, staring crowds along the route. (Above) The day compartment of her LNWR saloon, rebuilt in 1895. The walls and ceiling are quilted in silk. The Queen used this carriage until her death.

Victorias Salonwagen

Victoria fand Eisenbahnfahrten »bezaubernd«, nicht zuletzt, weil sie weite Strecken zurücklegen konnte, ohne dass lärmende, neugierige Menschenmengen den Weg säumten. (Oben) Das Wohnzimmer ihres Salonwagens bei der LNWR, 1895 neu ausgestattet. Wände und Decke sind mit Seide ausgeschlagen. Die Queen fuhr mit diesem Wagen bis an ihr Lebensende.

La voiture de la reine Victoria

Victoria était « charmée » par les voyages en train, notamment parce qu'elle pouvait parcourir de longues distances sans être importunée par des foules bruyantes et curieuses massées sur sa route. (Ci-dessus) Le compartiment de jour de sa voiture-salon du LNWR, reconstruit en 1895, présente des parois et un plafond tapissés de soie. La reine utilisa cette voiture jusqu'à sa mort.

Fishguard harbour

The railway companies did not confine themselves to dry land; they also operated a range of services to support their main business. Steamships were operated for both passengers and freight including services across the English Channel, the North Sea and to Ireland. The GWR ran a ferry service from Fishguard (above) to Rosslare, County Waterford, in 1906 and day excursions to Killarney in 1907. (Left) A GWR 'bulldog' 4–4–0 locomotive at Fishguard harbour.

Im Hafen von Fishguard

Die Bahngesellschaften beschränkten ihr Angebot nicht auf den Landverkehr, sondern ergänzten ihr Stammgeschäft mit einer Reihe von Dienstleistungen. Dampfschiffe für Passagiere wie für Frachtgut fuhren auf dem Ärmelkanal, der Nordsee und der Irischen See. Seit 1906 betrieb die GWR einen Fährdienst von Fishguard (oben) nach Rosslare in der irischen Grafschaft Waterford, und 1907 kamen Tagesausflüge nach Killarney hinzu. (Links) Eine 2 B »Bulldog«- Lokomotive der GWR im Hafen von Fishguard.

Le port de Fishguard

Les compagnies de chemin de fer ne se limitaient pas au transport terrestre mais offraient également toute une gamme de services venant compléter leur activité principale. Elles possédaient ainsi des navires à vapeur pour le transport des passagers comme du fret sur des liaisons en Manche, en mer du Nord et vers l'Irlande. En 1906, le GWR assurait un service de ferries entre Fishguard (ci-dessus) et Rosslare (comté de Waterford) et organisait en 1907 des traversées quotidiennes vers Killarney. (À gauche) Une « bulldog » 220 du GWR sur le port de Fishguard.

GWR poster publicity

The railway poster was to develop into a familiar feature of station booking halls and platforms during this decade. Some of the finest poster artists of the day were employed to advertise the places that could be reached by train. The GWR called itself the 'Holiday Line' and exploited its West Country resorts by comparing Cornwall with Italy, proclaiming 'See your own country first – the Cornish Riviera' and 'There is a great similarity between Cornwall and Italy in shape, climate and natural beauties. It was a simpler age. (Above and below) Examples of railway posters, illustrated and letterpress.

GWR-Poster

Plakate der Bahngesellschaften entwickelten sich in diesem Jahrzehnt zum vertrauten Bild in Schalterhallen und auf Bahnsteigen. Plakate von Orten, die sich als Reiseziele anboten, wurden von den besten Plakatkünstlern der Zeit entworfen. Die GWR nannte sich die »Urlaubslinie«, verglich Cornwall mit Italien und machte das Beste aus ihrem Streckennetz im englischen Westen. »Ferien zu Hause – die Riviera von Cornwall« lautete ein Slogan, »nicht nur in den Umrissen, auch in Klima und Schönheit der Natur ist die Ähnlichkeit von Cornwall und Italien groß«. Die Menschen waren damals leichtgläubiger als heute. (Oben und unten) Typische Eisenbahnplakate, illustriert oder mit Text.

Affiches de la GWR

L'affiche ferroviaire va faire partie du décor familier des salles de billets et des quais des gares au cours de cette décennie. Les compagnies de chemin de fer demandent alors à certains des plus talentueux affichistes de l'époque de faire la réclame des endroits accessibles en train. Le GWR y est présenté comme la « Holiday Line » (la voie des vacances) et fait la promotion des stations de villégiature de l'ouest de la Grande-Bretagne en associant la Cornouailles à l'Italie par des slogans tels que « Visitez d'abord votre pays – la Riviera cornouaillaise » ou « La Cornouailles et l'Italie se ressemblent quant à leurs paysages, à leur climat et à leur beauté naturelle ». L'époque sans doute était plus simple! (En haut et en bas) Exemples d'affiches des chemins de fer.

The train now departing…
At 10.30 every morning the *Cornish Riviera Express* left
Paddington Station on the seven-hour journey to Penzance,
Cornwall. Departing here from Platform 1, it took passengers
from London and the Home Counties to the holiday haunts
of the south west on the GWR.

Einsteigen und Türen schließen …
Jeden Vormittag um 10 Uhr 30 verließ der *Cornish Riviera
Express* den Bahnhof Paddington und fuhr binnen sieben
Stunden nach Penzance in Cornwall. Der Zug, hier zur Abfahrt
bereit auf Bahnsteig 1, brachte Reisende aus London und
den Home Counties zu den Ferienorten im Südwesten des
GWR-Netzes.

Le train au départ …
Le *Cornish Riviera Express* du GWR quittait la gare de
Paddington tous les jours à 10 h 30 pour rallier Penzance
(Cornouailles) en sept heures. Partant ici du quai numéro 1,
il emportait les passagers de Londres et des Home Counties
vers les lieux de villégiature du sud-ouest de l'Angleterre.

Passenger and goods porters

(Left) An assortment of porters and sack barrows, or trolleys. The first porters gave directions, carried luggage, unloaded it on a sack barrow and carried it out to waiting omnibuses. They answered questions and closed carriage doors before departure. Freight porters loaded and unloaded goods and at large stations would be responsible for such things as washing carriages, filling oil lamps and sorting panels. For an ambitious man it was the first step on the promotional ladder.

Kofferträger

(Links) Vier Fotos von Dienstmännern und ihren typischen Karren. Die Kofferträger gaben den Fahrgästen Auskünfte, trugen Gepäck und fuhren es auf ihren Sackkarren hinaus zu den wartenden Omnibussen. Sie schlossen auch die Abteiltüren, wenn der Zug bereit zur Abfahrt war. Für den Frachtbetrieb gab es Dienstmänner, die die Güter luden und entluden. Auf den großen Bahnhöfen waren sie auch für das Waschen der Waggons, das Nachfüllen der Öllampen und das Anstecken der Richtungsschilder verantwortlich. Für einen ehrgeizigen Mann war es die erste Stufe auf der Karriereleiter.

Passagers et porteurs

(À gauche) Portraits de porteurs de bagages. Les premiers porteurs indiquaient les directions aux voyageurs, portaient les bagages, les déchargeaient sur des chariots et les amenaient jusqu'aux omnibus. Ils répondaient aux questions et fermaient les portes des fourgons à bagages avant le départ. Les porteurs de colis chargeaient et déchargeaient les marchandises et, dans les grandes gares, étaient responsables notamment du lavage des voitures, du remplissage des lampes à huile et de la mise à jour des panneaux d'affichage. Pour un homme ambitieux, c'était une première marche dans le monde du travail.

Transatlantic luggage and travel
Luggage at Paddington Station after its arrival from the Boston to Southampton boat after approximately a week in transit. Passengers were advised to pack clothing and other necessaries in small flat boxes that could lie easily in cabins. The rest went in the hold.

Transatlantisches Gepäck
Das Gepäck der Passagiere eines Schiffes von Boston nach Southampton traf nach etwa einer Woche in Paddington Station ein. Den Reisenden wurde empfohlen, Kleidung und andere Notwendigkeiten in flache Koffer zu packen, die sich gut in den Kabinen verstauen ließen. Alles andere kam in den Laderaum.

Bagages et voyages transatlantiques
Les bagages sont rassemblés à la gare de Paddington après leur arrivée du bateau de la ligne Boston-Southampton, après une semaine de voyage environ. Il était conseillé aux passagers d'emballer leurs vêtements et autres affaires dans des mallettes plates pouvant facilement se ranger dans les cabines, le reste étant chargé en soute.

Keeping the passenger informed

As more lines opened, the companies felt the need to advertise their services and produced leaflets, handbills and guides. They went on to open up enquiry and booking offices at major stations (see Euston, below) and tried to ensure that train times were accessible (above). Booking was often quite complicated as passengers travelling any distance had to travel on the lines of more than one company.

Informiert sein ist alles

Als der Konkurrenzdruck wuchs, begannen die Gesellschaften für ihre Züge zu werben und brachten Broschüren, Handzettel und Fahrpläne heraus. In den größeren Bahnhöfen öffneten sie Buchungs- und Beratungsbüros (etwa in Euston, unten) und führten Fahrpläne ein (oben). Der Fahrkartenkauf war oft recht kompliziert, denn jeder, der eine längere Reise machte, nahm die Dienste mehrerer Gesellschaften in Anspruch.

L'information des voyageurs

Les compagnies de chemin de fer ont rapidement éprouvé le besoin de faire la publicité sur les services offerts et imprimèrent des prospectus, des brochures et des guides à mesure que de nouvelles lignes ouvraient. Ils ouvrirent des bureaux de réservation et de renseignements dans les grandes gares (comme à Euston, en bas) et s'efforcèrent de rendre les horaires des trains accessibles au public (en haut). Les réservations restaient souvent assez compliquées car les voyageurs parcourant de longues distances devaient emprunter des lignes appartenant à des compagnies différentes.

'That way, madam'

A porter at Leicester Central Station on the Great Central Railway goes about his clock indicator and finger board duties, c. 1900. The GCR – constructed by Sir Edward Watkin – was the last main line to be built.

»Hier entlang, Madam«

Ein Dienstmann der Great Central Railway stellt auf dem Bahnhof von Leicester Abfahrtszeiten ein und hängt Richtungsschilder aus, um 1900. Die GCR, erbaut von Sir Edward Watkin, entstand als letzte der großen britischen Linien.

« Par ici, madame »

Un porteur de la gare centrale de Leicester, du Great Central Railway, met à jour le tableau d'affichage des horaires et l'indicateur des départs, vers 1900. La ligne du GCR, construite par sir Edward Watkin, fut la dernière grande voie ferrée créée.

An integrated service

The railway companies did not limit themselves simply to operating the railways: they aimed to provide an integrated transport system. They had their own stables and horse-drawn vehicles (left and opposite, below), their own bus services to connect stations (opposite, above right) and their own tourist coaches. The GWR's sightseeing tour from Paddington (opposite, above left) began in 1907.

Komplettservice

Die Bahngesellschaften beschränkten sich nicht auf den Betrieb ihrer Eisenbahnstrecken – ihr Ziel war ein integriertes Transportsystem. Sie hatten ihre eigenen Ställe und Pferdewagen (links und gegenüberliegende Seite, unten), eigene Busse für den Verkehr zwischen den Londoner Bahnhöfen (gegenüberliegende Seite, oben rechts) und für Ausflugsfahrten. Die GWR bot erstmals 1907 vom Bahnhof Paddington aus eine Stadtrundfahrt an (gegenüberliegende Seite, oben links).

Un service complet

Les compagnies de chemin de fer ne se contentaient pas de l'exploitation ferroviaire mais visaien à fournir tout un système de transports intégrés. Elles possédaient notamment des voitures à cheval et des écuries (à gauche et ci-contre en bas), disposaient d'un service d'autobus pour relier les gares entre elles (ci-contre, en haut à droite) et de compagnies de fiacres. La visite guidée organisée par le GWR au départ de Paddington (ci-contre, en haut à gauche) fut lancée en 1907.

In the company's service…

Operating a railway was very labour intensive. Workers had a job for life but they also had to work long hours and endure strict discipline. The NER's company rulebook stated that 'Each man shall devote such time as may be required to the company's service'. Here we see (above) a signalman, (above right) a guard and (below right) a fireman doing just that.

Die Erfordernisse des Betriebs

Der Bahnbetrieb war sehr arbeitsintensiv. Wer einen Posten bei der Bahn bekam, hatte ausgesorgt, aber dafür wurde strikte Disziplin erwartet, und ein Arbeitstag war lang. Im Regelbuch der NER hieß es: »Jeder Mann hat soviel seiner Zeit einzusetzen, wie es die Erfordernisse des Betriebs verlangen.« Hier sehen wir (oben) einen Weichensteller in einem Stellwerk, (rechts oben) einen Schaffner und (rechts unten) einen Heizer, die alle drei diesen Grundsatz beherzigen.

Au service de la compagnie …

L'exploitation d'un chemin de fer nécessitait une main-d'œuvre importante. Si les ouvriers pouvaient garder toute leur vie leur emploi, ils devaient en revanche travailler de longues heures et se soumettre à une stricte discipline. Le règlement du NER stipulait notamment que « chaque homme doit consacrer autant de temps qu'il est nécessaire au service de la compagnie ». On voit ici un aiguilleur (ci-dessus), un chef de train (ci-dessus à droite) et un chauffeur (en bas à droite).

Universal pride

Devotion to the company was not a solely British phenomenon. The pride of these Swedish railway employees (below), and of the fireman (top left) and guard (top right) is evident. Medals and certificates were often given to long-serving employees; some started as young as fourteen and had worked their way to the top job of engine driver by the time they reached retirement.

Stolze Eisenbahner

Treue Bahnangestellte gab es auch auf dem Kontinent. Dass die Belegschaft dieses schwedischen Bahnhofes (unten), der Heizer (oben links) und der Schaffner (oben rechts) auf ihre Arbeit stolz sind, ist nicht zu übersehen. Langjährige Angestellte wurden oft mit Medaillen oder Urkunden ausgezeichnet; manche fingen schon mit 14 Jahren an, und wenn sie das Rentenalter erreichten, hatten sie sich zum Lokomotivführer hochgearbeitet, der angesehensten Position.

Une fierté universelle

L'attachement du personnel des chemins de fer à leur compagnie n'est pas un phénomène uniquement britannique et la fierté de ces cheminots suédois (en bas), de ce chauffeur (en haut à gauche) ou de ce chef de train (en haut à droite) est manifeste. Les cheminots ayant travaillé longtemps étaient fréquemment récompensés par des médailles et des diplômes. Certains étaient entrés dans la compagnie dès 14 ans et avaient exercé tous les emplois jusqu'à atteindre le sommet de l'échelle en devenant mécanicien à l'âge de la retraite.

EXIT

Grand American stations

The original Penn Station, New York (above), opened in 1910. Cathedral-like in dimension, it featured Doric columns, colonnades, sandstone eagles and bronze statues. Fifty years later, it was demolished to make way for Madison Square Garden and replaced by a smaller station underground. Union Station, Washington, DC (opposite), survived, however, and was extensively restored and remodelled in the 1980s.

Prachtbahnhöfe in Amerika

Die ursprüngliche Penn Station in New York (oben), eröffnet 1910, war groß wie eine Kathedrale und konnte mit dorischen Säulen, Kolonnaden, Adlern aus Sandstein und Bronzestatuen aufwarten. 50 Jahre später musste sie dem Madison Square Garden weichen, und der Bahnhof wurde in den Untergrund verbannt. Union Station in Washington, D.C., (gegenüberliegende Seite) überlebte hingegen und wurde in den 1980er Jahren aufwendig restauriert und neu gestaltet.

Grandes gares américaines

Abondamment ornée de colonnes doriques, de colonnades, d'aigles en grès et de statues en bronze, la gare new-yorkaise de Pennsylvania, inaugurée en 1910, avait les dimensions d'une cathédrale. Elle fut détruite cinquante ans plus tard pour laisser place au Madison Square Garden et à une gare souterraine plus modeste. Union Station, la gare de Washington (ci-contre), fut conservée après d'importants travaux de restauration et de transformation dans les années 1980.

Paddington Station

Inspired by the Crystal Palace and the main station in Munich, Paddington, opened in 1854, was the first London station to have a private entrance and waiting room for royalty. Although remembered for holiday traffic, it was important for milk traffic at the time. By 1900, Paddington was handling 3,000 milk churns daily as well as meat, fish, flowers and vegetables in season.

Paddington Station

Die vom Crystal Palace und dem Münchner Hauptbahnhof inspirierte, 1854 fertig gestellte Paddington Station war der erste Londoner Bahnhof mit einem eigenen Eingang und Warteraum für die Königsfamilie. Die Londoner haben Paddington als den Bahnhof im Gedächtnis, von dem aus man in die Ferien fuhr, aber seinerzeit war er auch wichtig für die Versorgung der Stadt. Im Jahr 1900 kamen dort 3000 Kannen Milch pro Tag an, dazu Fleisch, Fisch, Blumen und Gemüse der Saison.

La gare de Paddington

Inspirée par le Crystal Palace et la grande gare de Munich, la gare de Paddington, inaugurée en 1854, fut la première gare londonienne à disposer d'un accès privé et d'une salle d'attente réservés à la famille royale. Cette gare, très active en période de vacances, jouait également à l'époque un rôle important dans le trafic laitier. En 1900, Paddington voyait ainsi passer quotidiennement 3 000 bidons de lait mais aussi, en saison, de la viande, du poisson, des fleurs et des légumes.

Euston Station
Euston was London's first main line station. Built for the
London & Birmingham Railway under the supervision of
Robert Stephenson and designed by the architect Philip
Hardwick, it opened to the public on 20 July 1837. It is remem-
bered for its entrance portico (above), a Doric arch, and its
Great Hall which opened later, in 1849. Grand in its way, too,
was the GWR's Snow Hill Station, Birmingham, 1910 (opposite).

Euston Station
Euston, unter der Leitung von Robert Stephenson für die
London & Birmingham Railway erbaut und gestaltet von dem
Architekten Philip Hardwick, wurde am 20. Juli 1837 als erster
der Londoner Großbahnhöfe eingeweiht. Denkwürdig waren
der dorische Torbogen (oben) und die 1849 hinzugekommene
Schalterhalle Great Hall. Doch auch die Snow Hill Station der
GWR in Birmingham, 1910 (gegenüberliegende Seite), konnte
sich sehen lassen.

La gare d'Euston
Euston fut la première gare de grande ligne de Londres.
Construite pour le London & Birmingham Railway sous la
supervision de Robert Stephenson et dessinée par l'architecte
Philip Hardwick, elle fut ouverte au public le 20 juillet 1837.
On se souvient de l'arche dorique de son portique d'entrée
(ci-dessus) et de son grand hall, achevé en 1849. La gare GWR
de Snow Hill, à Birmingham, était également un édifice
majestueux (ci-contre en 1910).

Swedish winter weather
(Left and opposite) Winter was harsh. According to reports of an English engineer, Charles Broxup, who worked on the construction of the iron ore line from Gällivare to Luleå from 1884 to 1891, the winter weather conditions were extreme: 'In many places we had to cross bogs which were nothing less than liquid mud. One morning 51° C of frost was recorded.' (Above) A Swedish compound locomotive 0–6–0 built in 1895 by Nyqvist and Holm at Trollhättan.

Schwedisches Winterwetter
(Links und gegenüberliegende Seite) Ein harter Winter. Der englische Ingenieur Charles Broxup, der zwischen 1884 und 1891 beim Bau der Eisenerzbahn von Gällivare nach Luleå dabei war, beschreibt das Winterwetter: »An vielen Stellen mussten wir Sümpfe durchqueren, die schlicht und einfach flüssiger Schlamm waren. Einmal maßen wir morgens minus 51 Grad Celsius.« (Oben) Eine schwedische C Lokomotive, 1895 bei Nyqvist und Holm in Trollhättan gebaut.

Hiver suédois …
(À gauche et ci-contre) L'hiver est rude. D'après les comptes-rendus de Charles Broxup, un ingénieur anglais qui travailla de 1884 à 1891 à la construction de la ligne de transport du minerai de fer entre Gälliware et Luleå, les conditions climatiques hivernales étaient extrêmes : « En de nombreux endroits, nous devions franchir des tourbières qui n'étaient rien d'autre que de la boue liquide. Un matin, on enregistra -51 °C. » (Ci-dessus) Une locomotive 030 compound suédoise construite en 1895 par Nyqvist et Holm, à Trollhättan.

...and Swedish railways

Swedish railways got off to a slow start but by 1899 the demand for locomotives was so great that neither Swedish nor other European companies
could supply enough; engines were therefore imported from the USA.
By 1900, the Swedish network stretched to 11,000 kilometres, of which
1,500 were privately owned.

... und schwedische Eisenbahnen

Die schwedischen Eisenbahnen kamen nur langsam in Fahrt, doch 1899 war
der Bedarf an Lokomotiven schon so groß, dass weder die einheimischen
noch andere europäische Lieferanten ihn decken konnten, und so importierte
man Lokomotiven aus den USA. Im Jahr 1900 umfasste das schwedische
Streckennetz 11 000 Kilometer, davon 1500 in privater Hand.

... et chemins de fer suédois

Si le réseau ferré suédois se développa lentement, en 1899 la demande en
locomotives des chemins de fer était si forte qu'aucune entreprise, suédoise ou
européenne, ne pouvait en fournir suffisamment. Ces machines furent donc
importées des États-Unis. En 1900, les chemins de fer suédois s'étendaient sur
11 000 kilomètres, dont 1 500 appartenaient à des compagnies privées.

Shaping the landscape (overleaf)

Since the early days of the railways its architecture has reshaped the landscape. These two massive structures can be seen in north-eastern England,
the birthplace of the locomotive. Durham viaduct (above) was built as an
eleven-arch stone structure in 1857. The high level bridge in Newcastle (below)
opened in 1849. It had three tracks on the upper deck and a roadway on the
lower level.

Die Bahn prägt die Landschaft (folgende Doppelseite)

Von Anfang an hat der Eisenbahnbau die Landschaft umgestaltet. Diese
beiden Großbauten sind im Nordosten Englands zu bewundern, das als die
Wiege der Eisenbahn gilt: Das elfbögige, aus massivem Stein gebaute Viadukt
von Durham (oben) entstand 1857. Die Hochbrücke von Newcastle (unten)
eröffnete 1849 mit drei Bahntrassen auf der oberen Etage und einer Straße
in der unteren.

Transformer le paysage (pages suivantes)

L'architecture ferroviaire a transformé le paysage dès les débuts du chemin
de fer. Cela est particulièrement évident dans le nord-est de l'Angleterre, la
patrie de la locomotive, où furent construits ces deux ouvrages : le viaduc de
Durham, construit en 1857, franchissait une partie de la ville sur onze arches
de pierre (en haut) ; le pont surélevé de Newcastle, inauguré en 1849, offrait
trois voies au niveau supérieur et une route au niveau inférieur (en bas).

Bridging England and Scotland

The *Flying Scotsman* service, which operated between London and Edinburgh, celebrated its centenary in 1962. Here it is seen crossing the Royal Border Bridge at Berwick-upon-Tweed in Northumberland in 1903. The bridge was built in 1850 and featured twenty-eight arches. The photograph is by A.H. Robinson.

Von England nach Schottland

Der Schnellzug *Flying Scotsman*, der zwischen London und Edinburgh verkehrte, feierte 1962 sein hundertjähriges Jubiläum. In dieser Aufnahme von A. H. Robinson sehen wir ihn 1903 auf der Royal Border Bridge in Berwick-upon-Tweed, Northumberland. Die Brücke mit ihren 28 Bögen entstand 1850.

Relier l'Angleterre à l'Écosse

Le *Flying Scotsman*, qui assurait la liaison entre Londres et Édimbourg, célébra son centenaire en 1962. On le voit ici traverser le Royal Border Bridge à Berwick-upon-Tweed (Northumberland), en 1903. Ce pont, construit en 1850, comptait 28 arches. La photographie est due à A. H. Robinson.

The Transandine

The Transandine Railway runs between Los Andes, Chile, and Mendoza, Argentina. Many of the railways in South America were owned and funded by British companies seeking business with Argentine counterparts. Opened in 1910, the Transandine was a remarkable feat of engineering, not least because of the skill required in negotiating the steep gradients, and the frequent threat of avalanches.

Die Andenbahn

Die Andenbahn verläuft zwischen dem chilenischen Los Andes und Mendoza in Argentinien. Viele südamerikanische Strecken wurden von britischen Gesellschaften, die mit argentinischen Unternehmen ins Geschäft kommen wollten, betrieben und finanziert. Die 1910 eröffnete Andenbahn war eine Meisterleistung der Ingenieure, die starke Steigungen zu bewältigen hatte und ständiger Lawinengefahr ausgesetzt war.

Le Transandin

Le chemin de fer Transandin relie Los Andes (Chili) à Mendoza (Argentine). Une grande partie des chemins de fer d'Amérique du Sud furent créés et appartenaient à des compagnies britanniques qui désiraient travailler avec leurs équivalents argentins. Inauguré en 1910, le Transandin était un véritable exploit d'ingénierie, entre autres en raison des forts pourcentages des pentes et la fréquente menace d'avalanches.

Mountain railway system

A view of the Rimutaka Incline in North Island, New Zealand, 1920, which used the Fell railway system, named after its inventor, J.B. Fell. This operated using the friction between the wheels of specially designed locomotives and an additional centre rail. This passenger train is being pulled up a gradient by no less than four locomotives. The line operated between 1878 and 1955.

Bergfahrten

Eine Ansicht der Rimutaka-Steigung auf der neuseeländischen Nordinsel, 1920, wo Lokomotiven mit dem (nach dem Erfinder J. B. Fell benannten) Fell-System ausgerüstet waren, bei dem zusätzliche Triebräder auf eine dritte Mittelschiene griffen. Diesen Personenzug ziehen nicht weniger als vier Lokomotiven einen Berg hinauf. Die Linie war von 1878 bis 1955 in Betrieb.

Réseau ferré de montagne

Une vue du Rimutaka Incline, dans l'île du Nord (Nouvelle-Zélande), en 1920. Cette ligne, exploitée de 1878 à 1955, utilisait le système Fell (du nom de son inventeur, J. B. Fell), qui nécessitait l'emploi de locomotives spéciales disposant de roues venant serrer un rail central. La rampe est si forte que quatre locomotives au moins sont nécessaires pour tracter ce train de voyageurs.

The observation car

This was designed to be attached to the rear of the train so that passengers could enjoy the scenic routes. From the outside it was very much like a standard coach with extra large windows. (Top left) This one ran from Llandudno to Llanberis in North Wales. (Above left) An English Edwardian car. (Above right) An example of a Japanese '*Momoyamu*'.

Panoramawagen

Solche Wagen wurden auf landschaftlich schönen Strecken ans Ende des Zuges gehängt und boten den Fahrgästen einen besseren Ausblick. Von außen wirkten sie wie normale Waggons, nur dass die Fenster wesentlich größer waren. (Ganz oben) Dieses Exemplar fuhr in Nordwales von Llandudno nach Llanberis. (Oben links) Ein englischer Wagen aus edwardianischer Zeit. (Rechts) Ein Beispiel für den japanischen *Momoyamu*.

La voiture panoramique

Les voitures panoramiques étaient accrochées en queue de convoi des lignes touristiques afin que les voyageurs puissent profiter pleinement des paysages traversés. (En haut à gauche) Cette voiture était en service entre Llandudno et Llanberis, au nord du Pays de Galles. (Ci-dessus à gauche) Une voiture anglaise édouardienne. (À droite) Une « Momoyamu » japonaise.

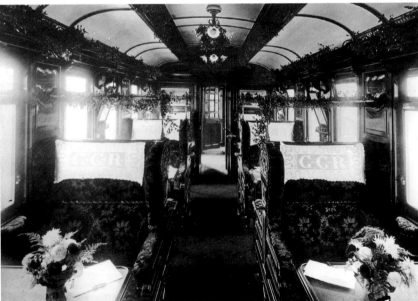

Railway catering

Influenced by the American Pullman cars, the first dining car was introduced to Britain by the Midland Railway in the 1870s. Before this passengers had to make a quick dash to refreshment rooms at designated stops for dining purposes, or book a luncheon basket. The first daily diners ran between Leeds and London in 1879. By this time they had kitchens and an adjacent smoking room.

Das leibliche Wohl

Nach dem Vorbild der amerikanischen Pullmanwagen führte die Midland Railway die ersten britischen Speisewagen in den 1870er Jahren ein. Zuvor hatten Züge an bestimmten Bahnhöfen zu Mahlzeiten länger gehalten, und die Fahrgäste drängten sich in den Teestuben, oder sie bestellten Lunchkörbe vor. Der erste tägliche Speisewagen, schon mit Küche und eigenem Rauchsalon, verkehrte 1879 zwischen Leeds und London.

Restauration en chemin de fer

La première voiture-restaurant, inspirée par les voitures Pullman américaines, fut introduite en Grande-Bretagne dans les années 1870 par le Midland Railway. Auparavant, les voyageurs devaient se précipiter au buffet des gares traversées afin de se restaurer ou de commander un panier-repas. Les premières voitures-restaurants, qui disposaient à l'époque de cuisines et d'un fumoir, furent exploitées en 1879 entre Leeds et Londres.

Down boy!

Dogs too travelled by and worked for the railways. Flossie (above) was a 'collecting dog'. From the end of the 19th to the mid-20th century, collecting dogs were a familiar sight at large stations where they collected money for railway charities. Cared for by station staff, they patrolled platforms to entice travellers to donate their loose change. Special carriages were set aside for dogs to travel to shows (below left and right) or go hunting (opposite).

Sitz!

Auch Hunde fuhren Bahn und arbeiteten bei der Bahn. Flossie (oben) war ein »Spendenhund«. Vom späten 19. bis in die Mitte des 20. Jahrhunderts waren solche Hunde, von der Belegschaft versorgt, ein vertrauter Anblick auf den großen Bahnhöfen, wo sie für wohltätige Zwecke Geld sammelten. Sie patrouillierten entlang der Bahnsteige, und Reisende steckten ihr Kleingeld in die Sammelbüchsen. Hunde, die zu Ausstellungen (unten links und rechts) oder auf die Jagd (gegenüberliegende Seite) fuhren, hatten ihre eigenen Wagen.

Couché !

Les chiens pouvaient également voyager en train et travaillaient pour les chemins de fer. Flossie (en haut) était un de ces « chiens collecteurs ». De la fin du XIXᵉ siècle jusqu'au milieu du XXᵉ siècle, ces chiens furent un spectacle familier des grandes gares, où ils collectaient de l'argent pour les œuvres de charité des chemins de fer. Soignés par les cheminots, ils patrouillaient ainsi sur les quais afin d'inciter les voyageurs à leur donner un peu d'argent. Des voitures spéciales étaient spécialement aménagées pour les chiens voyageant à l'occasion de concours (en bas à gauche et à droite) ou de parties de chasse (ci-contre).

Child's play

In 1903 *The Ballad of Casey Jones*, a folk song by T. Lawrence Siebert, was published and was a sheet music best-seller. Railways were a romantic attraction for children, a new toy and a source of free amusement. (Above) American youngsters climb onto a box car, oblivious of any dangers.

Ein Kinderspiel

Im Jahr 1903 kam T. Lawrence Sieberts Folksong *The Ballad of Casey Jones* als Notenheft heraus und verkaufte sich reißend. Für Kinder waren die Eisenbahnen eine neue Attraktion, ein Abenteuer, noch dazu kostenlos. (Oben) Junge Amerikaner klettern auf einen Güterwagen und kümmern sich um keine Gefahr.

Jeux d'enfants

En 1903, *The Ballad of Casey Jones*, une chanson populaire de T. Lawrence Siebert, devint rapidement un succès. Les chemins de fer exerçaient un attrait romantique sur les enfants, qui y voyaient un nouveau jouet et une source d'amusements. (En haut) Ces jeunes Américains grimpent sur un wagon de marchandises sans souci du danger.

Day trippers

The railways made day trips to the seaside easy and affordable for Londoners. Sea bathing increased in popularity and growing prosperity led to an increase in demand for travel. 'Trippers' were an important source of revenue. (Above) This London, Brighton & South Coast third class compartment carries children on an outing to Bognor in 1913.

Ausflügler

Den Londonern ermöglichte die Eisenbahn einfachere und erschwinglichere Tagesausflüge an die See. Im Meerwasser zu baden war beliebter denn je, höherer Wohlstand ließ die Nachfrage nach solchen Fahrten weiter steigen, und die Sonntagsausflügler füllten die Kassen der Bahngesellschaften. (Oben) Dieses Dritter-Klasse-Abteil der London, Brighton & South Coast Railway bringt 1913 junge Ausflügler nach Bognor.

Vacanciers d'un jour

Les chemins de fer permettaient aux Londoniens de se rendre plus facilement et à moindres frais au bord de la mer. Les stations balnéaires connaissant une popularité croissante grâce à une plus grande prospérité, la demande de voyages augmentait et les nouveaux vacanciers devenaient une source importante de profits pour les compagnies. (Ci-dessus) Des enfants partent en excursion à Bognor, en 1913, dans un compartiment de troisième classe du London, Brighton & South Coast.

'Happy as a sandboy'

The lure of the seaside cut across the classes. Working-class children took day trips to the seaside with Sunday schools (above) while the middle classes (left) took holidays by the sea. There were popular resorts such as Blackpool, Skegness and Clacton, and more genteel ones such as Lytham St Anne's and Southport. The latter provided an excursionists' day nursery where children under five could be left while their parents enjoyed themselves.

Jedem sein Schäufelchen

Das Meer war eine Attraktion für Arm und Reich. Arbeiterkinder machten Ausflüge mit der Sonntagsschule (oben), die Mittelschicht (links) konnte sich ganze Urlaube in den Badeorten leisten. Blackpool, Skegness und Clacton waren populäre Ziele, Orte wie Lytham St. Anne's oder Southport galten als vornehmer. Letzteres bot einen Kindergarten an, wo Kinder unter fünf den Tag verbringen konnten, während die Eltern sich amüsierten.

« Heureux comme un poisson dans l'eau »

Les bords de mer attiraient toutes les classes sociales. Ces enfants d'ouvriers se contentent d'aller à la mer avec leur école du dimanche (ci-dessus) tandis que les Anglais de la classe moyenne y passent leurs vacances (à gauche). Blackpool, Skegness et Clacton étaient des stations balnéaires populaires, tandis que Lytham St Anne's et Southport étaient plus élégantes, cette dernière disposant d'une garderie de jour pour les enfants de moins de cinq ans des vacanciers.

The Henley Royal Regatta
The Henley Regatta, an annual amateur rowing event, began in 1859. Held on the River Thames each year in July, it has long been patronised by the reigning monarch. (Above) Visitors arrive from Paddington on the Great Western Railway, 1911. By this time Henley had become an international sporting event.

Royal Regatta in Henley
Jährlich im Juli fand seit 1859 auf der Themse die Amateur-Ruderregatta von Henley statt, zu deren Gästen traditioneller-weise auch der Monarch gehörte. (Oben) Zuschauer treffen mit dem Zug der Great Western Railway von Paddington ein, 1911. Zu dieser Zeit war Henley bereits ein internationales Sportereignis.

La Henley Royal Regatta
Longtemps parrainée par le monarque régnant et organisée pour la première fois en 1859, la Henley Regatta est une compé-tition d'aviron amateur qui se déroule sur la Tamise chaque année en juillet. (Ci-dessus) Des spectateurs arrivent à Henley en provenance de Paddington par le Great Western Railway en 1911. Henley est à cette époque un événement sportif de renommée internationale.

Mobile propaganda

During times of political upheaval, the mobility of the railways offered great advantages. (Above) Two years after the Revolution, in 1919, workers in the Ukraine queue to visit a propaganda information coach. These were used to raise Lenin's profile and to spread his ideological message. (Below) Before the Revolution. A Russian church service on the Manchurian Railway, 1906.

Mobile Propaganda

In politisch unruhigen Zeiten war die Beweglichkeit der Eisenbahn ein großer Vorteil. (Oben) 1919, zwei Jahre nach der Revolution, stehen Arbeiter in der Ukraine an einem mobilen Informationsstand an. Mit solchen Ausstellungen machte man Lenin im Land bekannt und sorgte für die Verbreitung der revolutionären Ideen. (Unten) Vor der Revolution: eine rollende orthodoxe Kirche auf den Gleisen der Mandschurischen Eisenbahn, 1906.

Propagande mobile

Les chemins de fer offraient l'avantage d'une grande mobilité à une époque d'importants bouleversements politiques. (Ci-dessus) Deux ans après la révolution russe, en 1919, des ouvriers ukrainiens font la queue pour monter dans une voiture de propagande, où l'on glorifiait la personnalité de Lénine en propageant son idéologie. (En bas) Avant la Révolution, en 1906 : une messe de l'Église orthodoxe russe dans une voiture des chemins de fer de Mandchourie.

Railways reach Arabia

To improve communications, the Turks built the Hedjaz railway. (Right) The opening ceremony of the line from Damascus to Medina, a line which was completed in 1908. Under the arch the chief engineer, Mouktar Bey, gives the opening speech at the Ville sainte.

Bis nach Arabien

Die Türken bauten ihre Verkehrswege mit der Hedschasbahn aus. (Rechts) Die Eröffnungsfeier der 1908 fertig gestellten Linie von Damaskus nach Medina – unter dem Torbogen von der Ville sainte hält Chefingenieur Mouktar Bey die Festrede.

Le chemin de fer atteint l'Arabie

Les Turcs construisirent le chemin de fer du Hedjaz afin d'améliorer les communications à l'intérieur de leur empire. (À droite) Achevée en 1908, la ligne entre Damas et Médine fut inaugurée dans la Ville sainte par l'ingénieur en chef Mouktar Bey (sous l'arche).

Deluge and devastation

An American Pennsylvanian Railroad freight train derailed and tipped over by floodwater. In 1913 the Ohio River valley flooded: many towns were submerged and more than 500 people died. The cost of reconstruction to the Pennsylvania Railroad and its affiliates was over $5,500,000.

Zerstörerische Fluten

Ein Güterzug der amerikanischen Pennsylvania Railroad ist auf einem unterspülten Streckenabschnitt umgekippt. 1913 gab es im Tal des Ohio schwere Überschwemmungen; ganze Städte standen unter Wasser, über 500 Menschen kamen um. Mehr als 5½ Millionen Dollar waren notwendig, um die Pennsylvania Railroad und ihre Nebenstrecken wieder instand zu setzen.

Déluge et dévastation

Ce train de marchandises de l'American Pennsylvania Railroad a déraillé à cause des inondations. En 1913, l'Ohio débordait, submergeant de nombreuses villes en faisant plus de 500 victimes. Le coût de la reconstruction du Pennsylvanian Railroad et de ses filiales dépassa les 5 500 000 dollars.

Berlin crash

Accidents happened in the city too. In September 1908, two trains collided on the Berlin overhead, leaving both precariously balanced above concerned onlookers. If nothing else the picture shows how standards of safety at the site of an accident have changed down the years.

Berliner Unglück

Auch in den Städten ging es nicht ohne Unfälle ab. Im September 1908 stießen zwei Züge der Berliner Hochbahn zusammen, und beide hängen bedrohlich wackelig über den Schaulustigen. Zumindest die Sicherungsmaßnahmen am Unfallort haben sich in den Jahren seither gebessert.

Accident à Berlin

Les accidents de chemin de fer pouvaient également se produire en ville. En septembre 1908, deux trains entrèrent en collision sur un viaduc de Berlin et restèrent suspendus au-dessus des spectateurs. La photographie montre bien l'évolution des normes de sécurité sur le lieu d'un accident.

Britain goes to war

Railways were vital in times of war, not least for transporting troops. Britain declared war on Germany on 4 August 1914; one hour later the Railway Executive took control of the railways from 35 Parliament Street, Westminster. The railways were now under State control. For the first time, Britain's railways were run as a single system and would have to work together in the national interest. (Above left and right) Soldiers embark, some after fond farewells.

Die Briten ziehen in den Krieg

In Kriegszeiten waren Eisenbahnen von entscheidender Bedeutung, nicht zuletzt für den Truppentransport. Am 4. August 1914 erklärte Großbritannien Deutschland den Krieg; schon eine Stunde später übernahm das Kriegsministerium das Kommando über das Eisenbahnnetz. Erstmals fuhren alle britischen Bahnen unter gemeinsamer Leitung und mussten im nationalen Interesse zusammenarbeiten. (Oben links und rechts) Soldaten rücken ein, mancher zärtlich verabschiedet.

La Grande-Bretagne entre en guerre

Les chemins de fer étaient vitaux en période de conflit, entre autres pour transporter les troupes. Une heure après que la Grande-Bretagne déclare la guerre à l'Allemagne, le 4 août 1914, l'État prend le contrôle du réseau ferré par l'intermédiaire de la Direction des Chemins de fer, installée au 35 Parliament Street, à Westminster. Pour la première fois de leur histoire, les compagnies de chemin de fer britanniques sont unifiées pour concourir ensemble à l'intérêt national. (Ci-dessus à gauche et à droite) Des soldats embarquent pour le front, certains après de touchants adieux.

'Goodbyee, goodbyee...'
With the country's railways providing mass transportation for troops from Britain to the Continent, troop trains were coordinated by army area commands; many soldiers, like these (above), passed through London Victoria on their way to France and beyond. For those who never returned, it was a true soldier's farewell.

»Auf Wiederseh'n ...«
Britische Truppen fuhren mit der Bahn auf den Kontinent; die Rekrutierungsbehörden stellten die Züge in ihren Bereichen zusammen, und viele einrückende Männer passierten auf ihrem Weg an die Front die Londoner Victoria Station (oben). Für diejenigen, die nicht zurückkamen, wenigstens ein Gruß zum Abschied.

« Au revoir, au revoir ... »
Les différents commandements militaires des régions britanniques coordonnent la circulation des trains pour assurer le transport des troupes entre la Grande-Bretagne et le continent. Nombre des soldats passaient par la gare londonienne de Victoria pour se rendre en France et sur les fronts (ci-dessus). L'au revoir devint un adieu pour tous ceux qui ne revinrent jamais au pays.

Wartime livery

A camouflaged German artillery train (above) and an Austro-Hungarian armoured train (below), c. 1916. During the First World War, railway operating and construction corps were formed on both sides. Some locomotives were especially built for military service while others were requisitioned and adapted. Because huge steam locomotives and their exhaust made excellent targets for artillery spotters, trains had to be both armoured and camouflaged.

Tarnen und täuschen

Ein deutscher Artilleriezug mit Tarnanstrich (oben) und ein österreichischer Panzerzug (unten) ca. 1916. Im Ersten Weltkrieg wurden auf beiden Seiten spezielle Divisionen für den Bau und den Betrieb der Eisenbahnen gegründet. Einige Lokomotiven entstanden speziell für den Kriegseinsatz, andere wurden requiriert und umgebaut. Da die großen Loks mit ihren Dampfwolken gute Ziele für die Artillerieschützen waren, panzerte und tarnte man die Züge.

Décorations de guerre

Un convoi d'artillerie allemand camouflé (en haut) et un train blindé austro-hongrois (en bas), vers 1916. Chacun des adversaires créa des unités spéciales chargées de la construction et de l'exploitation des chemins de fer au cours de la Première Guerre mondiale. L'armée fit construire spécialement des locomotives ou modifier celles qu'elle réquisitionnait pour les adapter à ses besoins, notamment en les faisant blinder et camoufler car la fumée des cheminées des locomotives à vapeur en faisait d'excellentes cibles pour les observateurs de l'artillerie.

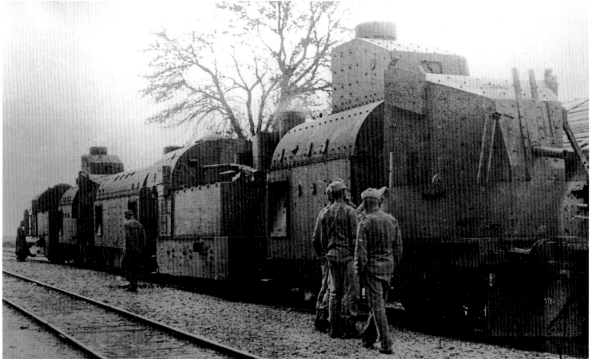

Transporting troops and equipment
(Above) French gunners hoist a shell on to a large camouflaged gun which is to be moved around by rail, c. 1918. (Below) Aftermath of the worst rail disaster in Britain. A troop train collided with a passenger train at Gretna Green in Scotland, killing 227 people. Here firemen douse the last of the flames.

Männer und Waffen für die Front
(Oben) Französische Kanoniere hieven eine Granate auf ein großes, mit Tarnfarben bemaltes Geschütz, das per Bahn an die Front kommt, um 1918. (Unten) Das schlimmste britische Eisenbahn-unglück aller Zeiten: Beim schottischen Gretna Green prallte ein Truppentransportzug mit einem Personenzug zusammen; 227 Menschen fanden den Tod. Hier löschen Feuerwehrmänner die letzten Flammen.

Transport des troupes et du matériel
(En haut) Des artilleurs français hissent un obus sur un canon d'artillerie camouflé monté sur bogies, vers 1918. (En bas) Les pompiers noient les dernières flammes d'un convoi de transport de troupes entré en collision avec un train de voyageurs à Gretna Green (Écosse), faisant 227 victimes ; c'est à ce jour le plus important accident de chemin de fer en Grande-Bretagne.

Railways at war

War necessitated the movement of vast armies and their machines from place to place. Military campaigns relied on supplies and good communications and the railways facilitated all this for the first time in the war. (Above left) Russian troops deserting, 1916; (above right) German troops heading for the Front, 1915. (Opposite, clockwise from top left) Soldiers on the move: British; French; Canadian; Italian.

Kriegsbetrieb

Der Krieg machte den Transport ganzer Armeen und ihres Geräts erforderlich. Feldzüge waren auf Nachschub und gute Nachrichtenverbindungen angewiesen, und all das bewerkstelligte die Eisenbahn ungleich leichter als zuvor. (Oben links) Desertierende russische Truppen, 1916; (oben rechts) deutsche Soldaten auf dem Weg an die Front, 1915. (Gegenüberliegende Seite, im Uhrzeigersinn von oben links) Soldaten unterwegs: Briten, Franzosen, Kanadier, Italiener.

Les chemins de fer en guerre

Le chemin de fer facilite le déplacement de troupes nombreuses et de leur équipement, ainsi que leur approvisionnement, que nécessitent les mouvements du front et les différentes campagnes militaires. (En haut à gauche) Les troupes russes désertent en 1916. (En haut à droite) Les troupes allemandes se rendent sur le front, en 1915. (Ci-contre) Les soldats en déplacement: britanniques (en haut à gauche), français (en haut à droite), canadiens (en bas à droite) et italiens (en bas à gauche).

Ambulance trains
First introduced during the American Civil War, ambulance trains saw much service in the Great War. (Above and below) American army trains at London St Pancras, 1 January 1918. Repatriated casualties were conveyed by ambulance train from ports to local stations and then by road to hospitals near their homes. Movements of such trains were announced in the press and at stations so that local people could bring gifts of food, flowers and newspapers for the wounded.

Lazarettzüge
Lazarette auf Schienen, wie sie erstmals im amerikanischen Bürgerkrieg zum Einsatz kamen, waren im Weltkrieg allgegenwärtig. (Oben und unten) Züge der U.S.-Armee auf dem Londoner Bahnhof St. Pancras, 1. Januar 1918. Zurückkehrende Verwundete wurden per Lazarettzug von den Häfen zu lokalen Bahnhöfen und von dort mit Ambulanzen in heimatnahe Krankenhäuser gebracht. Die Fahrpläne wurden in der Presse und an Bahnhöfen bekannt gemacht, sodass die Bevölkerung Nahrungsmittel, Blumen und Zeitungen für die Verwundeten bringen konnte.

Les trains sanitaires
Mis en service pour la première fois lors de la guerre de Sécession, les trains sanitaires furent très utilisés pendant la Grande Guerre. (En haut et en bas) Des trains militaires américains à la gare londonienne de St Pancras, le 1er janvier 1918. Les blessés rapatriés étaient transportés en train sanitaire des ports jusqu'aux gares locales puis par la route vers les hôpitaux les plus proches de leur domicile. Les déplacements de ces trains étaient annoncés dans la presse et dans les gares afin que les habitants puissent venir offrir nourriture, fleurs et journaux aux blessés.

Nursing the wounded

Ambulance trains meant the employment of women on the railways. They were manned by British and American nurses who tended the wounded and provided them with sustenance. Although such trains were treated as priority traffic, many of the wounded nonetheless died en route.

Hilfe für die Opfer

Mit den Lazarettzügen kam erstmals weibliches Bahnpersonal. Britische und amerikanische Krankenschwestern pflegten und versorgten die Verwundeten an Bord. Solche Züge hatten stets Vorfahrt, doch trotzdem starben viele Soldaten unterwegs.

Les soins aux blessés

De nombreuses femmes étaient employées dans les trains sanitaires. Il s'agissait en général d'infirmières américaines et britanniques, chargées de soigner les blessés et de leur fournir un réconfort. Malheureusement, même si ces trains circulaient en priorité, nombre des blessés transportés mouraient en cours de route.

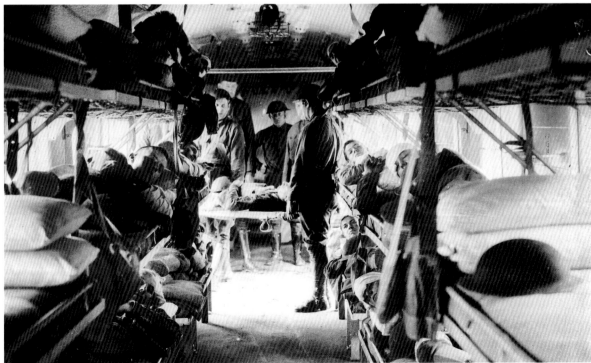

Cape to Cairo

The Mashonaland railway in Rhodesia. On 22 May 1909 the
newly completed Umtali (now Mutare) to Salisbury (now
Harare) route was opened, giving Fort Salisbury transport links
with the rest of Rhodesia. The wood-fuelled locomotive is a
Cape 4th class 4–6–0 No. 1, built by Robert Stephenson in 1882.

Vom Kap nach Kairo

Die Maschonalandbahn in Rhodesien. Am 22. Mai 1909 wurde
die neue Strecke von Umtali (heute Mutare) nach Salisbury
(heute Harare) eröffnet, mit der Fort Salisbury Bahnanschluss
an das restliche Rhodesien bekam. Die Lokomotive mit
Holzfeuerung ist die Cape 4. Klasse 2 C Nr. 1, 1882 von Robert
Stephenson erbaut.

Du Cap au Caire

Le chemin de fer du Mashonaland en Rhodésie. La ligne, tout
juste achevée entre Umtali (l'actuelle Mutare) et Salisbury
(l'actuelle Harare), fut ouverte le 22 mai 1909 pour relier Fort
Salisbury au reste de la Rhodésie. Cette locomotive à bois est
la Cape 230 de classe 4 n°1, construite par Robert Stephenson
en 1882.

Going nowhere?

Somewhere in Africa in 1906... If the photograph opposite showed a sense of purpose, this conveys anything but optimism. Whether the scene is of a man-made or natural disaster or construction in progress is hard to say. Whatever, it illustrates the difficulty inherent in driving the railways through rugged terrain.

Das Ende der Strecke?

Irgendwo in Afrika, 1906 ... Hier ist nichts von dem Optimismus zu spüren, den das Bild gegenüberliegende Seite ausstrahlt. Ob es sich um ein von Menschenhand verursachtes Unglück oder eine Naturkatastrophe oder nur um eine Strecke im Bau handelt, lässt sich nicht sagen. Jedenfalls vermittelt die Aufnahme einen Begriff davon, wie mühevoll es war, in solchem Terrain Bahnlinien anzulegen.

Vers nulle part ?

Quelque part en Afrique en 1906 ... Si la photographie ci-contre témoigne d'un certain optimisme, ce n'est pas le cas de celle-ci. Même s'il est difficile de dire s'il s'agit d'un désastre naturel (ou dû à l'homme) ou du chantier de construction d'une voie ferrée, elle illustre toutefois les difficultés qu'ont pu rencontrer les ingénieurs des compagnies ferroviaires en terrain accidenté.

The war effort

The shortage of male railway workers due to enlistment was so bad by 1915 that for the first time women were encouraged to work on the railways as guards (opposite, right), clerks, ticket collectors, carriage cleaners and porters (opposite, left, above and below). Those men not called up did the heavy work such as digging (and carrying) potatoes (above), while prisoners of war (below) were also expected to contribute to the war effort.

Die Heimatfront

Schon 1915 waren so viele Bahnangestellte zum Kriegsdienst eingezogen worden, dass nun auch Frauen angeworben wurden – als Schaffnerinnen (gegenüberliegende Seite, rechts), Bürokräfte, Fahrkartenkontrolleure, zum Putzen und als Kofferträgerinnen (gegenüberliegende Seite, links oben und unten). Die verbliebenen Männer verrichteten die körperlich schwereren Arbeiten, machten zum Beispiel Kartoffeln aus (und trugen die Säcke, oben), und auch die Kriegsgefangenen (unten) hatten ihren Beitrag zu leisten.

L'effort de guerre

La pénurie de main-d'œuvre masculine, provoquée par la mobilisation, était si grande en 1915 que des femmes furent incitées pour la première fois à travailler dans les chemins de fer, que ce soit comme chef de train (ci-contre, à droite), employées, contrôleuses, chargées de l'entretien des voitures ou porteuses (ci-contre, à gauche, en haut et en bas). Ces hommes, qui n'ont pas été mobilisés, font des travaux plus pénibles comme le ramassage (et le transport) des pommes de terre (en haut), tandis que des prisonniers de guerre contribuent à leur manière à l'effort de guerre (en bas).

Giant's Causeway tramway

The first railways in Ireland were built to carry passengers rather than goods. The Giant's Causeway tramway, seen here in c. 1900, was the first electric railway in Ireland built by the German company Siemens in 1882; it carried holiday-makers from Portrush along the famous North Antrim coast.

Auf dem Giant's Causeway

Die ersten irischen Eisenbahnen dienten dem Personen-, nicht dem Güterverkehr. Die Trambahn auf dem Giant's Causeway, hier um die Jahrhundertwende, war die erste elektrische Bahn in Irland. Die 1882 bei Siemens in Deutschland gebauten Züge beförderten Touristen von Portrush die berühmte Küste von Nord-Antrim entlang.

Le tramway de la Chaussée des Géants

Les premiers chemins de fer d'Irlande furent construits plutôt pour le transport des voyageurs que des marchandises. Le tramway de Giant's Causeway (la Chaussée des Géants), que l'on voit ici vers 1900, fut le premier chemin de fer électrique d'Irlande. Construit par la compagnie allemande Siemens en 1882, il longeait la célèbre côte nord de l'Antrim au départ de Portrush.

8906.

L.S.&.P.C

The Franco-British Exhibition
The Renard Road train ferries visitors around the site of the Franco-British Exhibition, London, 1908. The exhibition was intended to display and promote the artistic and industrial achievements of both countries. Since the exhibition was spread over a 140-acre site, the train, even if it was a novelty in keeping with the spirit of the venture, was also a necessity.

Die franko-britische Ausstellung
Die Straßen-Eisenbahn von Renard fuhr im Jahr 1908 die Besucher durch das Gelände der Londoner franko-britischen Ausstellung, die die künstlerischen und technischen Leistungen beider Länder feierte. Die Bahn war ein Kuriosum, das zum Geist des Unternehmens passte; bei einer Ausstellungsfläche von 57 Hektar war sie allerdings auch dringend notwendig.

L'Exposition franco-britannique
Le Renard Road transportait les visiteurs pendant l'Exposition franco-britannique de 1908 à Londres. Cette manifestation avait pour but de présenter et de promouvoir les réalisations artistiques et industrielles des deux pays. Comme le site occupait près de 57 hectares, ce train était non seulement une nouveauté, dans l'esprit même de l'exposition, mais également une nécessité.

British Commonwealth

In 1919 the Prince of Wales (later Edward VIII) left Britain to make a cross-country tour of Canada aimed at bringing unity and strength to the Commonwealth. While there, he laid the foundation stone of the tower of the new Parliament building in Ottawa. Here he stands on a cowcatcher in conversation with a locomotive driver. The same year, the Canadian National Railways were also founded.

Dienst am Commonwealth

1919 unternahm der Prince of Wales (der spätere Edward VIII.) eine ausgedehnte Kanadareise, die für mehr Solidarität im British Commonwealth sorgen sollte. In Ottawa legte er den Grundstein für den Turm des neuen Parlamentsgebäudes. Hier sehen wir ihn auf dem Gleisräumer eines Zuges im Gespräch mit dem Lokomotivführer. Im selben Jahr wurden auch die Canadian National Railways gegründet.

Le Commonwealth britannique

En 1919, le prince de Galles – et futur Edouard VIII – quitte la Grande-Bretagne pour effectuer un tour du Canada visant à renforcer l'unité et la puissance du Commonwealth. Il en profita pour poser la première pierre du nouveau bâtiment du Parlement d'Ottawa. On le voit ici, debout sur le chasse-bœufs, en grande conversation avec le mécanicien de la locomotive. Le Canadian National Railways fut fondé cette même année.

Anti-suffragette campaign
In London, Emmeline Pankhurst was organising the Women's Social and Political Union to campaign for the right to vote. Although both Canada and the US wanted female immigrants, they did not want suffragettes, as this Canadian Pacific billboard poster hoarding in Cockspur Street, London, in 1913 makes clear. Canada wanted wives and homemakers – not bluestockings.

Keine Suffragetten
In London organisierte Emmeline Pankhurst die Women's Social and Political Union, die für das Frauenwahlrecht kämpfte. Wie die USA warb auch Kanada um weibliche Einwanderer, aber Suffragetten sollten es nicht sein – wie diese Schutzwand am Canadian-Pacific-Büro in der Londoner Cockspur Street verdeutlicht, aufgenommen 1913. Die Kanadier wollten Mütter für ihre Kinder, keine Blaustrümpfe.

Campagne anti-suffragettes
Emmeline Pankhurst organisait à Londres la Women's Social and Political Union pour faire campagne en faveur du droit de vote des femmes. Bien que le Canada et les États-Unis désiraient également des immigrantes, ils ne voulaient pas des suffragettes, comme l'indiquent clairement ces affiches devant la vitrine londonienne du Canadian Pacific, dans Cockspur Street, en 1913. Le Canada avait besoin de femmes et de maîtresses de maison et non de bas bleus.

Curiosities

Unusual railway innovations of the era; (above) an Austrian 4 combined cylinder locomotive built in Vienna by Karl Gölsdorf in 1906, better known for his armoured train designs; (below) a Central London electric tube locomotive, 1900. These were withdrawn in 1906 due to excessive vibration. (Opposite, above) A slide pulled by two men in Funchal, Madeira, c. 1900, a method of transport still in use today; (opposite, below left) the Brennan monorail, 1910. In 1903 Louis Brennan applied for a master patent for his Gyroscopic Monorail; (opposite, below right) the *Cannonball Express,* a wood-fuelled express which ran between Peru and Chile.

Kuriositäten

Ungewöhnliche Konstruktionen dieser Ära: (Oben) Eine österreichische Lokomotive mit Vierzylinder-Verbundtriebwerk, gebaut 1906 in Wien von Carl Gölsdorf, den man vor allem für seine Panzerzüge kennt; (unten) eine elektrische U-Bahn-Lok der Central London Railway, 1900. Diese Baureihe wurde 1906 wegen zu großer Vibrationen außer Dienst gestellt. (Gegenüberliegende Seite, oben) Eine von zwei Männern gezogene Rutsche in Funchal, Madeira, ca. 1900 – ein Transportmittel, das es bis heute gibt; (gegenüberliegende Seite, unten links) die Brennan-Einschienenbahn, 1910 – das System mit stabilisierenden Kreiseln ließ Louis Brennan sich 1903 patentieren; (gegenüberliegende Seite, unten rechts) der *Cannonball Express* (Kanonenkugel-Express), der, von einer holzbefeuerten Dampfmaschine getrieben, zwischen Peru und Chile verkehrte.

Curiosités

Innovations insolites de l'époque : (en haut) une locomotive autrichienne à 4 cylindres combinés, construite à Vienne en 1906 par Karl Gölsdorf, plus connu pour ses blindages de trains ; (en bas) une motrice électrique du métro de Central London en 1900. Ces machines furent retirées de la circulation en 1906 en raison de leurs vibrations excessives. (Ci-contre en haut) Une glissoire poussée par deux hommes à Funchal (Madère) vers 1900, une méthode de transport toujours employée de nos jours. (Ci-contre, en bas à gauche) Le monorail Brennan en 1910, dont Louis Brennan avait déposé le brevet d'un Monorail gyroscopique en 1903. (Ci-contre, en bas à droite) Le *Cannonball Express,* un train express fonctionnant au bois, circulait entre le Pérou et le Chili.

Birthplace of the locomotive
An official works record photograph of the North Eastern Railway's Darlington locomotive works, c. 1910. Darlington, in the industrial north east of England, and the birthplace of the locomotive, was an extensive railway centre with workshops, iron foundries and heavy engineering works.

Die Geburtsstätte der Lokomotive
Eine offizielle Aufnahme aus den Lokomotivenwerken der North Eastern Railway in Darlington, um 1910. Darlington im industriellen Nordosten Englands, wo die erste Lokomotive überhaupt gebaut wurde, entwickelte sich zu einer Eisenbahnmetropole mit Werkstätten, Gießereien und Schwermaschinenbau.

La naissance d'une locomotive
Une photographie officielle de l'usine du North Eastern Railway à Darlington, vers 1910. Ville natale de la locomotive, Darlington, située dans le bassin industriel du nord-est de la Grande-Bretagne, était un grand centre ferroviaire qui comptait de nombreux ateliers mécaniques, des fonderies et de grandes usines d'assemblage.

—— 3 ——
Shrinking the World

The ravages and extensive use of the railways during the 1914–18 war left the European railway structure in urgent need of attention. The damaged lines of mainland Europe had to be rebuilt and during this period of restoration vast improvements and technical innovations also took place. For the first time the railways of Continental Europe had a superior system to Britain, the birthplace of the locomotive. However, shortages of funds, material and manpower were affecting all Europe. After the end of the First World War the release of thousands of ex-army lorries helped to establish the road haulage business and such competition to the railways was slowly becoming a serious issue.

To put the railways in Britain to rights, plans were made to amalgamate the one hundred and twenty or so independent companies into just four large companies. These companies came into being on 1 January 1923 and were known as the 'Big Four'. Their names reflected the geographical areas they served – the London, Midland & Scottish railway (LMS) the London & North Eastern Railway (LNER), the Great Western Railway (GWR) and the Southern Railway (SR). They varied in size and character. The LMS was the largest, covering 6,911 miles; the LNER was the most innovative and experimental; the GWR the only one to retain its name and continuity; and the SR the smallest, at just 2,153 miles but covering central London commuting passenger traffic. The LMS and LNER were rivals for the Anglo-Scottish passenger traffic that was to be the subject of later competition. Incidentally, the term 'Big Four' in the United States had quite a different meaning. It referred to the four operating brotherhoods which were similar to unions: the Brotherhood of Railroad Trainmen; the Order of Railroad Conductors; the Brotherhood of Locomotive Fireman; and the Engineers and Brotherhood of Locomotive Engineers.

Gradually, life on the railways returned to relative normality after the war. From 1923 onwards the SR carried out extensive suburban electrification in and around London, using the third rail direct current system. In America by 1924 eight out of ten people who travelled did so by train. The benefits of improved transit for freight and passengers were felt all over what was now a shrinking world. As travelling times fell, demand for travel grew and people looked for new and different places to go to. Sports events mushroomed: football teams could now be followed around the country and horse racing took on national and international dimensions. The railways were now turning everyone into trippers and holiday makers. With statutory holidays established, factory workers could go away for two weeks a year. It was now usual for benevolent firms to take their employees for days out at the company's expense, their philosophy being that a contented, well-treated workforce would be loyal and work harder. In Britain this was common practice with such companies as Huntley and Palmer, Colman's and Boots. Fresh food was now increasingly distributed over long distances so that diets generally improved and became more varied. Without the railways the traditional British fish and chip shop would not have been so ubiquitous, nor for that matter would the concept of the rush hour or the expression 'strap hanging' have come into being.

The Roaring Twenties meant yet more luxurious trains for those who could afford such travel. The *Golden Arrow* was of French origin, the Chemin de Fer du Nord introducing the *Flèche d'Or* service between London and Paris in 1926. The counterpart English train between Victoria and Dover was called the *Continental Express*. In 1929 the SR changed its name to the *Golden Arrow* when Pullman coaches were added. A new boat was constructed for this service with private de luxe cabins and a Palm Court. On the alternative Night Ferry service the entire train was shipped across the Channel from Dover to Dunkirk. On the Canadian National Railways the *Continental Limited* ran from Montreal to Vancouver over the Rockies. Between Jasper, Alberta, and Kamloops, British Columbia, an open observation car was attached so that passengers could view the spectacular scenery. In 1927 the *Etoile du Nord*, or *North Star*, Pullman began between Paris and Brussels or Amsterdam. The *Edelweiss Pullman* and *Rheingold Mitropa* (a subsidiary of the Reichsbahn) began in 1928, running from England to Switzerland. The facilities of these 'hotels on wheels' were of the highest standard and dinner in the dining car was an important part of the journey. During these years catering also reached new heights. The luxury trains would have especially built, ultra-stylish dining cars with catering vehicles staffed at all times. Cocktails and crusted port, epitomizing the image and style of the period, were *de rigueur*.

In Britain under the leadership of C.B. Collett the GWR developed the 'King' and 'Castle' class locomotives for express passenger work. The 'Castle' class was introduced in 1924. *Caerphilly Castle* was displayed at the British Empire Exhibition in Wembley, London, and the first 'King' class locomotive, *King George V*, was exhibited at the Baltimore & Ohio centenary celebrations in 1927.

The Edmonson ticket machine was first introduced in 1929 in England. The major railway companies had their own printing works and tickets were issued for passengers... as well as dogs, bicycles and racing pigeons. During this period too country rambling became a popular pastime, fresh air being plentiful, healthy and cheap. A total eclipse of the sun on 29 June 1927 meant that both the LMS and the LNER could take trippers to experience 'the thrill of a lifetime'. Naturally, both companies claimed that the best views would be seen from the part of the country served by their trains.

Just as the railways in Britain had unified to support the country's war efforts in 1914 they did so again in 1926 to support the General Strike, but this time it was against the government. The railways were extremely disciplined with their workforce and there were carefully drawn up rules and regulations and a strict hierarchy that was reflected in pay differentials and rank. Uniforms further reflected such rank and enabled passengers and employees to recognise a man's status immediately. Staff took pride in their work and reflected the company image. Therefore, their participation in the General Strike came as something of a shock to railway company officials and directors. The Prime Minister Stanley Baldwin had pronounced that 'constitutional government is being attacked. Let all good citizens whose livelihood and labour have thus been put in peril bear with fortitude and patience the hardship with which they have been so suddenly confronted. The General Strike is a challenge to Parliament and is the road to anarchy and ruin.' He therefore co-opted volunteers to do the vital jobs affected by the strike, including railway work. On the second day of the strike, the GWR announced 'the distribution of milk and food is being methodically carried forward. Volunteers of every kind are being brought in. The nation remains calm and contented.' Many of the volunteers were middle-class students who had no sympathy with the labour force. Terence Cuneo, the railway artist, who drove a Lyons delivery van in London during the strike, wrote in his biography, 'to think that we are free; out for the day with a damned great lorry to drive'. The strike only lasted from 3 to 12 May and the miners gained nothing but longer hours and lower pay, but it made the government realise how important economically the rail network had become to the country and how much people suffered when it was in disarray.

The railways made an impact on camera and cinema history during this era. Photography was becoming increasingly pop-

ular as cameras became less expensive, lighter to carry and easier to use. The Railway Photographic Society was founded by Maurice Early in 1927. Photojournalism was also becoming more professional, sophisticated and political. The 35mm film camera was introduced into Britain in 1925 when the first Leicas were imported from Germany.

From the start cinema film directors saw the cinematic and artistic potential of the steam locomotive. In 1895 the Lumière brothers showed train scenes in one of the first demonstrations of the moving picture, *L'Arrivée d'un train en gare de la Ciotat*. One of the first films to tell a story was *The Great Train Robbery* of 1903. Buster Keaton's classic *The General* was released in 1927. In France Abel Gance produced the silent film *La Roue* between 1919 and 1923, made in the Nice railway yards with PLM, and in Germany Fritz Lang's 1928 film *Spione* (*Spies*) showed a spectacular railway crash. The railways were catching on in more ways than one.

Nach den Verwüstungen des Ersten Weltkriegs und der starken Beanspruchung im Kriegsbetrieb waren umfassende Instandsetzungsarbeiten am europäischen Schienennetz erforderlich. Auf dem Kontinent mussten ganze Strecken neu aufgebaut werden, was sie zugleich auf den neuesten technischen Stand brachte. Erstmals waren die kontinentalen Bahnen damit denjenigen Großbritanniens, des Mutterlands der Eisenbahn, überlegen. Mit fehlendem Kapital, Material und mangelnden Arbeitskräften hatte allerdings ganz Europa zu kämpfen. Zudem kamen nach Kriegsende Tausende von Militärlastwagen auf den Markt, und ein Straßen Speditionssystem entstand, das allmählich zur ernsthaften Konkurrenz für die Bahn heranwuchs.

Zur Sanierung wurden die etwa einhundertzwanzig unabhängigen britischen Bahnbetreiber zu vier großen Gesellschaften verschmolzen. Am 1. Januar 1923 erblickten die »Big Four« das Licht der Welt. Ihre Namen entsprachen den Regionen, die sie bedienten – London, Midland & Scottish (LMS), London & North Eastern Railway (LNER), Great Western Railway (GWR) und Southern Railway (SR). In der Größe variierten sie, und jede hatte einen eigenständigen Charakter. Mit einem Streckennetz von 11 120 Kilometern war die LMS die größte; die LNER war die innovativste und experimentierfreudigste; die GWR war die einzige, die Namen und Netz unverändert behielt; und die Kleinste unter den Großen war mit 3464 Kilometern die SR, die jedoch den Großteil der Pendlerstrecken nach London bediente. Im anglo-schottischen Personenverkehr waren LMS und LNER Rivalen und lieferten sich manchen Wettstreit. In den Vereinigten Staaten hatte »Big Four« übrigens eine ganz andere Bedeutung; dort bezog es sich auf die vier Bruderschaften, die dort die Funktion von Gewerkschaften erfüllten: die Brotherhood of Railroad Trainmen, die Order of Railroad Conductors, die Brotherhood of Locomotive Fireman und die Engineers and Brotherhood of Locomotive Engineers.

Allmählich kehrten die Eisenbahnen nach dem Krieg zum Normalbetrieb zurück. Von 1923 an elektrifizierte die SR die Londoner Vorortlinien im großen Stil; eine dritte Schiene, die Gleichstrom führte, kam hinzu. In Amerika fuhren 1924 acht von zehn Reisenden mit der Bahn. Je besser die Verbindungen für Fracht und Fahrgäste wurden, desto kleiner schien die Welt. Mit schnelleren Fahrtzeiten stieg die Nachfrage, und Leute sahen sich nach neuen Reisezielen um. Sport-

veranstaltungen häuften sich – Fußballteams konnte man nun überall im Lande begleiten und Pferderennen wurden zu nationalen und internationalen Ereignissen. Die Eisenbahnen machten alle Welt zu Urlaubern und Ausflüglern, zumal den Fabrikarbeitern nach einem neuen Gesetz nun zwei Wochen Jahresurlaub zustanden. Bei den sozialeren Betrieben wurde es üblich, Tagesausflüge mit der ganzen Belegschaft zu machen, denn – so die Philosophie dieser Betriebe – ein zufriedener, gut behandelter Arbeiter arbeitete mehr und engagierte sich stärker. In Großbritannien waren Huntley and Palmer, Colman's und Boots für diese Einstellung bekannt. Frische Lebensmittel konnten schneller und über größere Entfernungen geliefert werden, und die Ernährung wurde damit überall gesünder und vielfältiger. Ohne die Eisenbahn hätten die Briten keinen Fish-and-Chips-Laden an jeder Ecke; es gäbe aber auch keine Rushhour.

In den Goldenen Zwanzigern konnten diejenigen, die das Geld dazu hatten, mit mehr Luxuszügen fahren denn je. Die französische Chemin de Fer du Nord nahm den *Flèche d'Or*-Service von London nach Paris 1926 auf. Das englische Gegenstück von London Victoria nach Dover hieß zunächst *Continental Express* – erst als er 1929 mit Pullmanwagen ausgestattet wurde, nannte die SR ihn in *Golden Arrow* um. Für diese Verbindung wurde auch eine neue Fähre gebaut, mit privaten De-luxe-Kabinen und einem Palmensalon. Für die Nachtzug-Verbindung wurden die kompletten Waggons auf die Fähre Dover–Dünkirchen verladen. Der *Continental Limited* der Canadian National Railways verkehrte über die Rocky Mountains von Montreal nach Vancouver. Zwischen Jasper in Alberta und Kamloops in British Columbia wurde ein offener Aussichtswagen angehängt, damit Fahrgäste die prachtvolle Landschaft bewundern konnten. Von 1927 an verkehrte der Pullmanzug *Étoile du Nord* von Paris nach Brüssel und Amsterdam. Der *Edelweiss Pullman* und der *Rheingold Mitropa* der Reichsbahn fuhren seit 1928 zwischen England und der Schweiz. Die Einrichtungen dieser »rollenden Hotels« entsprachen den höchsten Ansprüchen, und die Mahlzeiten im Speisewagen waren Höhepunkte jeder Fahrt. Die Luxuszüge hatten speziell für sie gebaute, hochelegante Restaurantwagen, die rund um die Uhr besetzt waren. Cocktails und ehrwürdiger Portwein, Inbegriffe des Lebensstils jener Zeit, waren *de rigueur*.

In Großbritannien entwickelte die GWR unter der Leitung von C. B. Collett die Expresslokomotiven der »King«- und

»Castle«-Klasse. *Caerphilly Castle,* die erste der »Castle«-Baureihe, wurde 1924 auf der British Empire Exhibition, Wembley, London, vorgestellt, die erste »King«-Lokomotive, *King George V,* war 1927 zur Hundertjahrfeier der Baltimore & Ohio Railroad zu sehen.

Der erste Edmonson-Fahrkartenautomat wurde 1929 in England aufgestellt. Die großen Bahngesellschaften hatten ihre eigenen Druckereien, und es gab nicht nur Karten für Personen, sondern auch für Hunde, Fahrräder und Brieftauben. Zu dieser Zeit kam auch das Wandern in Mode, denn frische Landluft war gesund, billig und reichlich vorhanden. Zur totalen Sonnenfinsternis vom 19. Juni 1927 überboten sich LMS und LNER mit Fahrten zum »größten Tag Ihres Lebens«: Beide Gesellschaften warben damit, dass das Naturschauspiel in Gegenden, die mit ihren Zügen zu erreichen waren, am besten zu sehen sein würde.

1914 hatten die britischen Eisenbahnen ihre Kräfte vereint, um dem Land im Krieg zu dienen, und dasselbe galt für den Generalstreik von 1926, nur dass diesmal der Gegner aus den eigenen Reihen kam. Die Bahngesellschaften sorgten für strenge Disziplin bei ihren Angestellten, es gab bis ins Kleinste ausgearbeitete Regeln und eine feste Hierarchie, die sich auch im Lohn für die verschiedenen Dienstgrade niederschlug. Uniformen drückten diese Rangunterschiede aus, und Reisende wie Angestellte erkannten an der Uniform sofort, wen sie vor sich hatten. Angestellte waren stolz auf ihre Arbeit und repräsentierten die Firma nach außen. Deshalb war es auch ein gewisser Schock für Direktoren und Führungskräfte, dass die Belegschaften am Generalstreik teilnahmen. Premierminister Stanley Baldwin hatte den Streik zum »Angriff auf den Staat« erklärt. »Alle aufrechten Bürger, deren Wohlstand und Arbeit nun in Gefahr sind, sollen tapfer und geduldig die Belastungen ertragen, die ihnen so unvermutet aufgebürdet sind. Der Generalstreik ist eine Herausforderung an die Regierung, der Weg in Anarchie und Untergang.« Er rief nach Freiwilligen, die die Arbeit in den vom Streik betroffenen Bereichen übernehmen sollten, darunter auch dem der Eisenbahn. Am zweiten Tag des Streikes meldete die GWR: »Die Versorgung mit Milch und Lebensmitteln ist gesichert. Freiwillige Helfer verschiedenster Herkunft gehen ans Werk. Das Land bleibt ruhig und friedlich.« Viele Helfer waren Studenten aus der Mittelschicht, die keine Solidarität mit den Arbeitern kannten. Der Eisenbahnmaler Terence Cuneo, der während des Streiks in London einen Lyons-Lieferwagen fuhr, schreibt in seiner Autobiogra-

phie: »Wenn man sich das ausmalt! Nichts stand uns im Wege, den ganzen Tag lang konnten wir mit einem mächtig großen Lastwagen spazieren fahren.« Der Streik dauerte nur vom 3. bis zum 12. Mai, und das Einzige, was die Bergarbeiter davon hatten, waren längere Arbeitszeiten und niedrigerer Lohn, aber den Politikern brachte er zu Bewusstsein, wie wichtig der Wirtschaftsfaktor Eisenbahn inzwischen geworden war und welche Folgen es für die Bevölkerung hatte, wenn ihr Betrieb gestört war.

Die Eisenbahn jener Epoche spielt auch ihre Rolle in Film- und Fotogeschichte. Die Fotografie setzte sich immer stärker durch, je preisgünstiger, leichter im Gewicht und einfacher in der Bedienung die Apparate wurden. Maurice Early gründete 1927 die Railway Photographic Society. Der Fotojournalismus wurde professioneller, anspruchsvoller und politischer. 1925 kamen die ersten deutschen Leicas nach Großbritannien und mit ihnen der 35-mm-Film.

Von Anfang an sahen Filmregisseure das künstlerische Potential der Dampflokomotive. 1895 zeigten die Brüder Lumière in einem der ersten Filme überhaupt Bahnszenen, *L'Arrivée d'un train en gare de la Ciotat.* Einer der ersten Filme, die eine Geschichte erzählten, war *The Great Train Robbery (Der große Eisenbahnraub)* von 1903. Buster Keatons Klassiker *The General (Der General)* kam 1927 heraus. In Frankreich produzierte Abel Gance zwischen 1919 und 1925 auf dem Bahngelände von Nizza *La Roue,* und in *Spione,* Fritz Langs Film von 1928, war ein spektakuläres Zugunglück zu sehen. Die Bahn setzte sich in allen Bereichen des Lebens durch.

Le réseau ferroviaire d'Europe continentale n'a pas échappé aux ravages de la Première Guerre mondiale et se trouve dans un tel état de délabrement qu'il nécessite d'urgence des réparations. Les compagnies profitent de ce qu'il faut reconstruire les voies endommagées pour procéder à un certain nombre d'améliorations et d'innovations techniques. Pour la première fois de leur histoire, les chemins de fer de l'Europe continentale disposent d'un réseau supérieur à celui des Britanniques, berceau de la locomotive. Cependant, le manque d'argent, de matériaux et de main-d'œuvre qui affecte toute l'Europe constitue un handicap pour les chemins de fer, qui se trouvent alors sérieusement concurrencés par les transports routiers, qu'a permis de développer le déclassement de milliers de camions militaires à la fin de la Première Guerre mondiale.

En Grande-Bretagne, le gouvernement s'efforce de remettre en ordre les chemins de fer et élabore un plan de restructuration visant à fusionner les cent vingt et quelques compagnies indépendantes en quatre grands réseaux. Créées le 1er janvier 1923, et aussitôt surnommées les « Big Four », elles sont désignées par la région du Royaume-Uni qu'elles desservent : London, Midland & Scottish (LMS), London & North Eastern Railway (LNER), Great Western Railway (GWR) et Southern Railway (SR). Leur dimension et leur caractère sont très différents : le LMS dispose du réseau le plus étendu, couvrant près de 11 000 km ; le LNER est le plus innovant et moderniste ; le GWR, le seul à garder sa désignation d'origine, reste conservateur et traditionnel ; le SR, enfin, gère le plus petit réseau ferroviaire du pays (3 500 km seulement) mais assure tout le trafic de la région de Londres. Une certaine émulation va naître de la concurrence entre le LMS et le LNER, qui traitent tous deux le trafic de voyageurs entre l'Angleterre et l'Écosse. Incidemment, le terme de « Big Four » a une signification très différente aux États-Unis et désigne les quatre corporations de cheminots (comparables à des syndicats) américains : la Brotherhood of Railroad Trainmen, l'Order of Railroad Conductors, la Brotherhood of Locomotive Fireman et les Engineers and Brotherhood of Locomotive Engineers.

Les chemins de fer reviennent progressivement à un fonctionnement relativement normal. À partir de 1923, le SR se lance dans une vaste opération d'électrification du réseau urbain et suburbain de Londres en adoptant le principe du troisième rail d'alimentation. Aux États-Unis, en 1924, huit voyageurs sur dix empruntent le chemin de fer pour se déplacer. Le monde semble désormais plus petit à mesure que s'améliore le transport des voyageurs et des marchandises. Les temps de trajet ayant diminué, de plus en plus de gens peuvent et veulent aller dans des endroits nouveaux et différents. Malgré la multiplication des événements sportifs, il est désormais possible de suivre partout les équipes de football ou les courses de chevaux, qui prennent alors une dimension autant nationale qu'internationale. Les chemins de fer transforment chacun en vacancier, d'autant que les congés payés permettent aux ouvriers de partir deux semaines par an. Certaines entreprises – comme Huntley and Palmer, Colman's ou Boots en Grande-Bretagne – ont également pris l'habitude d'organiser des excursions pour leurs employés, suivant le principe que plus la main-d'œuvre est satisfaite et bien traitée plus elle est fidèle et meilleur est son travail. L'amélioration des liaisons ferroviaires permet aussi aux populations les plus éloignées des centres de production de bénéficier de produits frais, de sorte qu'on constate une amélioration et une plus grande diversité du régime alimentaire. Toutefois, sans les chemins de fer, il n'y aurait pas autant de fish and chips et on ne connaîtrait pas l'expression « heures d'affluence ».

C'est pendant les années folles que se multiplient les trains de luxe (pour ceux qui ont les moyens). La Compagnie du Nord inaugure le service de la *Flèche d'Or* entre Londres et Paris en 1926, sa contrepartie anglaise entre la gare de Victoria et Douvres étant alors appelée *Continental Express*. En 1929, le SR le débaptise en *Golden Arrow*, y met en service des voitures Pullman et construit un nouveau navire disposant de cabines de luxe et d'un « thé dansant ». Quelques années plus tard, les Anglais lanceront le Night Ferry, où l'ensemble des voitures est embarqué de Douvres à Dunkerque. En 1927, l'*Étoile du Nord*, un autre train Pullman, est mis en service entre Paris et Bruxelles ou Amsterdam, tandis que l'année suivante l'*Edelweiss Pullman* et le *Rheingold Mitropa* (une filiale du Deutsche Reichsbahn) assurent la relation Grande-Bretagne–Suisse. En Amérique, le *Continental Limited* des Canadian National Railways, qui assure la liaison de Montréal à Vancouver en franchissant les Rocheuses, est complété par une voiture panoramique ouverte permettant aux voyageurs de profiter des spectaculaires paysages traversés entre Jasper (Alberta) et Kamloops (Colombie britannique). Le service à bord des trains atteint alors de nouveaux sommets, les trains de luxe étant équipés de voitures-restaurants très élégantes, où l'on sert des repas à toute heure ; cocktails et vieux porto, symboles s'il en est du raffinement de l'époque, sont alors de rigueur. Les aménagements de ces «hôtels sur roues» sont du meilleur niveau et le dîner dans la voiture-restaurant représente une étape importante du voyage.

Sous la direction de Charles B. Collett, le GWR adopte les locomotives de classes «King» et «Castle» pour la traction des trains de voyageurs. La première «Castle», la *Caerphilly Castle*, est présentée à l'Exposition de l'Empire britannique à Wembley, près de Londres, et mise en service régulier en 1924; la première classe «King», la *King George V,* fut expédiée en 1927 aux États-Unis pour participer aux célébrations du centenaire du Baltimore & Ohio Railroad.

C'est en 1929 qu'est installé en Grande-Bretagne le premier distributeur de billets Edmonson. Les principales compagnies de chemin de fer, qui disposent alors de leurs propres imprimeries, délivrent des billets non seulement aux voyageurs mais aussi aux chiens, aux bicyclettes et aux pigeons de compétition. C'est à cette époque que la randonnée pédestre connaît un certain engouement, l'air alors pur de la campagne étant jugé excellent pour la santé. L'éclipse totale de soleil du 29 juin 1927 fut l'occasion pour le LMS et le LNER de proposer un train spécial pour faire l'expérience «du frisson d'une vie», chacune des deux compagnies annonçant que c'est depuis la région qu'elle dessert que l'on aurait la meilleure vision du phénomène.

De même que les chemins de fer britanniques s'étaient regroupés en 1914 pour soutenir l'effort de guerre, les cheminots des Big Four s'unirent de nouveau en 1926 pour soutenir la grève générale, cette fois contre le gouvernement. Les compagnies ferroviaires maintenaient alors une sévère discipline, édictant des règles strictes et s'appuyant sur une hiérarchie rigoureusement graduée, qui se manifestait notamment par la différence de salaire et de responsabilité. L'adoption d'uniformes distinctifs selon le grade permit ensuite aux voyageurs, et aux employés entre eux, de reconnaître immédiatement la qualité et le niveau de compétence de chacun. Les cheminots se montrant généralement fiers de leur travail, un sentiment dont bénéficiait l'image de la compagnie, leur participation massive à la grève générale fut un choc pour les directeurs des compagnies de chemin de fer. La crise était si grave que le Premier Ministre Stanley Baldwin prononça un discours alarmant: «Le gouvernement constitutionnel est attaqué. Que les bons citoyens, dont le mode de vie et le travail ont été ainsi mis en péril, supportent avec courage et patience les difficultés auxquelles ils sont soudain confrontés. La grève

générale est un défi au Parlement et ne peut que mener à la ruine et à l'anarchie.» Il fit donc appel à des volontaires pour remplacer les grévistes, cheminots compris, dans toutes les activités vitales pour le pays. Le second jour de la grève, le GWR annonçait que «la distribution de lait et de nourriture sera méthodiquement poursuivie. Des volontaires sont au travail. La nation reste calme et satisfaite.» Nombre de ces volontaires sont des étudiants de la classe moyenne qui n'ont en réalité aucune sympathie pour les forces ouvrières. Terence Cuneo, un peintre des chemins de fer, qui conduisait un camion de livraison de la Lyons à Londres pendant la grève, écrivit dans sa biographie «et dire que nous sommes libres! dehors toute la journée avec un sacré gros camion à conduire.» La grève ne dure que du 3 au 12 mai, et les mineurs ne gagnent rien d'autre qu'une augmentation des horaires de travail et une diminution de leur salaire. Mais elle permit au gouvernement de se rendre mieux compte de l'importance économique des chemins de fer pour le pays et des difficultés qu'entraînait leur désorganisation.

Les chemins de fer eurent également une certaine influence sur l'histoire de la photographie et du cinéma. Les appareils devenant plus légers, plus facile à utiliser et plus abordables, la photographie connaît alors une incroyable popularité. L'appareil photo 35 mm arrive en Grande-Bretagne en 1925 avec l'importation des premiers Leica allemands. Le photojournalisme devient également plus professionnel, plus raffiné et plus politique, et la Railway Photographic Society est fondée par Maurice Early en 1927.

Les réalisateurs de films ont tout de suite vu l'intérêt cinématographique et artistique des chemins de fer à vapeur: les frères Lumière créent l'événement en présentant dès 1895 un petit film, *L'Arrivée d'un train en gare de la Ciotat.* L'un des premiers films à utiliser un train dans le cadre d'une histoire est *Le Vol du rapide,* réalisé en 1903; en France, *La Roue,* un film muet réalisé entre 1919 et 1923 par Abel Gance fut tourné dans les dépôts niçois du PLM; le grand classique de Buster Keaton – *Le Mécano de la Général* – sort en 1927; en Allemagne, Fritz Lang filme un spectaculaire accident de chemin de fer dans *Les Espions,* de 1928. Les chemins de fer deviennent alors de plus en plus populaires ... à plus d'un titre.

In Berlin one of the results of the First World War was a huge housing and accommodation shortage. At Berlin Station railway sleeping cars were used as emergency hotel facilities.

In Berlin waren nach dem Ersten Weltkrieg Wohnungen und Unterkünfte äußerst knapp. Schlafwagen dienten auf den Bahnhöfen als Hotelersatz.

L'une des conséquences de la Première Guerre mondiale fut une gigantesque pénurie de logements à Berlin, conduisant à aménager des voitures-lits en hôtel de dépannage.

Waiting for the milk train

Platform 1, King's Cross Station, 7 May 1926, on the fourth day of the General Strike. The milk porters are on strike and as a result the platform is congested with empty churns awaiting return to the dairies. The familiar metal milk churn was soon to be a thing of the past, on the railways at least. Glass-lined milk tanks were introduced in 1928 and eventually replaced the milk churn altogether.

Warten auf den Milchzug

Bahnsteig 1, King's Cross, 7. Mai 1926, am vierten Tag des Generalstreiks. Auch die Milchmänner streiken, und auf dem Bahnsteig warten leere Kannen auf ihre Rückkehr zu den Molkereien. Die vertrauten Metallkannen waren zumindest auf der Eisenbahn bald Geschichte – 1928 wurden mit Glas ausgekleidete Tanks eingeführt und ersetzten die Milchkannen schließlich ganz.

L'attente du train de lait

Gare de King's Cross, quai n°1, le 7 mai 1926, au quatrième jour de la grève générale. Les trains sont en grève et les bidons de lait vides encombrent le quai en attendant d'être réexpédiés aux laiteries. Ces bidons en métal ordinaires allaient bientôt disparaître, dans les chemins de fer au moins, pour être remplacés en 1928 par des bidons en verre.

King's Cross dairy
A surreal picture of a less frequently reported consequence of the General Strike on Platform 2 at King's Cross, 1926. Generally, much livestock was transported by train during this period but because of the strike this cow found itself stranded in London. Volunteer railway workers take turns to serve as emergency milkmaids.

Milchversorgung, King's Cross
Eine surreale Aufnahme von Bahnsteig 2, King's Cross 1926, zeigt weniger bekannte Seiten des Streiks. Vieh wurde damals häufig per Zug transportiert, und als der Verkehr zum Erliegen kam, strandete diese Kuh in London. Freiwillige Bahnhelfer versuchen sich als Milchmädchen in der Not.

La laiterie de King's Cross
Cette photo surréaliste, prise sur un quai de la gare de King's Cross, illustre une conséquence peu connue de la grève générale de 1926. La majorité du bétail étant transporté par train à cette époque, cette malheureuse vache s'est trouvée bloquée à Londres à cause de la grève et des cheminots volontaires ont dû se mobiliser chacun à leur tour pour la traire.

Southern goods deliveries

The railways carried most foodstuffs from town to town and country to country and they were especially busy at Christmas. (Above) Italian cheese (the barrels suggest Parmesan), from Milan being unloaded at Bishopsgate goods station in London, November 1924. (Below) A consignment of bacon arriving at Nine Elms shed, London, December 1922, from the Home Counties.

Von Nah und Fern

Wenn Lebensmittel von Stadt zu Stadt oder von einem Land zum anderen transportiert wurden, geschah das meist per Eisenbahn. Besonders großer Betrieb herrschte vor Weihnachten. (Oben) Italienischer Käse (die Körbe lassen Parmesan vermuten) trifft aus Mailand im Londoner Güterbahnhof Bishopsgate ein, November 1924. (Unten) Eine Lieferung Speck aus den Home Counties wird im Dezember 1922 im Lagerhaus Nine Elms, London, entladen.

Livraisons des marchandises dans le Sud

Les chemins de fer transportaient la plupart des denrées alimentaires de ville à ville et de pays à pays, la période de Noël étant une période particulièrement chargée. (En haut) Des fromages italiens (les caisses font penser à du parmesan) en provenance de Milan sont déchargés à la gare de marchandises de Bishopsgate, à Londres, en novembre 1924. (En bas) Une expédition de bacon arrive dans les entrepôts londoniens de Nine Elms, en décembre 1922, en provenance des Home Counties.

A northern goods station

The Midland Railway Canal Road goods yard in Bradford, 1921. The goods here are most probably wool. Bradford had a thriving wool trade and the goods yard had a bonded warehouse. Leeds and Bradford demanded huge supplies of wool and fuel for their factories and the railways were the means of delivering the finished goods to all parts of the country.

Güterverkehr im Norden

Der Güterbahnhof Canal Road der Midland Railway im nordenglischen Bradford, 1921. In den Ballen steckt vermutlich Wolle. Bradford betrieb einen blühenden Wollhandel, und zum Bahnhof gehörte ein Zolllagerhaus. Der Bedarf an Wolle und Brennmaterial für die Webereien in Leeds und Bradford war groß, und die fertigen Produkte wurden per Bahn ins ganze Land geliefert.

Une gare de marchandises du Nord

La gare de marchandises du Midland Railway, à Canal Road (Bradford), en 1921. Bradford, qui disposait d'entrepôts sous douane, était un centre commercial lainier florissant (il s'agit ici probablement de balles de laine). Le chemin de fer, qui alimentait les usines de Leeds et Bradford en laine et en carburant, permettait également d'acheminer dans tous les coins du pays les produits finis qu'elles produisaient.

London's quietest station

Marylebone, the London terminus of the Great Central Railway, opened in 1899 and was the last main line into London. It never ran to capacity and was a quiet, almost suburban station. By 1928, it was owned by the LNER and only came to life on Cup Final day when trains departed for Wembley Stadium every few minutes.

Londons ruhigster Bahnhof

Der Bahnhof Marylebone eröffnete 1899 als Endstation der Great Central Railway, der letzten großen Linie in die Hauptstadt. Er erreichte nie die Zahl von Fahrgästen, für die er geplant war, und die Stimmung war ruhig, beinahe schon vorstädtisch. Als dieses Bild 1928 entstand, gehörte er bereits der LNER und erwachte nur am Tag des Pokalfinales zum Leben, wenn die Züge im Abstand von wenigen Minuten zum Wembley-Stadion fuhren.

La gare la plus paisible de Londres

Inaugurée en 1899, la gare de Marylebone était le terminus londonien du Great Central Railway, dernière ligne à pénétrer dans Londres. Elle ne fut jamais utilisée à pleine capacité et aurait pu passer pour une paisible gare de banlieue. Reprise par le LNER en 1928, elle connaissait un peu plus d'animation les jours de finale de la Coupe de football, lorsque des trains en partaient toutes les quelques minutes à destination du stade de Wembley.

Penn Station, New York, 1925
The Great Gate room of the neo-classical Penn Station, opened on
27 November 1910. The Gate room was modelled on the Roman Baths
of Caracalla and built of travertine marble. It took thirteen months to
complete and occupied 28 acres. The main waiting room was the
world's largest at the time.

Penn Station, New York, 1925
Die große Schalterhalle der neoklassizistischen Penn Station eröffnete
nach 13 Monaten Bauzeit am 27. November 1910. Den römischen
Caracalla-Thermen nachempfunden und aus Travertin erbaut, bedeckte
sie eine Fläche von 14 Hektar und war damals die größte der Welt.

Penn Station, New York, 1925
La Great Gate de la gare néoclassique de Penn Station, inaugurée le
27 novembre 1910. Ce hall, construit en travertin, reprenait le plan des
bains romains de Caracalla et occupait une superficie de 14 hectares.
Il fallut 13 mois pour achever cette grande salle des pas perdus, la plus
vaste de son époque.

The Forth Bridge
A passenger express steams through the Forth Bridge in 1927, crossing the Firth of Forth between Granton and Burntisland. With main spans of 1,700 feet, it was the first major British bridge to be made from steel. By this time it was owned by the LNER.

Die Forth Bridge
Ein Expresszug dampft im Jahr 1927 über die Forth Bridge zwischen Granton und Burntisland. Mit Spannweiten von 518 Metern war die Brücke über den Firth of Forth die erste größere Stahlbrücke in Großbritannien. Als diese Aufnahme entstand, gehörte sie bereits der LNER.

Le pont de Forth
Un train express traverse le Forth Bridge, jeté au-dessus du Firth of Forth entre Granton et Burntisland. D'une travée principale de 518 mètres, ce fut le premier grand pont britannique à être réalisé en acier. À cette époque, en 1927, il appartenait au LNER.

Providing a better service – progress

Each of the big four railway companies initiated its own revitalising scheme after the grouping of 1923 in Britain. Here we see the widening of the LNER main line between Fletton Junction and Peterborough in September 1924.

Für die Zukunft gerüstet

Nach der Neuordnung des britischen Bahnwesens im Jahr 1923 begannen alle vier großen Gesellschaften mit Ausbaumaßnahmen. Hier sehen wir die Erweiterung der LNER-Hauptstrecke zwischen Fletton Junction und Peterborough im September 1924.

Le progrès : fournir un meilleur service

Chacune des quatre grandes compagnies de chemin de fer britanniques a lancé un programme de rénovation après leur regroupement en 1923. On voit ici les travaux d'élargissement de la ligne principale du LNER entre Fletton Junction et Peterborough, exécutés en septembre 1924.

Diamond crossing

Newcastle Central Station was built by local architect John Dobson and opened by Queen Victoria in 1893. The famous 'Diamond Crossing' (above), seen in 1924, is at the east end of the station and was introduced to increase traffic capacity through the station.

Rautenkreuzung

Den Hauptbahnhof von Newcastle erbaute der dortige Architekt John Dobson; Königin Victoria eröffnete ihn 1893. Die berühmte »Rautenkreuzung«, hier (oben) in einem Bild von 1924, liegt am Ostende des Bahnhofs und sollte die Zahl der möglichen Durchfahrten erhöhen.

Le croisement en diamant

La gare centrale de Newcastle fut construite par John Dobson, un architecte local, et inaugurée par la reine Victoria en 1893. Elle est célèbre notamment pour son « Diamond Crossing », ici en 1924 (ci-dessus), aménagé à la sortie est de la gare pour augmenter la capacité du trafic ferroviaire.

Signal success

(Above) German students in the control office at Manchester, c. 1925, view what was considered to be the best electrical signal office in the world. (Below) Signalman Rogers waits in his Liverpool Street signal box for the centralized timing signal sent twice a day across the LNER network. At 10 o'clock morning and evening a small lever would send a signal to each box in the system to synchronise railway time.

Die Signale stimmen

(Oben) Deutsche Studenten besichtigen etwa 1925 das elektrische Stellwerk in Manchester, das damals als modernstes der Welt galt. (Unten) Bahnwärter Rogers wartet in seinem Stellwerk am Bahnhof Liverpool Street auf das Signal, das zweimal täglich die Uhren im gesamten LNER-Netz synchronisierte. Das Signal wurde jeweils um zehn Uhr morgens und abends mit einem kleinen Hebel an alle Stellwerke des Systems geschickt und sorgte für einheitliche »Eisenbahnzeit«.

Les progrès de la signalisation

(En haut) Des étudiants allemands en visite au poste de contrôle de Manchester, vers 1925, examinent ce qui était alors considéré comme le meilleur centre de signalisation électrique du monde. (En bas) Dans son poste de Liverpool Street, l'aiguilleur Rogers attend de recevoir le signal centralisé envoyé deux fois par jour – à 10 heures et à 22 heures – à tous les postes du réseau du LNER afin de synchroniser leurs horloges.

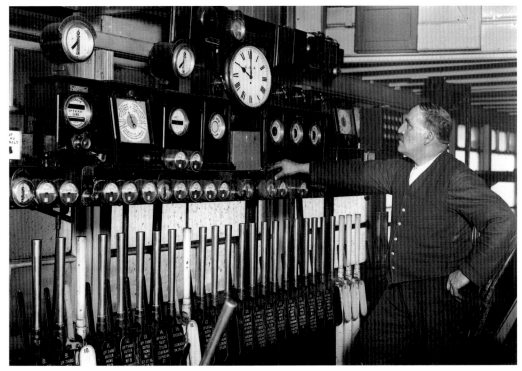

Signal manoeuvres

A signalman operating a manual signal lever frame in Ambergate signal box in the late 1920s. An old Midland Railway locomotive can be seen in the background. The Midland Railway opened a branch line from Ambergate to Rowsley in the Peak District in 1849. Ambergate is one of the few country stations still being used today in rural Britain.

Alles im Griff

Ein Bahnwärter zieht einen mechanischen Signalhebel im Stellwerk von Ambergate, Ende der zwanziger Jahre. Im Hintergrund eine alte Lokomotive der Midland Railway. Die Midland-Nebenstrecke von Ambergate nach Rowsley im Peak District wurde 1849 eröffnet, und Ambergate ist einer der wenigen britischen Landbahnhöfe, die auch heute noch in Betrieb sind.

Manœuvres d'aiguillage

Un aiguilleur du poste d'Ambergate actionne à la main un levier d'aiguillage, à la fin des années 1920. On peut distinguer à l'arrière-plan une vieille locomotive du Midland Railway. Le Midland Railway avait ouvert en 1849 une ligne secondaire entre Rowsley, dans le Peak District, et Ambergate, l'une des rares gares de campagne britanniques encore en service de nos jours.

Trainspotting

This mirror was positioned to help the signalman looking down the line from Stratford Central on the old Great Eastern Railway, which had been taken over by the LNER by the time this photograph was taken in August 1923. The signalman's view from his box was obscured by the waiting room roof and chimney stacks. The locomotive in the mirror is a 0–6–2; empty stock can be seen in the background.

Ein Blick zurück

Der Bahnwärter im Hauptbahnhof Stratford an der alten Great Eastern Railway behält über einen Spiegel den Verkehr hinter sich im Auge, denn Schornsteine und das Dach des Haupt-gebäudes verstellten ihm den Blick zurück. Die Lokomotive im Spiegel ist eine C 1, und im Hintergrund sind Wagen und Loks auf dem Abstellgleis zu sehen. Als diese Aufnahme im August 1923 entstand, war die Great Eastern schon in den Besitz der LNER übergegangen.

Surveillance des trains

Ce miroir est placé de telle sorte que l'aiguilleur puisse voir les trains provenant de Stratford Central, sur l'ancienne ligne du Great Eastern Railway, repris par le LNER au moment où cette photographie a été prise, en août 1923. La vision de l'aiguilleur depuis son poste est toutefois gênée par la toiture de la salle des pas perdus et les souches de cheminées. La locomotive que l'on aperçoit dans le miroir est une 031 et on peut distinguer du matériel roulant vide à l'arrière-plan.

Works tours

The railway industry was justifiably proud of its workshops and craftsmen, and visits from dignitaries and school parties were not unusual. (Above) A party of German students is given an instructive tour of the Great Western Railway works in Swindon in 1927. Here they are shown in the foundry. (Opposite) Boys from Eton College tour the Swindon works. This is a 'star' class locomotive, *Knight Templar*, being lifted especially so that they can view the locomotive's precision engineering.

Werksbesichtigungen

Die Eisenbahnindustrie war zu Recht stolz auf ihre Fabriken und Facharbeiter, und nicht selten kamen Würdenträger oder Schulgruppen zu Besuch. (Oben) Eine Gruppe deutscher Studenten wird 1927 durch das Betriebswerk der Great Western Railway in Swindon geführt. Hier besichtigen sie die Gießerei. (Gegenüberliegende Seite) Schüler von Eton besuchen das Werk in Swindon, und die Lokomotive *Knight Templar* wird eigens für sie in die Höhe gehievt, damit sie die Präzisionsarbeit am Unterbau bewundern können.

Visites d'usines

L'industrie ferroviaire, fière à juste titre de ses ateliers et de ses ouvriers, accueillait fréquemment des visites de personnalités et d'écoliers. (Ci-dessus) Un groupe d'étudiants allemands découvre la fonderie des ateliers du Great Western Railway à Swindon, en 1927. (Ci-contre) Des écoliers du collège d'Eton admirent la mécanique de précision d'une locomotive de classe Star, la *Knight Templar*, que l'on a soulevée spécialement à leur intention.

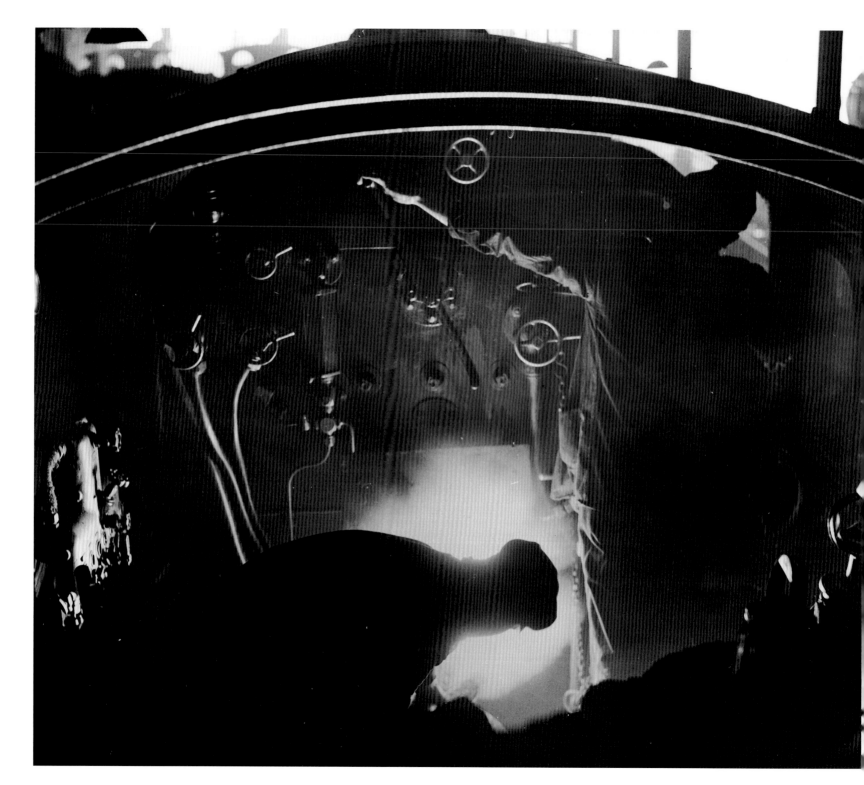

Camera compositions

(Opposite) A posed photograph celebrates the end of a work to rule protest at Stratford repair shop, 1927, when 'between 150 and 200' men returned to work. The photograph shows how the fireman and guard return to their footplate once again. The photographer would have had to crouch in the coal to take this evocative shot. (Right) Another poser? A Great Northern Atlantic firebox being cleaned by two unusually pristine firemen for the LNER.

Für die Kamera

(Gegenüberliegende Seite) Ein gestelltes Foto aus dem Ausbesserungswerk Stratford, wo die Männer im Jahre 1927 nach einem Dienst-nach-Vorschrift-Protest wieder an die Arbeit gehen; »zwischen 150 und 200« waren in den Ausstand getreten. Im Bild nehmen Heizer und Lokomotivführer ihren Dienst auf – der Fotograf muss in den Kohlenkasten gekrochen sein, um diese stimmungsvolle Aufnahme zu machen. (Rechts) Ist es echt? Zwei verdächtig saubere Heizer der LNER putzen den Feuerraum einer Great-Northern-Atlantic-Lokomotive.

Compositions

(Ci-contre) Cette image du chauffeur et du mécanicien sur leur plate-forme célèbre la fin de la grève du zèle de « 150 à 200 ouvriers » des ateliers de réparation de Stratford, en 1927. Le photographe a probablement dû s'allonger sur le charbon du tender pour prendre cette photographie évocatrice. (À droite) Deux chauffeurs du LNER, étrangement propres, nettoient la chaudière d'une Atlantic du Great Northern Railway.

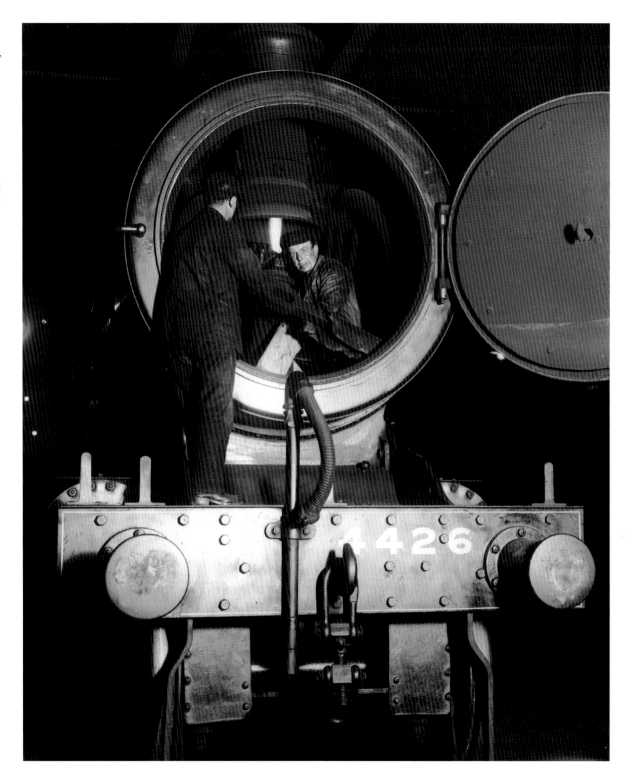

Railway operations

It was a guard's job to signal to the driver when it was safe to move off and when to stop. He was also responsible for the safety of the trains and its passengers or goods. The language of the guard was universal. (Above) A French guard sounds his horn and raises his flag to give the all-clear to the driver to move out at the Gare du Nord, Paris. (Below) In England, Richard Jarvis of the GWR whistles and raises his flag to relay the same message to the train on the opposite platform. (Right) An LNER passenger express pulled by an ex-Great Eastern (Holden 4-6-0) locomotive in East Anglia, c. 1928.

Bahnbetrieb

Der Schaffner gab dem Lokomotivführer Zeichen zur Abfahrt und zum Halten. Er war auch für die Sicherheit der Züge, der Fahrgäste und der Güter verantwortlich. Die Sprache der Signale war international. (Oben) Ein französischer Schaffner stößt ins Horn und hebt seine Fahne, für den Maschinisten im Pariser Gare du Nord die Aufforderung zur Abfahrt. (Unten) In England gibt Richard Jarvis von der GWR mit Trillerpfeife und Flagge für den Führer des Zugs am Bahnsteig gegenüber dasselbe Signal. (Rechts) Ein Expresszug der LNER in East Anglia, um 1928. Die Lokomotive ist eine Holden 2 C der ehemaligen Great Eastern.

Fonctionnement du chemin de fer

Le chef de train, responsable de la sécurité du convoi, de ses passagers et des marchandises qu'il transporte, donne au conducteur le signal du départ et lui indique quand il doit s'arrêter en utilisant des gestes conventionnels et quasi universels. (En haut) À la gare du Nord, à Paris, un chef de train français sonne de la trompe en levant son drapeau pour annoncer le départ du train. (En bas) En Grande-Bretagne, Richard Jarvis, du GWR, fait le même geste et siffle pour transmettre le même message au mécanicien du train sur le quai opposé. (À droite) Un express de voyageurs du LNER tracté par une Holden 230, de l'ancien Great Eastern Railway, en East Anglia, vers 1928.

Universal maintenance

Building and repairing the track was a vital part of railway operations. (Above) Platelayers check the alignment, known as doing the 'pencil drill', for the GWR, 1928. (Opposite, clockwise from left) Trackwalkers checked the line for defects: here 'Jo' works on the Pennsylvania Railroad in 1920; Chinese workers lay it on the line on the Shanghai to Nanking Railway, 1924; Japanese workers play it up for the camera, c. 1928.

Bahnarbeit in aller Welt

Bau und Instandhaltung der Gleise waren entscheidende Bestandteile des Bahnbetriebs. (Oben) Schienenleger der GWR prüfen 1928 die Ausrichtung. (Gegenüberliegende Seite, im Uhrzeigersinn von links) Streckenwärter, hier »Jo« auf der Pennsylvania Railroad 1920, gingen die Strecke ab und prüften sie auf Schäden; chinesische Arbeiter auf der Linie Schanghai–Nanking beschränken sich auf die akustische Prüfung, 1924; japanische Streckenarbeiter setzen sich für die Kamera in Szene, ca. 1928.

Entretien universel

La construction et la réparation des voies est une des activités essentielles dans les chemins de fer. (Ci-dessus) Des poseurs de rails rectifient l'alignement des rails d'une voie du GWR, en 1928. (Ci-contre, à gauche) Les agents de parcours étaient chargés de détecter d'éventuels défauts, comme ici Jo sur le Pennsylvania Railroad, en 1920. (En haut à droite) Des ouvriers chinois se reposent sur la voie ferrée Shanghai–Nankin, en 1924. (En bas à droite) Des ouvriers japonais saluent pour l'objectif, vers 1928.

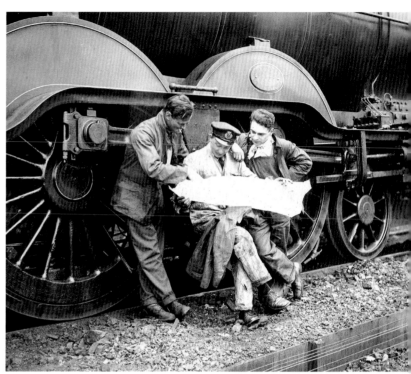

All hands to the pump

The May 1926 General Strike began with a miners' dispute which was supported by the trades unions who called on all workers in key industries, including the railways, to strike. The Government's response was to call in the volunteers. (Opposite, clockwise from left) Women take over as footplate crew; drivers and fireman study a route map; handling luggage at King's Cross; (above) inappropriately shod lady firemen set to work.

Alle Mann an die Pumpen

Der britische Generalstreik vom Mai 1926 begann mit einem Ausstand der Bergarbeiter; die Gewerkschaften schlossen sich an und riefen die Arbeiter in den Schlüsselindustrien, darunter auch den Bahnen, zum Streik auf. Die Regierung organisierte Freiwillige. (Gegenüberliegende Seite, im Uhrzeigersinn von links) Frauen übernehmen den Führerstand; Lokführer und Heizer studieren den Streckenplan; Gepäcktransport in King's Cross. (Oben) Heizerinnen mit nicht ganz passendem Schuhwerk.

Tout le monde au travail

La grève générale de mai 1926 avait pour origine un conflit dans les mines. Lorsque les syndicats lancèrent le mot d'ordre de grève dans tous les secteurs clés de l'économie, dont les chemins de fer, pour soutenir les mineurs, le gouvernement fit appel à des volontaires. (Ci-contre, à gauche) Des femmes-mécaniciens ; (en haut à droite) des mécaniciens et un chauffeur étudient une carte ; (en bas à droite) la manutention des bagages à la gare de King's Cross. (Ci-dessus) Deux femmes-chauffeurs.

Victoria Railway Station, Bombay

The original Victoria Station was opened in 1888 for the Great Indian Peninsula Railway, designed by F.W. Stevens in a medieval Italian Gothic style. It was named for Queen Victoria's Golden Jubilee on 20 June 1887. The new building opened in 1929 to deal with main line traffic. Bombay (now Mumbai) takes its name from the goddess Mumba Devi, and the earliest temple dedicated to her was formerly on the station site.

Victoria Railway Station, Bombay

Die erste Victoria Station der Great Indian Peninsula Railway, von F. W. Stevens im italienisch-gotischen Stil erbaut, wurde 1888 eingeweiht und aus Anlass des Goldjubiläums der Königin am 20. Juni 1887 nach ihr benannt. 1929 war der neue Bahnhof fertig gestellt, der dem wachsenden Verkehr Rechnung trug. Der Name Bombay (heute Mumbai) leitet sich von der Göttin Mumba Devi her, und der Bahnhof entstand auf einem Gelände, auf dem einst der älteste ihr geweihte Tempel stand.

Gare Victoria à Bombay

Conçue par F. W. Stevens dans le style gothique médiéval italien, la première gare Victoria de Bombay fut construite à l'emplacement d'un des plus anciens temples consacrés à la déesse Mumba Devi (qui a donné son nom actuel – Mumbai – à la ville de Bombay). Cette gare, baptisée du nom de la reine Victoria à l'occasion de son jubilée d'or, le 20 juin 1887, fut ouverte en 1888 pour le Great Indian Peninsula Railway. Elle fut réaménagée en 1929 pour accueillir le trafic ferroviaire de la ligne principale.

Stettin Station, Berlin

Berlin's Stettin Station was built to serve the lines from Berlin to the northern ports of Rostock and Stettin (now Szczecin, in Poland), both of which were important points of emigration and saw thousands of eastern Europeans leave for America in the last century and earlier. Opened on 1 August 1842, Stettin was at one time Berlin's largest station. Today, cosmetically restored, it serves as a storage depot.

Stettiner Bahnhof, Berlin

Vom Stettiner Bahnhof in Berlin aus gingen die Linien zu den nördlichen Hafenstädten Rostock und Stettin (heute Szczecin in Polen), beides wichtige Auswandererhäfen, von denen sich im vorigen Jahrhundert und schon früher Tausende von Osteuropäern nach Amerika einschifften. Am 1. August 1842 eröffnet, war er zeitweise der größte Bahnhof Berlins; heute dient er, kosmetisch restauriert, als Depot.

Gare de Stettin, Berlin

La gare de Stettin fut construite pour desservir les lignes entre Berlin et les ports de Rostock et de Stettin (aujourd'hui Szczecin, en Pologne), au nord de l'Allemagne, deux points d'émigration importants d'où des milliers d'Européens de l'Est partirent vers les États-Unis. Inaugurée le 1er août 1842, la gare de Stettin fut un temps l'une des plus importantes de Berlin. Elle sert aujourd'hui d'entrepôt après une restauration superficielle.

Big boys' games

Trains have always inspired a passionate following, spanning class, creed and race. (Opposite, clockwise from top left) A model engineering exhibition at the Horticultural Hall; an exhibitor at the Railway Model Club Annual Exhibition, Kingsway Hall, London; J.H. Thomas and his miniature locomotive in the gardens of Sir Edward Nichol's home, 1927. (Above) Young trainspotters at Victoria Station, London, 1928.

Für große Jungs

Eisenbahnen hatten seit jeher über alle sozialen Schranken hinweg ihre begeisterten Anhänger. (Gegenüberliegende Seite, im Uhrzeigersinn von oben links) Eine Modellbahnausstellung in der Horticultural Hall und ein Teilnehmer der jährlichen Ausstellung des Railway Model Club, Kingsway Hall, beide in London; J. H. Thomas mit seiner Miniaturlok im Garten von Sir Edward Nichol, 1927. (Oben) Junge Eisenbahnfreunde, Victoria Station, London, 1928.

Des jouets pour grands enfants

Les trains ont toujours suscité les passions, au-delà des classes sociales, des croyances et des races. (Ci-contre, en haut à gauche) Une exposition de maquettes à l'Horticultural Hall ; (à droite) un participant à l'exposition annuelle du club des amateurs de maquettes ferroviaires, à Kingsway Hall (Londres) ; (en bas à gauche) J. H. Thomas et sa locomotive miniature dans les jardins de la demeure de sir Edward Nichol, en 1927. (Ci-dessus) De jeunes admirateurs à la gare Victoria, à Londres, en 1928.

Cinema coaches

In 1924 the *Flying Scotsman* did its best to cater for all tastes. Along with a hairdressing salon, Louis XVI-style restaurant and a cocktail bar, it also boasted a cinema coach showing the latest films. (Above) *Black Oxen*, adapted from the best-selling novel by Gertrude Artherton, was released in 1924 and starred Corinne Griffith and Clara Bow. (Below) Passengers could also catch up on the latest Gary Cooper film. Later, in association with Pathé News, the LNER also attached a mobile news cinema to its trains with an advertised weekly programme.

Film im Zug

Der *Flying Scotsman* war ein Zug, der jedem etwas bot. 1924 konnte er neben dem Friseursalon, dem Restaurant im Louis-XVI-Stil und der Cocktailbar auch mit einem Kinowagen aufwarten, der die neuesten Filme zeigte. (Oben) *Black Oxen*, eine Verfilmung des Bestsellerromans von Gertrude Atherton, kam in jenem Jahr heraus; die Hauptrollen spielten Corinne Griffith und Clara Bow. (Unten) Auch der neueste Gary-Cooper-Film war zu sehen. Später richtete die LNER zusammen mit Pathé ebenfalls Wochenschaukinos in ihren Zügen ein und warb mit den wöchentlich wechselnden Programmen.

Des voitures-cinéma

En 1924, le *Flying Scotsman* proposait, outre un salon de coiffure, un restaurant de style Louis XVI et un bar, une voiture-cinéma où des films récents étaient projetés pendant le trajet : (en haut) *Black Oxen*, un film de 1924 avec Corinne Griffith et Clara Bow, adapté du best-seller de Gertrude Artherton, ou (en bas) le dernier film avec Gary Cooper. Le LNER, associé avec Pathé News, accrocha également une voiture de cinéma d'actualité, accompagnée d'un programme publié chaque semaine.

Cinema production

Film companies were quick to see the benefits of featuring trains in their films and news programmes: they were used as props, scenery, settings and atmosphere. (Above) An American train being filmed by Paramount Pictures in 1928 in a documentary about the lives of hobos who lived on and around the railroads. (Below) A British cameraman perched on the tender of a locomotive filming the footplate crew of an express train in 1930.

Zug im Film

Es dauerte nicht lange, bis die Studios merkten, dass Züge in ihren Filmen und Wochenschauen die Aufmerksamkeit der Zuschauer fesselten – schon bald lieferte die Eisenbahn Dekor, Hintergrund, Schauplatz und Atmosphäre. (Oben) Paramount Pictures nehmen im Jahr 1928 einen amerikanischen Zug für eine Dokumentation über die Hobos auf, Landstreicher, die auf den Bahnen und Bahnhöfen lebten. (Unten) Der britische Kameramann, 1930, ist oben auf den Kohlenwagen geklettert, um die Arbeit im Führerstand dieses Expresszuges zu filmen.

Production cinématographique

Les producteurs de cinéma comprirent rapidement l'intérêt de montrer des trains dans leurs films et leurs programmes d'actualité, et s'en servirent fréquemment comme accessoires, comme décor ou pour leur atmosphère. (En haut) Un train américain est filmé en 1928 dans un documentaire de la Paramount Pictures sur la vie des « hobos », ces vagabonds qui vivaient et se déplaçaient en chemin de fer aux États-Unis. (En bas) En 1930, un opérateur britannique juché sur le tender d'une locomotive filme l'équipe de conduite d'un express.

'South for Sunshine'
Happy crowds en route to the south coast from Waterloo
Station, 1927. The SR produced hundreds of guidebooks offering,
among other delights, 'Hints for Holidays'. It called itself the
'Sunshine Line' and coined the phrase 'South for Sunshine'.
The *Bournemouth Belle*, *Atlantic Coast Express* and *Devon Belle*
all ran from Waterloo to such resorts as Eastbourne, Bexhill-
on-Sea, Southsea and Folkestone.

»In den sonnigen Süden«
Glückliches Gedränge auf dem Weg an die Südküste, Waterloo
Station 1927. Die SR brachte Hunderte von Broschüren heraus,
darunter viele mit Ferientipps. Sie nannte sich »Die Sonnen-
scheinlinie« und warb mit dem Slogan »In den Süden, in die
Sonne«. *Bournemouth Belle*, *Atlantic Coast Express* und *Devon
Belle* fuhren von Waterloo aus zu Badeorten wie Eastbourne,
Bexhill-on-Sea, Southsea und Folkestone.

« Le Sud pour le soleil »
En 1927, une foule de voyageurs se presse à la gare de Waterloo
pour partir sur la côte sud de l'Angleterre. Le SR, qui se faisait
appeler la « Sunshine Line » et avait inventé le slogan « Le Sud
pour le soleil », publia des centaines de guides offrant, entre
autres promesses, des « Astuces de vacances ». Les trains *Bournemouth Belle*, *Atlantic Coast Express* et *Devon Belle* partaient de
Waterloo pour rallier des stations balnéaires britanniques
comme Eastbourne, Bexhill-on-Sea, Southsea et Folkestone.

All packed up and ready to go

The excitement and anticipation of the annual holiday away at the seaside was still a novelty in this period. The 1920s saw the advent of the mass market and industries to service it prospered. As standards of living improved, families had more time and money to spend on leisure. (Above) Packed benches at Waterloo, August 1923. (Below) Transferring luggage from taxi to train at Paddington, August 1929.

Alle Koffer gepackt

Der Sommerurlaub an der See war damals noch eine neue Errungenschaft, und entsprechend groß waren Vorbereitungen und Vorfreude. In den zwanziger Jahren entwickelten sich der Massentourismus und die Reiseindustrie, die ihn bediente. Der Lebensstandard stieg, und Familien hatten mehr Zeit und Geld zur freien Verfügung. (Oben) Vollbesetzte Bänke in Waterloo, August 1923. (Unten) Gepäcktransport vom Taxi zum Zug in Paddington, August 1929.

Bagages bouclés, et prêt au départ

C'est dans les années 1920 que l'on assiste au développement d'un marché de masse et d'industries de service prospères. Les vacances balnéaires sont encore une nouveauté mais l'amélioration de leur niveau de vie permettra ensuite aux familles de consacrer plus de temps et d'argent à leurs loisirs. (En haut) En août 1923, les bancs de la gare de Waterloo sont pleins. (En bas) Le transfert des bagages entre le taxi et le train, à la gare de Paddington, en août 1929.

The 'Penny Express'
To encourage weekend travel, the Hungarian State Railways introduced the 'Penny Express' for tourists in the late 1920s. Passengers paid only 25 per cent of the normal ticket price, getting the other 75 per cent free. The first 'Penny Express' ran one Easter Sunday between Budapest and Szeged.

Der »Pfennigexpress«
Um am Wochenende mehr Fahrgäste anzulocken, führten die ungarischen Staatsbahnen Ende der zwanziger Jahre den »Pfennigexpress« ein. Die Reisenden zahlten bei 75 % Rabatt nur ein Viertel des Fahrpreises. Der erste dieser Züge fuhr an einem Ostersonntag von Budapest nach Szegedin.

Le « Penny Express »
À la fin des années 1920, les chemins de fer de l'État hongrois lancent le « Penny Express » en offrant un billet touristique à 25 % du tarif normal afin d'encourager les excursions de fin de semaine. Le premier « Penny Express » fut mis en service le dimanche de Pâques entre Budapest et Szeged.

Special excursions

The railways offered the opportunity for all sorts of excursions for people from various walks of life. (Above) An excursion train from Nottingham carrying Boots employees to the British Empire Exhibition at Wembley in 1924. (Below) A group of 'bright young things' at Cannon Street Station ready to party. The ticket reads 'Inside Information from Mademoiselle d'Armentières'. Armentières was a rest area behind British lines in northern France in the First World War which lent its name to a song.

Sonderfahrten

Die Eisenbahn bot Ausflugsmöglichkeiten für Gruppen aller Art. (Oben) Ein Sonderzug aus Nottingham brachte im Jahr 1924 die Belegschaft der Firma Boots zur Empire-Ausstellung in Wembley. (Unten) Die wilden Zwanziger – Partygäste auf dem Bahnhof Cannon Street. Auf dem Schild heißt es »Nähere Auskünfte von Mademoiselle d'Armentières«. Armentières war im ersten Weltkrieg ein Erholungslager der britischen Armee, hinter den Linien in Nordfrankreich; ein Schlager machte es berühmt.

Excursions spéciales

Les chemins de fer offraient la possibilité de voyager à des voyageurs aux modes de vie très différents. (En haut) Un train d'excursion emmène des employés de Boots, à Nottingham, à l'exposition de l'Empire britannique organisée à Wembley en 1924. (En bas) Un groupe de «joyeuses jeunes personnes» s'apprête à partir de la gare de Cannon Street. L'inscription sur leur panneau fait référence à la ville d'Armentières, une ville du nord de la France appréciée des soldats britanniques de la Première Guerre mondiale venus s'y reposer et rendue célèbre par la chanson «Mademoiselle d'Armentières».

Sporting trains

The railways catered for all popular sporting activities; they ran excursions to sporting events, issued special tickets and programmes and carried the teams to their destinations. (Left) The Australian cricket team leaves Paddington on the GWR locomotive *Windsor Castle* in 1926 to join the Canadian Pacific liner SS *Montrose* at Liverpool to travel home. (Above) Football trains in San Francisco, 1929. These Southern Pacific trains took thousands of football fans to the Stanford games each weekend.

Sportbegeistert

Eisenbahnen trugen zu Sportereignissen bei. Es gab Sonderzüge zu den Arenen, spezielle Fahrkarten und Programme, und auch die Mannschaften kamen per Zug ans Ziel. (Links) Die australische Kricketmannschaft 1926 auf dem Rückweg mit der *Windsor Castle* der GWR vom Bahnhof Paddington nach Liverpool, wo sie an Bord der Canadian Pacific SS *Montrose* gingen. (Oben) Fußballzüge in San Francisco, 1929. Die Züge der Southern Pacific brachten jedes Wochenende Tausende von Fans zu den Spielen nach Stanford.

Trains de sportifs

Les chemins de fer proposaient leurs services lors de nombreux événements sportifs populaires. Ils transportaient fréquemment les équipes sur le lieu des rencontres. (À gauche) En 1926, l'équipe australienne de cricket quitte la gare de Paddington à bord du *Windsor Castle* du GWR pour rejoindre à Liverpool le paquebot SS *Montrose* de la Canadian Pacific qui les ramènera chez eux. (En haut) Ces trains du South Pacific, ici à San Francisco en 1929, amenaient chaque week-end des milliers de supporters des équipes de football aux compétitions de Stanford.

Watch the birdie
The British Ryder Cup team pose with Sam Ryder (centre, holding hat) at Waterloo Station just before leaving to catch a Cunard liner to America before their unsuccessful bid for the 1927 Ryder Cup. Sam Ryder was known as 'the world's best loser'.

Und lächeln!
Die britische Golfmannschaft im Wettbewerb um den Ryder-Cup, 1927, mit Stifter Sam Ryder (Mitte, mit Hut in der Hand) auf dem Bahnhof Waterloo vor dem Zug zum Cunard-Atlantikliner. Gegen die amerikanische Konkurrenz blieben sie erfolglos – Sam Ryder galt als »bester Verlierer der Welt«.

Regardez le petit oiseau!
L'équipe des golfeurs britanniques de la Ryder Cup pose avec Sam Ryder (au centre, tenant son chapeau) juste avant leur départ de la gare de Waterloo pour prendre le paquebot de la Cunard qui les emmènera aux États-Unis. Sam Ryder fut surnommé « le meilleur perdant du monde » après avoir échoué lors de la Ryder Cup de 1927.

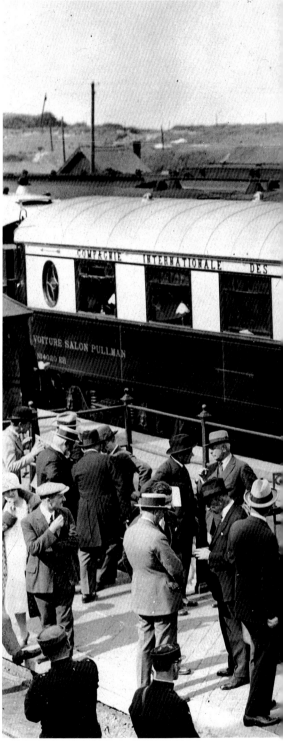

To the Continent

The SR in Britain had the advantage of being the major continental carrier, with its Channel crossing connections. The *Golden Arrow* was a de luxe train for first class Pullman passengers between London and Paris. These photographs were taken on its trial run on 17 May 1929. (Above) Sir Herbert Walker, general manager of Southern Railways, and Mr L.C. Cook, chief operating superintendent. (Right) Passengers milling around on the platform.

Auf den Kontinent

Die SR mit ihren Anschlüssen an die Kanalfähren war für britische Reisende die wichtigste Verbindung zum Kontinent. Der Luxus-Pullmanzug *Golden Arrow* verkehrte für Erster-Klasse-Passagiere von London nach Paris. Diese Aufnahmen entstanden am 17. Mai 1929 bei seiner Probefahrt. (Oben) Sir Herbert Walker, Generaldirektor von Southern Railways, und Mr L. C. Cook, Geschäftsführer. (Rechts) Fahrgäste auf dem Bahnsteig.

Vers le continent

En Grande-Bretagne, la compagnie des Southern Railways avait l'avantage d'être le plus gros transporteur européen grâce à ses liaisons trans-Manche. (Ci-dessus) Sir Herbert Walker, directeur général des Southern Railways, et L.C. Cook, superviseur en chef des opérations, sont photographiés lors du voyage inaugural du *Golden Arrow*, le 17 mai 1929. Ce luxueux train Pullman, qui assurait la relation Londres-Paris, était réservé à des voyageurs de première classe (à droite).

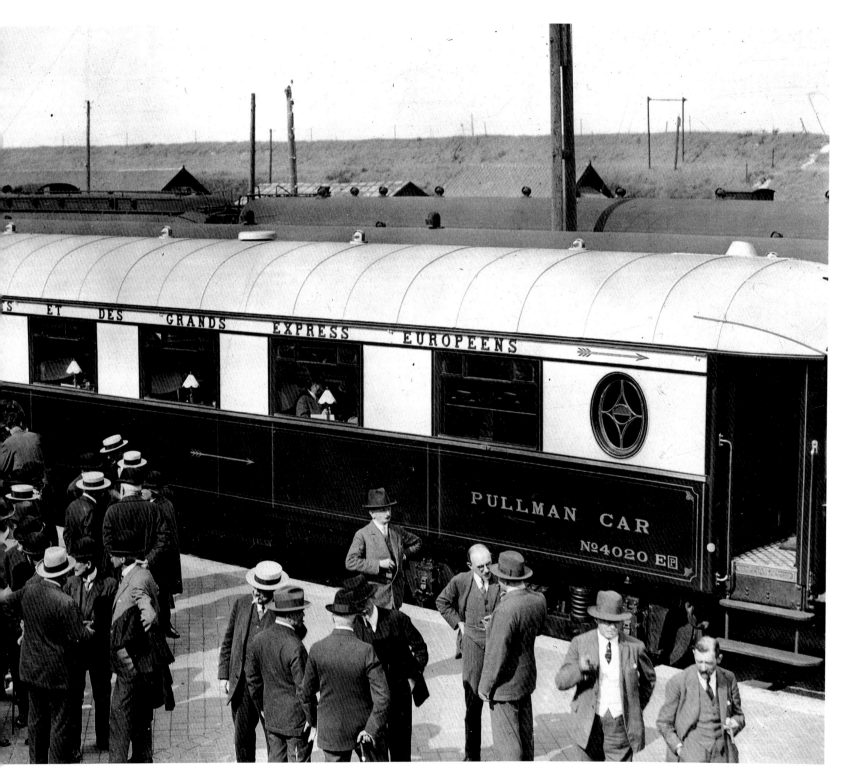

Luxury travel to and from the States

It was now possible to travel in comfort to and from the USA by train and liner. (Left) Scottish tea magnate Sir Thomas Lipton leaving London for New York in 1929 to take part in the Americas Cup. (Above) In 1927 the GWR advertised its 'Land Cruises' in the USA. Tickets were offered for holiday tours very much like the package holiday of today. The intention was to 'make haste slowly'; progress was indeed leisurely.

Stilvoll in die USA

Die Kombination aus Dampfer und Bahn machte Luxusreisen über den Atlantik möglich. (Links) Der schottische Teemagnat Sir Thomas Lipton bricht 1929 zur Teilnahme am Americas Cup von London nach New York auf. (Oben) 1927 warb die GWR für »Landausflüge« in die Vereinigten Staaten, ähnlich den heutigen Pauschalreisen. Das Motto war »Mit Muße in die Ferne«, und tatsächlich waren diese Reisen sehr gemächlich.

Voyage luxueux de et vers les États-Unis

Il était désormais possible de voyager confortablement de et vers les États-Unis en combinant train et paquebot. (À gauche) En 1929, le magnat écossais du thé, sir Thomas Lipton, quitte Londres pour se rendre à New York où il participera à la Coupe de l'America. (Ci-dessus) En 1927, le GWR fait aux États-Unis la publicité de ses « Croisières terrestres », qui annoncent déjà les actuels voyages organisés à forfait, en lançant le slogan « se dépêcher lentement ». Le progrès passe à l'évidence par les loisirs.

Throwing a lifeline

The railway networks were not just playthings for the rich but were used as lifelines in times of poverty and famine. (Above) Thousands of people left Tashkent, Uzbekistan, during the famine of 1921–22 by the Trans Caspian Railway. (Below) Jackie Coogan, the child actor best remembered for his role of Uncle Fester in *The Addams Family*, gives his support to the American Near East Refugee Aid in 1928. Their mission was to reduce poverty and relieve suffering in the Middle East. Blankets, tents and condensed milk were sent by rail.

Ein Funken Hoffnung

Bahnen waren nicht nur Spielzeuge für die Reichen, sondern konnten in Zeiten von Armut und Hunger auch die letzte Rettung sein. (Oben) Tausende flohen während der Hungerkatastrophe von 1921–1922 mit der Transkaspischen Eisenbahn aus Taschkent, Usbekistan. (Unten) Kinderstar Jackie Coogan, vor allem für seine Rolle als Onkel Festus in der *Addams-Familie* im Gedächtnis geblieben, macht 1928 Werbung für die amerikanische Nahost-Flüchtlingshilfe, die Armut und Leiden der in Not Geratenen lindern sollte. Decken, Zelte und Kondensmilch wurden per Zug verschickt.

Une ligne de vie

Les chemins de fer n'étaient pas uniquement un jouet pour gens riches mais jouaient parfois un rôle vital en période de misère et de famine. (En haut) Des milliers de personnes quittent Tashkent (Ouzbékistan) par le Transcaspien lors de la famine de 1921–1922. (En bas) En 1928, Jackie Coogan – l'enfant-acteur dont on se souvient notamment pour son rôle d'oncle Fester dans *La Famille Addams* – vient soutenir l'action de l'American Near East Refugee Aid, dont la mission était de réduire la misère et de soulager les souffrances des peuples du Moyen-Orient en leur distribuant couvertures, tentes et lait condensé, expédiés par chemin de fer depuis les pays riches.

Camping coaches, Germany 1920
Whilst first class carriages were turned into hotels for
tourists during German's post-war crisis, many ordin-
ary homeless families resorted to using old railway
freight trucks as temporary living quarters. A mother
is doing the household washing with her children outside their railway carriage home. Many of these were
later turned into chicken coops.

Notquartiere, Deutschland 1920
In den schwierigen Nachkriegsjahren dienten in
Deutschland Erster-Klasse-Wagen als Hotels für die
Reisenden, und manche obdachlose Familie suchte
sich in einem ausrangierten Güterwagen ein notdürftiges Quartier. Eine Mutter mit Kindern wäscht
vor einem solchen Heim die Wäsche. Später dienten
die Waggons oft noch als Hühnerställe.

Des voitures de camping, Allemagne 1920
Tandis que les voitures de première classe sont trans-
formées en hôtels pour touristes pendant la crise de
l'après-guerre en Allemagne, nombre de familles sans
domicile s'installent dans des wagons de marchandises abandonnés (plus tard transformés en poulaillers).

Germany at war

Railways have played a prominent role in the history of Germany. (Above) The 1918 Armistice was signed in a railway carriage at Rethondes. One of the conditions of the surrender was that Germany had to hand over 150,000 railway carriages to the Allies. German soldiers also understood the important role the railways were playing in the war. (Below) Soldiers sabotage their own locomotive at Düsseldorf in 1923.

Deutschland im Krieg

In der deutschen Geschichte haben Eisenbahnen eine wichtige Rolle gespielt. (Oben) Der Waffenstillstand von 1918 wurde in einem Eisenbahnwagen im Wald von Compiègne unterzeichnet. Zu den Bedingungen der Kapitulation gehörte, dass Deutschland den Alliierten 150 000 Waggons zu überlassen hatte. Deutsche Soldaten wussten auch, welche wichtige Rolle Eisenbahnen für den Krieg spielten. (Unten) Soldaten sabotieren ihre eigene Lokomotive, Düsseldorf 1923.

L'Allemagne en guerre

Les chemins de fer ont joué un rôle essentiel dans l'histoire de l'Allemagne. (En haut) L'Armistice de 1918 fut signé à Rethondes dans une voiture de chemin de fer. L'une des conditions du traité était que l'Allemagne fournisse 150 000 wagons aux Alliés. Les soldats allemands, comme ceux-ci qui sabotent leur propre locomotive à Düsseldorf en 1923 (en bas), ont également vite compris l'importance des chemins de fer en période de guerre.

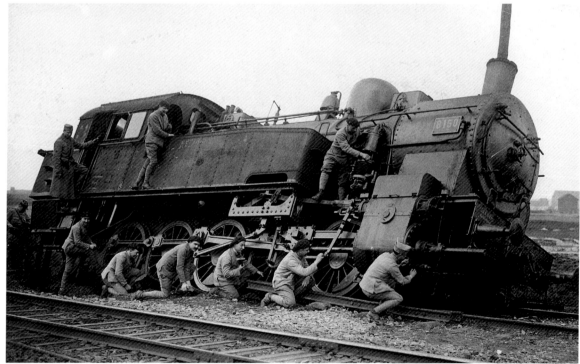

War reparations

France demanded heavy reparations from post-war Germany. She gained the right to occupy the Rhine for fifteen years and, when payments were defaulted, she occupied the Ruhr. This French soldier stands guard on a pile of coke near Cologne, c. 1920.

Reparationen

Nach dem Weltkrieg forderten die Franzosen von Deutschland schwere Reparationen. Der Friedensvertrag sah eine 15-jährige Besetzung des Rheinlandes vor, und als die Zahlungen ausblieben, wurde zudem das Ruhrgebiet okkupiert. Hier bewacht ein französischer Soldat in der Nähe von Köln einen Zug mit Briketts, um 1920.

Réparations de guerre

La France exigea de lourds dommages de guerre à l'Allemagne et, ayant obtenu le droit d'occuper le Rhin pendant 15 ans, occupa la Ruhr lorsque l'Allemagne interrompit le paiement de sa dette. Ce soldat français monte la garde sur un wagon de briques de coke près de Cologne, vers 1920.

Going home…
In the mid-Twenties Germany returned to the international scene. The Allied troops left the Rhineland in 1930.
(Left) Eleven years of occupation ends with a passionate kiss before the troop train leaves.

In die Heimat …
Ab Mitte der zwanziger Jahre kehrte Deutschland auf das internationale Parkett zurück. 1930 verließen die Alliierten schrittweise das besetzte Rheinland. (Links) 11 Jahre Besatzungszeit enden mit einem leidenschaftlichen Kuss, dann dampft der Zug mit den Soldaten davon.

De retour …
Au milieu des années 1920, l'Allemagne réapparut sur le devant de la scène internationale. En 1930, les troupes alliées ont quitté pas à pas la Rhénanie occupée.
(À gauche) Ces onze années de présence s'achèvent par un baiser passionné avant le départ du train.

...home to Blighty

Germany had plumbed the depths of human misery after the war; Britain had experienced the General Strike in 1926 which reflected dire unemployment at home, among other things. Young German girls say goodbye to troops, both sides exuding a degree of optimism. The dog has seen enough.

... reif für die Insel

Der Krieg hatte Deutschland in tiefes Elend gestürzt; Großbritannien war vom General-streik von 1926 erschüttert, nicht zuletzt ein Ausdruck der allgegenwärtigen Arbeitslosig-keit. Deutsche Mädchen verabschieden die Besatzer. Die Szene strahlt auf beiden Seiten einen gewissen Optimismus aus. Nur dem Hund wird es zu viel.

... en Angleterre

Si l'Allemagne a connu des années de profon-de misère après-guerre, la Grande-Bretagne a subi en 1926 une grève générale, consécutive entre autres à un taux de chômage désastreux. Mais ces soldats britanniques des troupes d'occupation et ces jeunes Allemandes venues leur dire adieu font chacun assaut d'optimis-me. Quant au chien, il en a déjà bien trop vu !

Go to gaol

IRA prisoners en route to incarceration in Britain via the Great Western Railway, c. 1922. In this period it was perfectly usual to imprison Irish political prisoners across the water in England so as to remove them from the main areas of conflict and influence.

Gehe ins Gefängnis

IRA-Gefangene werden mit der Great Western Railway in britische Haftanstalten gebracht, ca. 1922. Damals war es durchaus üblich, politische Gefangene aus Irland auf der Hauptinsel unterzubringen, wo sie weit ab von den Konflikt-herden waren und ihr Einfluss schwand.

En prison

Ces prisonniers de l'IRA sont emmenés sur leur lieu d'incarcé-ration, en Grande-Bretagne, dans une voiture du Great Western Railway. À cette période, vers 1922, il était fréquent d'incarcérer les prisonniers politiques irlandais en Angleterre afin de les éloigner des zones principales de conflit et les soustraire à toute influence indépendantiste.

The difficult years
The years between 1900 and 1925 were not easy ones for the Dublin and South Eastern Railways in Ireland. When the IRA decided to turn its attention to the railways, stations were blown up, trains ambushed or derailed, as was the fate of this one at Killuvin, which alone suffered four attacks in 1922.

Schwierige Jahre
Die Jahre zwischen 1900 und 1925 waren für die irische Dublin and South Eastern Railways nicht leicht. Als die IRA die Eisenbahnen erst einmal als Ziel entdeckt hatte, wurden Bahnhöfe in die Luft gesprengt und Züge beschossen oder zum Entgleisen gebracht, wie hier in Killuvin; diese Strecke war allein 1922 viermal Ziel solcher Anschläge.

Les années difficiles
La période entre 1900 et 1925 fut difficile pour les Dublin and South Eastern Railways irlandais. L'IRA, ayant en effet décidé de s'attaquer aux chemins de fer, fit sauter des gares et dérailler des trains, comme ici à Killuvin, où la ligne subit quatre attaques successives en 1922.

The train approaching roof top number...

At 6.42 on Friday 15 August 1926 a train from Shepperton left the track and derailed four coaches. Luckily, the train was practically empty and there were no casualties. It caused a delay of between ten and fifteen minutes to nearby trains but how long the brewery it ran into was inconvenienced was not reported. The locomotive is an SER 4-4-4.

Der Zug hat Einfahrt auf das Dach Nummer ...

Am Freitag dem 15. August 1926 um 6.42 Uhr entgleisen vier Wagen eines aus Shepperton kommenden Zuges. Zum Glück war er fast leer, und es kam niemand zu Schaden. Die nachfolgenden Züge fuhren mit 10–15 Minuten Verspätung; wie lange es dauerte, bis die Brauerei, die er gerammt hatte, wieder instand gesetzt war, ist nicht überliefert. Die Lokomotive im Bild ist eine SER 2 B 2.

Le train en approche du toit numéro ...

C'est à 6 h 42 du matin, le vendredi 15 août 1926, qu'un train venant de Shepperton quitte la voie en provoquant le déraillement de quatre voitures. Le convoi étant heureusement pratiquement vide, l'accident ne fit pas de blessés mais provoqua un retard de dix à quinze minutes des trains voisins. On ne sait pas combien de temps dut fermer la brasserie que heurta cette locomotive de type 222 du SER.

Tragic derailment

In the same year a night express travelling from Berlin to Cologne to connect with the Flushing–Folkestone boat train was derailed at Lehrte, killing twenty and injuring many more. German policemen and their dogs examine the wreckage.

Ein tragischer Fall

Im selben Jahr entgleiste ein Expresszug von Berlin nach Köln, wo er Anschluss an die Fähre Vlissingen–Folkestone haben sollte, bei Lehrte; 20 Personen kamen ums Leben, und es gab zahlreiche Verletzte. Deutsche Polizisten und ihre Hunde erkunden den Unfallort.

Déraillement tragique

La même année, l'express de nuit Berlin-Cologne assurant la correspondance avec le train-bateau Flushing-Folkestone déraille à Lehrte, provoquant la mort de 20 voyageurs et de nombreux blessés. Des gendarmes allemands accompagnés de chiens examinent le lieu du désastre.

The *Flying Scotsman*

By the time this photograph was taken, on 9 July 1929, the *Flying Scotsman* was the world's most famous express and the world's longest daily non-stop run. The train left King's Cross at 10 a.m. every day and reached Edinburgh Waverley Station just over 8 hours later, having covered 392.7 miles. The train first ran in 1862 and still runs today. The first non-stop run was on 1 May 1928.

Flying Scotsman

Als dieses Bild am 9. Juli 1929 entstand, war der *Flying Scotsman* der berühmteste Expresszug der Welt, und keiner fuhr Tag für Tag eine längere Nonstopstrecke. Der Zug verließ jeweils um 10 Uhr morgens King's Cross und traf etwas über acht Stunden später auf dem Waverley-Bahnhof in Edinburgh ein, eine Strecke von 631,9 Kilometern. Der Zug fuhr erstmals 1862 und er verkehrt bis heute. Die erste Nonstopfahrt fand am 1. Mai 1928 statt.

Le *Flying Scotsman*

À l'époque où cette photographie a été prise, le 9 juillet 1929, le *Flying Scotsman* était l'express le plus célèbre du monde. Il assurait alors le plus long trajet quotidien sans arrêt (631,9 kilomètres), quittant la gare londonienne de King's Cross tous les jours à 10 heures du matin pour atteindre la gare de Waverley, à Édimbourg, à peine plus de 8 heures plus tard. Ce train, mis en service en 1862, fonctionne toujours aujourd'hui. Le premier trajet sans arrêt eut lieu le 1er mai 1928.

The dining car

The *Flying Scotsman* was also the ultimate in luxury passenger travel. New coaches were added in 1929 for the non-stop run and Sir Charles Allom, an interior decorator, advised on the decor of the first class restaurant car. The car contained light, moveable chairs to suggest a private dining room, and concealed lighting with matching wall coverings and curtains.

Der Speisewagen

Der *Flying Scotsman* galt auch als luxuriösester aller Züge. Für die Nonstopfahrt kamen im Jahr 1929 neue Wagen dazu, und die Ausstattung des Speisewagens der ersten Klasse entstand unter Mitarbeit des Inneneinrichters Sir Charles Allom. Der Wagen war mit leichten, frei beweglichen Stühlen ausgestattet, mit denen er wie ein privates Esszimmer wirkte, dazu mit indirekter Beleuchtung, passender Wandbespannung und passenden Vorhängen.

La voiture-restaurant

Le *Flying Scotsman* était le parangon du luxe pour les voyages en chemin de fer. De nouvelles voitures furent mises en service en 1929 lorsque le parcours fut effectué sans arrêt. Sir Charles Allom, un architecte d'intérieur, chargé de la décoration de la voiture-restaurant de première classe, fit installer un éclairage indirect, couvrir les parois de tentures, accrocher des rideaux aux fenêtres et installer des fauteuils mobiles pour que les voyageurs aient l'impression d'être dans une salle à manger.

Royal transport

King George V opened the British Empire Exhibition at Wembley on St George's Day, 23 April 1924. It was designed to show the world the wealth, resources and unity of the British Empire. In the amusement park at the exhibition King George and Queen Mary ride in a model train.

Der König amüsiert sich

König Georg V. eröffnete die British Empire Exhibition in Wembley am Sankt-Georgs-Tag, dem 23. April 1924. Die Ausstellung sollte der Welt den Wohlstand, die Ressourcen und die Einigkeit des britischen Weltreiches vor Augen führen. Im Vergnügungspark des Geländes unternahmen der König und seine Gemahlin Mary eine Fahrt auf der Miniatureisenbahn.

Transport royal

Le 23 avril 1924, jour de la Saint-Georges, le roi George V inaugura à Wembley l'Exposition de l'Empire britannique, destinée à présenter au monde les richesses, les ressources et l'unité de l'Empire britannique. On voit ici le roi George et la reine Mary juchés sur le train miniature du parc de loisirs de l'Exposition.

Palaces on wheels

Royal trains played an important part in the travel arrangements of royalty and resulted in some of the most sumptuous carriages ever built. (Above) After their wedding at Westminster Abbey on 28 February 1922, Princess Mary and Viscount Lascelles travelled in this honeymoon train. (Below) The Queen's day saloon, 1928. Built in 1908 at Doncaster for Edward VII, and originally the King's saloon, it was redesigned in 1924 for Queen Mary and used by HM the Queen Mother. It was withdrawn from service in 1978.

Rollende Paläste

Königliche Züge spielten eine wichtige Rolle, und wenn Monarchen auf Reisen gingen, enstanden zu diesem Zweck einige der prächtigsten, jemals gebauten Wagen. (Oben) Nach der Zeremonie in der Westminster-Abtei am 28. Februar 1922 fuhren Prinzessin Mary und Viscount Lascelles mit diesem Hochzeitszug in die Flitterwochen. (Unten) Der Salon der Königin, 1928. Der Wagen war 1908 in Doncaster für Edward VII. gebaut worden; 1924 wurde er für Königin Mary neu ausgestattet, später nutzte ihn Ihre Majestät die Königin-mutter. 1978 wurde er außer Dienst gestellt.

Palais sur bogies

Le chemin de fer était un mode de locomotion fréquemment utilisé par les membres de la famille royale d'Angleterre, le train royal disposant des voitures les plus somptueuses jamais réalisées. (En haut) Après leur mariage à l'abbaye de West-minster, le 28 février 1922, la princesse Mary et le vicomte Lascelles partirent en train pour leur lune de miel à bord de cette voiture. (En bas) Le salon de la reine, en 1928 ; construite en 1908 à Doncaster pour Edward VII, et à l'origine la voiture-salon du roi, elle fut redécorée en 1924 pour la reine Mary et utilisée par Sa Majesté la reine Mère. Elle fut retirée du service en 1978.

Monkey business

Monkeys associated with the Hindu monkey god Hanuman wait on the low, earth-built platform at Ayodhya on the Faizabad loop for food provided by the rail passengers. The guards are about to check their platform tickets.

Eine Affenschande

Affen, die mit dem hinduistischen Affengott Hanuman in Verbindung gebracht werden, erbetteln auf dem flachen Lehmbahnsteig von Ayodhya auf der Faizabad-Strecke von den Reisenden Essen. Die Schaffner werden gleich die Bahnsteigkarten kontrollieren.

Singeries

Des singes, associés au dieu hindou Hanuman, attendent sur le quai en terre d'Ayodhya, dans la boucle de Faizabad, que les voyageurs leur donnent à manger, tandis que les chefs de train s'apprêtent à contrôler les billets.

Hills and dams, tea and textiles

(Above) The first train to pass over the Blue Nile Dam. Built by the British in 1925, the Blue Nile, or Sennar, Dam enabled the textile industry in the Sudan to prosper. (Below) A contrast of the old with the new: a train on the Darjeeling Railway (an outstanding example of a hill passenger railway) in the foothills of the Himalayas passes bullock carts on its way down to Darjeeling.

Berge, Dämme, Tee und Textilien

(Oben) Der erste Zug überquert den Staudamm am Blauen Nil. Der von den Briten 1925 erbaute Nil- oder Sennardamm ermöglichte erst den Ausbau der sudanesischen Textilindustrie. (Unten) Alt und Neu begegnen sich: Ein Zug der Darjeelingbahn trifft auf seinem Weg hinab nach Darjeeling am Fuße des Himalaja zwei Ochsenkarren. Die Darjeelingbahn war eine Meisterleistung des Bergbahnbaus.

Collines et barrages, thé et tissus

(En haut) Construit par les Britanniques en 1925, le barrage du Nil Bleu (ou Sennar), que franchit ici pour la première fois un train, permit le développement de l'industrie textile soudanaise. (En bas) Contraste entre tradition et modernisme : un train du Darjeeling Railway (formidable exemple de chemin de fer de montagne) croise des chars à bœufs dans les contreforts des cols de l'Himalaya lors de sa descente vers Darjeeling.

Hotels on wheels
Every effort was made to ensure that passengers travelled in comfort and style. (Above) Cleaners preparing a saloon in the Royal train, c. 1928. (Below) The lounge bar of the *Royal Scot* where passengers could enjoy the comfort of a first-class hotel with wonderful views of Britain. The *Royal Scot* was an LMS train that ran between London Euston and Glasgow.

Hotels auf Rädern
Kein Aufwand war zu groß für ein stilvolles und komfortables Reisen. (Oben) Ein Salonwagen des königlichen Zuges wird auf Hochglanz gebracht, ca. 1928. (Unten) Die Bar des *Royal Scot*, wo die Fahrgäste den Komfort eines Erster-Klasse-Hotels und zugleich die schönsten Aussichten auf die britische Landschaft genießen konnten. Der *Royal Scot* der LMS verkehrte zwischen dem Londoner Bahnhof Euston und Glasgow.

Hôtels sur bogies
Tout était mis en œuvre pour offrir un cadre élégant et confortable aux voyageurs. (En haut) Le personnel de nettoyage prépare un salon du train royal, vers 1928. (En bas) Le salon-bar du *Royal Scot* du LMS, qui reliait la gare londonienne d'Euston à Glasgow, offrait aux passagers non seulement un confort équivalent à celui d'un hôtel quatre étoiles mais également des vues magnifiques sur la campagne britannique.

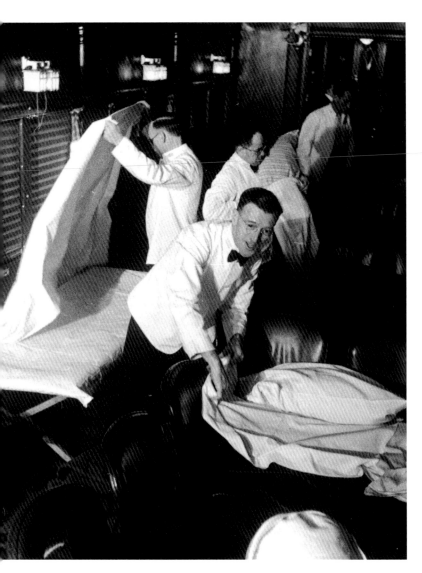

Sleeping arrangements

Many trains had accommodation for overnight travel either in berths or apartments. Most also had lavatories and an attendant to serve refreshments. (Above left) Sleeping was not only for passengers. Here stewards make up their own beds on couches in the dining car in 1929. (Above right) Sleeping accommodation in America was essential because of the distances covered. Here a lady elegantly adorns a coach in 1928. No doubt fashion dictated that she have the kimono-style dressing gown and fur-trimmed coat.

Schlafquartiere

Viele Züge waren auf Übernachtungen eingerichtet, mit Kojen oder eigenen Abteilen. Die meisten verfügten auch über Waschräume, und ein Kellner servierte Erfrischungen. (Oben links) Nicht nur die Passagiere schliefen im Zug. Hier richten Kellner sich im Speisewagen ihre Feldbetten her, 1929. (Oben rechts) Amerikanische Entfernungen waren ohne Übernachtung nicht zu bewältigen. Auf diesem Bild schmückt eine elegante Dame ein Abteil von 1928; der Kimono-Morgenrock und der Mantel mit Pelzkragen entsprachen zweifellos der neuesten Mode.

Trains de nuit

La plupart des trains de nuit disposaient de voitures avec cou-chettes ou cabines, souvent équipés de toilettes, et où un garçon assurait le service des rafraîchissements. (Ci-dessus à gauche) Les employés pouvaient également dormir à bord pendant les longs voyages. On voit ici les serveurs préparer leur couchette dans la voiture-restaurant, en 1929. (Ci-dessus à droite) Les trains américains, qui assuraient des liaisons sur de grandes distances, offraient également de confortables compartiments avec lit, comme celui où repose cette élégante jeune femme, en 1928. Le kimono et l'étole de fourrure étaient alors à la mode.

Experimental engines

Railways had always been keen to use an alternative fuel to coal to operate locomotives. (Opposite, clockwise from top left) An American petrol electric articulated rail motor car, c. 1920; an LNER electric locomotive at Newcastle quayside, 1924; an LNER petrol-driven locomotive; an LMS heavy oil or diesel locomotive; (above) an oil electric locomotive being used by the Canadian National Railways.

Neue Wege im Lokomotivenbau

Von Anfang an waren die Bahngesellschaften auf der Suche nach einer Alternative zur Kohlenfeuerung ihrer Lokomotiven. (Gegenüberliegende Seite, im Uhrzeigersinn von oben links) Ein amerikanischer Triebwagen mit Benzin-Elektro-Antrieb, um 1920; eine Elektrolok der LNER im Hafen von Newcastle, 1924; ein LNER-Schienenbus mit Benzinmotor; eine mit Schweröl oder Diesel betriebene Lok von LMS; (oben) eine dieselelektrische Lokomotive der Canadian National Railways.

Machines expérimentales

Les compagnies de chemin de fer ont toujours cherché à utiliser d'autres forces motrices que la vapeur pour faire fonctionner leurs locomotives. (Ci-contre, en haut à gauche) Une locomotive pétroléo-électrique articulée, vers 1920 ; (en haut à droite) une locomotive électrique du LNER, 1924 ; (en bas à droite) une locomotive à moteur à essence du LNER ; (en bas à gauche) une locomotive diesel ou à fuel lourd du LMS. (Ci-dessus) Une locomotive électro-diesel des Canadian National Railways.

Engine cleaning

Locomotives had to be cleaned and prepared for operating. (Opposite) A US army locomotive being cleaned in a maintenance depot. (Above left) A cleaner at the King's Cross sheds, c. 1928. (Above right) A British locomotive being positioned over an ashpit ready for ashing out, c. 1928.

Großreinemachen

Dampflokomotiven mussten regelmäßig gereinigt und für den nächsten Einsatz vorbereitet werden. (Gegenüberliegende Seite) Eine Lok der US-Armee wird in einem Betriebswerk geputzt. (Oben links) Ein Arbeiter im Lokschuppen von King's Cross, ca. 1928. (Oben rechts) Eine britische Lokomotive wird über die Aschgrube gefahren, bereit zum Ausleeren der Asche, um 1928.

Nettoyage des machines

Les locomotives étaient lavées et préparées avant leur mise en service. (Ci-contre) Une locomotive de l'armée américaine en cours de nettoyage dans les ateliers d'entretien. (Ci-dessus à gauche) Un ouvrier nettoyeur du dépôt de King's Cross, vers 1928. (Ci-dessus à droite) Une locomotive britannique vient vider ses cendres au-dessus de la fosse à cendrier, vers 1928.

The American Dream
Two photographs radiating the
optimism of immigrants who
travelled to the USA hoping for
a better, brighter future.
(Above) A family studies the
departure board at the Southern
Pacific Railroad station Oakland
Pier in San Francisco, 1926.
(Right) Six magnificent K4 Pacifics
on the Pennsylvania Railroad. They
were built between 1914 and 1928 by
the Pennsylvania Railroad.

Der amerikanische Traum
Zwei Bilder bringen den Optimismus der Einwanderer zum Ausdruck, die in der Hoffnung auf eine
schönere und bessere Zukunft in
die Vereinigten Staaten kamen.
(Oben) Eine Familie studiert
die Abfahrtstafel des Southern-
Pacific-Bahnhofs, Oakland Pier,
San Francisco, 1926. (Rechts) Sechs
prachtvolle K4-Pacifics der Pennsylvania Railroad, sie wurden von
1914 bis 1928 gebaut.

Le Rêve américain
Ces deux photographies témoignent
de l'optimisme des immigrants, qui
se rendaient aux États-Unis dans
l'espoir d'un avenir meilleur et plus
radieux. (Ci-dessus) En 1926, une
famille consulte le panneau des
horaires de la gare du Southern
Pacific Railroad, Oakland Pier, à
San Francisco. (À droite) Ces six
magnifiques Pacific de classe K4
furent construites entre 1914 et 1928
par le Pennsylvania Railroad.

Porter!

Uniformed baggage handlers (and a few straw-hatted onlookers) meet the camera's eye as they wait on the curb outside the Gare du Nord, Paris, in 1928, for the arrival of passengers and luggage.

Gepäckträger

Uniformierte Gepäckträger (und einige Zuschauer mit Strohhüten) warten vor dem Gare du Nord auf Fahrgäste und ihr Gepäck, Paris, 1928.

Porteur !

Des porteurs en uniforme (et quelques spectateurs avec des chapeaux de paille) attendent des passagers et leurs bagages à l'entrée de la Gare du Nord, Paris, 1928.

The Nord Express

The main concourse of the Gare du Nord Station, Paris, 1929.
Built by Jacques-Ignace Hittorff and opened in 1864, the station
served local areas, such as Pontoise, and was the point of departure for trains to Belgium, Holland, nothern Germany and the
Scandinavian countries. Visible in the photograph are the rows
of cast-iron columns that support the glass roof of the station.

Der Nordexpress

Die Bahnhofshalle der Pariser Gare du Nord, 1929. Die von
Jacques-Ignace Hittorff erbaute, 1864 eröffnete Station bediente
lokale Strecken, etwa nach Pontoise, und war Kopfbahnhof für
die Verbindungen nach Belgien, Holland, Norddeutschland und
Skandinavien. Das Bild zeigt die gusseisernen Säulenreihen,
auf denen das Glasdach ruht.

Le Nord Express

Le grand hall de la gare du Nord, à Paris en 1929, construite
par Jacques-Ignace Hittorff et inaugurée en 1864. Ses trains
assuraient la desserte locale du nord de la capitale, comme la
ville de Pontoise, ainsi que la Belgique, les Pays-Bas, le nord
de l'Allemagne et le pays scandinaves. On remarque sur la
photographie les colonnades de fonte qui soutiennent la
grande verrière.

North American peculiarities

(Opposite) A Union Pacific 9000 locomotive, 1926. The only surviving locomotive of its kind, it is now cared for by the Southern Californian Chapter Railway. In its day it broke new ground with twelve drive wheels powered by three cylinders and a wheelbase of over 30 feet. (Above) The CPR commissioned photographers specifically to record the progress of the railways, providing them with a special darkroom car and giving them complimentary passes.

Amerikanische Schaustücke

(Gegenüberliegende Seite) Eine 9000er-Lok der Union Pacific, 1926. Das Bild zeigt das einzige erhaltene Exemplar, heute in der Obhut der Southern Californian Chapter Railway, seinerzeit eine bahnbrechende Konstruktion mit drei Zylindern, zwölf Antriebsrädern und einem Radstand von über neun Metern. (Oben) Die CPR leistete sich eigene Fotografen, die den Ausbau des Streckennetzes festhielten und neben der Freifahrkarte auch ihre eigene Dunkelkammer im Wagen hatten.

Particularités nord-américaines

(Ci-contre) Une locomotive n° 9000 de l'Union Pacific, en 1926. Il ne reste qu'un seul exemplaire de ce type, aujourd'hui entretenu par le Southern Californian Chapter Railway. Très moderne pour son époque, cette machine d'un empattement de plus de 9 mètres de longueur disposait de 12 roues motrices actionnées par 3 cylindres. (Ci-dessus) Ayant demandé à des photographes d'immortaliser les progrès du chemin de fer, le CPR mit à leur disposition une voiture spéciale équipée d'une chambre noire.

4

The Age of Travel

In the 1930s railway travel reached its zenith in terms of style, speed and availability. The atrocities and terror of the First World War were put behind and the threat of another war, the rise of fascism and the potential effect on the future were largely ignored until the late thirties. People were determined to look to the future and live life to the full. The opening photograph in this chapter (pp. 224–225), showing New York's Grand Central Station in 1930 by Hal Morey, epitomises this decade of railway history. Reflected in this image are the pride, optimism and confidence at the beginning of the thirties.

Luxurious, named trains and steam and diesel records were an important feature of this era. One of the fastest services in North America was the *International Limited*, the first of the Canadian National's super expresses, which ran from Montreal to Chicago via Toronto, a distance of 849 miles, in seventeen and a half hours. It was the ultimate in luxury with a sleeping chambrette (a small private bedroom), a dining car with special menus for children and colonialist coaches which were similar to European third class. In these coaches the seats could be converted into sleeping accommodation and passengers could cook their own meals on a range. The *Continental Limited* was already running between Montreal and the Pacific Coast (Vancouver), and the *Canadian National Maritime Express* ran from Halifax to Nova Scotia and Montreal via Quebec. They were pulled by Hudson or 5700 type locomotives with six coupled driving wheels and could pull up to 1,000 tons. They also had 'booster' power, an extra steam engine driving the rear bogie wheels under the locomotive cab which was used for starting up. The US Pennsylvania Railroad ran the exclusive *Broadway Limited* which was rivalled by the New York Central Railroad's *Twentieth Century Limited*. In 1935 the largest stretch of electrified line was opened on the Chicago, Milwaukee, St Paul and Pacific Railroad and in May of the same year the Burlington Railroad's Pioneer *Zephyr* reached 112.5mph and earned the world railway speed record. The three-coach stainless steel streamlined train also ran the 1,015 miles between Denver and Chicago non-stop, at an overall average speed of 77.6mph. Not only was the railroad station now a centre of social activity, it was also an architectural expression of collective urban life. With competition from road and air transport looming, stations took on an international style and mass consumption was embraced. The original lofty station built to allow the dispersal of steam and smoke now became a symbol of modernity. Architecture now developed a new international style and used space more rationally and productively so that the station became the functional hub of many major cities.

In Germany the Zeppelin on rails was developed. Constructed by Kruckenberg of Hamburg, its streamlined frame reduced air restriction to a minimum. The concept of this Zeppelin led to the Reichsbahn developing the *Fliegender Hamburger*. Inside there were no separate compartments but one saloon with seats for up to fifty people. There was a luggage room at the front of the unit and a bar in the middle. In France the Bugatti railcars of the PLM and state railways were being developed and the major named trains were the *Nord Express*, which was a transcontinental train with wagon lits and Pullman carriages, and the *Sud Express*, which ran on the Paris–Orleans–Midi line between Paris and the Spanish frontier. In South Africa in 1939 the *Blue Train* was introduced on the 1,540 km stretch between Cape Town and Pretoria and is now regarded as the most luxurious train in the world.

In Britain the 'Big Four' started to give their trains names as a way of fostering their competitive services. The GWR express train was named the *Cheltenham Spa Express* but soon came to be known by its nickname, the 'Cheltenham Flyer'. In 1931 it was advertised as 'the fastest train in the world' and its quickest journey was recorded on 6 June 1932. The locomotive pulling this train was the four cylinder 4-6-0 No. 5006 *Tregenna Castle*. The train consisting of six coaches weighed 196 tons, including passengers and luggage. By 1935 the GWR *Cornish Riviera Express* was operating twice a day. The SR ran commuter trains such as the electric *Brighton Belle* which was composed of Pullman cars. The SR also had the first electric main line in Britain. However, the greatest rivalry during the 1930s was between the Anglo-Scottish services provided by the LNER and LMS. In 1937 LMS and LNER trains left Glasgow Central and Euston simultaneously at 1.30 pm and reached their destinations at 8.00 pm. The LMS *Coronation Scot* claimed a maximum speed of 114mph and was the first streamlined express to travel between the two stations. Five locomotives operated the service – *Coronation, Queen Elizabeth, Princess Alice, Princess Alexandra* and *Queen Mary* – all of them designed by William Stanier and built by the LMS at Crewe works. The rival LNER *Coronation Express* ran between King's Cross and Edinburgh and was pulled by A4 Pacific locomotives, of which *Mallard* is an example, and were built by Nigel Gresley. Both the *Coronation Scot* and the *Coronation Express*, with their own locomotives and carriages, were highly distinctive and extremely popular and they generated an enormous amount of interest and revenue. Although the *Flying Scotsman* made its debut in 1862 it was still running in the 1930s. By this time it too was being hauled by an A4 Pacific and was, in effect, a travelling hotel. It had independent hot water, a hairdressing salon, a ladies' rest room and a cocktail bar. The restaurant car was decorated in the style of Louis XVI and the train had its name emblazoned in white letters on the roof.

Another memorable (though less successful) form of transport at this time was the Bennie Railplane system. George Bennie was an engineer and inventor who constructed a railplane system over a quarter of a mile near Glasgow. It was a form of monorail with a carriage on an overhead track suspended on a framework of steel girders. It was driven by aircraft propellers and was lavishly decorated. It officially opened on 8 July 1930. The event attracted visitors and transport engineers from all over the world and the railplane was hailed as a 'wonderful product of British brains'. Sadly George Bennie was unable to find the financial backing for the system and, after running out of his own money, he was declared bankrupt in 1937.

Some of the world's most memorable advertising posters were produced in this decade. 1931 saw Tom Purvis's famous 'East Coast Joys' set of posters produced in flat blocks of colour which formed a continuous scene when placed alongside each other. They portrayed the holiday pleasures of rambling, sunbathing, sandcastle-building, bathing, fishing and sailing. Adolphe Mouron Cassandre produced the renowned poster advertising the *Nord Express* in six languages. The poster was symbolic of the movement and power of this famous train.

However, this seemingly endless decade of grandeur, fast trains and pleasure was to come to an abrupt end with the escalation of events leading up to the outbreak of the Second World War. On 4 March 1938 the *Railway Gazette* reported that three of the largest bridges on the Chinese railways had been demolished either by retreating Chinese troops or by Japanese bombs. At first Britain took little notice, feeling secure in its insularity, but by November 1939 the railway companies were moving extra food supplies as well as introducing wartime passenger services and carrying war supplies.

On the outbreak of war all advertising was removed and all across Europe luxury trains ceased to run, making way for the austerity that war conditions imposed.

Locomotive maintenance could be dirty and dangerous: here a fire dropper cleans out the fire box of a locomotive at London King's Cross. He wears the new regulation goggles to protect his eyes from ash dust and cinders.

Lokomotiven instand zu halten war ein schmutziges und gefährliches Geschäft. Hier räumt ein Arbeiter die Feuerbüchse einer Lokomotive in King's Cross, London, aus. Nach neuesten Bestimmungen trägt er eine Schutzbrille, die seine Augen vor Asche und Funken schützt.

L'entretien des locomotives était un travail sale et dangereux : ici, un cheminot des ateliers de King's Cross, à Londres, équipé de lunettes de protection réglementaires contre les cendres et les braises, nettoie la boîte à feu d'une locomotive au-dessus de la fosse du cendrier.

In den dreißiger Jahren war eine Eisenbahnreise schneller und eleganter denn je, und nie war das Angebot größer. Die Schrecken des Weltkriegs waren vergessen, und die mit dem Aufstieg des Faschismus drohende Gefahr des nächsten nahm man bis zum Ende des Jahrzehnts kaum wahr. Die Menschen hatten den Blick nach vorn gerichtet und waren fest entschlossen, das Beste aus ihrem Leben zu machen. Das erste Bild dieses Kapitels (Seite 224–225), Hal Moreys Aufnahme der Grand Central Station in New York, 1930 – die Art, wie es Stolz, Optimismus und Selbstvertrauen zum Ausdruck bringt –, ist geradezu ein Sinnbild dieser Ära.

Es war eine Zeit der Luxuszüge mit den großen Namen sowie der Dampf- und Dieselrekorde. Eine der schnellsten Verbindungen in Nordamerika war der *International Limited,* der erste Superexpress der Canadian National; er legte die 1366 Kilometer von Montreal über Toronto nach Chicago in 17½ Stunden zurück. Die Reisenden fuhren in allem erdenklichen Luxus, jeder mit seiner chamberette (einem kleinen eigenen Schlafzimmer) und einem Speisewagen, in dem es sogar Kindermenüs gab. Der Zug führte aber auch *colonialist coaches,* der europäischen dritten Klasse vergleichbar; hier ließen sich die Sitze zu Liegen umklappen, und auf einem Herd konnten die Fahrgäste sich ihr eigenes Essen kochen. Schon länger fuhr der *Continental Limited* von Montreal nach Vancouver an der Pazifikküste, und der *Maritime Express* der *Canadian National* verkehrte von Halifax über Neuschottland und Quebec nach Montreal. Als Zugmaschinen dienten Lokomotiven der Hudson- oder 5700-Klasse mit sechs gekoppelten Antriebsrädern, die bis zu 1000 Tonnen bewegen konnten. Sie verfügten über eine zweite Dampfmaschine für die hinteren Stützräder, die zusätzliche Kraft für die Anfahrt lieferte. In den USA setzte die Pennsylvania Railroad als Konkurrenz für den *Twentieth Century Limited* der New York Central den exklusiven *Broadway Limited* ein. 1935 nahm die Chicago, Milwaukee, St Paul and Pacific Railroad die bis dahin längste elektrifizierte Strecke in Betrieb, und im Mai desselben Jahres fuhr der Pioneer *Zephyr* der Burlington Railroad mit 181 km/h einen Geschwindigkeitsweltrekord. Der dreiteilige Edelstahl-Stromlinienzug bewältigte die 1633 Kilometer von Denver nach Chicago nonstop mit einer Durchschnittsgeschwindigkeit von 124,9 km/h. Bahnhöfe dienten inzwischen nicht nur der An- und Abreise: Sie waren architektonischer Ausdruck des kollektiven urbanen Lebens. Je mehr die Konkurrenz durch Straßen- und Luftverkehr wuchs, desto kommerzieller und internationaler wurden die Bahnstationen. Ursprünglich hoch gebaut, damit Dampf und Qualm sich verziehen konnten, wurden sie nun zum Symbol der Modernität. In der Architektur setzte sich der internationale Stil mit seiner funktionaleren Nutzung des Raumes durch, und der Bahnhof entwickelte sich zur Drehscheibe vieler großer Städte.

In Deutschland kam der Schienenzeppelin heraus. Die Konstruktion des Hamburgers Kruckenberg reduzierte durch ihre Stromlinienform den Luftwiderstand auf ein Minimum. Parallel zu seinen Versuchsfahrten entwickelte die Reichsbahn den *Fliegenden Hamburger.* Er war nicht mehr in Abteile aufgeteilt, sondern in Einheiten für jeweils bis zu 50 Fahrgäste. Vorn gab es einen Gepäckraum, in der Mitte des Zuges eine Bar. In Frankreich entwickelte Bugatti Triebwagen für die PLM und die Staatsbahnen, und die beiden wichtigsten Züge mit eigenem Namen waren der *Nord Express* mit Pullman- und Schlafwagen und der *Sud Express* Paris–Orléans–Midi bis zur spanischen Grenze. Südafrika stellte 1939 für die 1540 Kilometer lange Strecke von Kapstadt nach Pretoria den *Blue Train* vor, der heute als luxuriösester Zug der Welt gilt.

In Großbritannien gaben die »Großen Vier« immer mehr Zügen Namen und versprachen sich Wettbewerbsvorteile davon. Der Expresszug der GWR hieß *Cheltenham Spa Express,* war aber überall als »Cheltenham Flyer« bekannt. 1931 wurde er als »schnellster Zug der Welt« beworben. Seine schnellste Fahrt absolvierte er am 6. Juni 1932. Die Zugmaschine war die vierzylindrige C Nr. 5006, *Tregenna Castle.* Der Zug mit seinen sechs Wagen wog 196 Tonnen einschließlich Fahrgästen und Gepäck. Von 1935 an setzte die GWR den zweimal täglich verkehrenden *Cornish Riviera Express* ein, SR hatte Pendlerzüge mit Pullmanwagen, etwa die elektrische *Brighton Belle.* Die SR richtete auch die erste elektrische Hauptstrecke in Großbritannien ein. Die größte Rivalität herrschte in den dreißiger Jahren jedoch auf den Schottlandrouten zwischen LNER und LMS. 1937 liefen Züge beider Gesellschaften parallel um 13.30 Uhr von Glasgow Central und London Euston aus und erreichten ihr jeweiliges Ziel um 20 Uhr. Der *Coronation Scot* der LMS, der erste stromlinienförmig gestaltete Zug auf dieser Strecke, warb mit einer Spitzengeschwindigkeit von 183 km/h. Fünf Lokomotiven waren im Einsatz – *Coronation, Queen Elizabeth, Princess Alice, Princess Alexandra* und *Queen Mary* –, allesamt von William Stanier konstruiert und gebaut in den LMS-Lokomotivenwerken in Crewe. Die LNER-Alternative zwischen King's

Cross und Edinburgh boten die von Nigel Gresley entworfenen A4-Pacific-Lokomotiven als Zugmaschinen, darunter die *Mallard. Coronation Scot* und *Coronation Express,* beide mit eigenen Loks und Wagen, waren höchst individuelle und ausgesprochen populäre Züge und fuhren gute Gewinne ein. Auch der *Flying Scotsman,* schon 1862 eingeführt, verkehrte nach wie vor. Inzwischen sorgte auch hier eine A4-Pacific-Lokomotive für Kraft, und der Zug war im Grunde ein Hotel auf Rädern. Es gab fließendes warmes Wasser, einen Friseursalon, einen Ruheraum für die Damen und eine Cocktailbar. Das Restaurant war im Louis-XVI-Stil gehalten, und der Name des Zuges stand in großen weißen Lettern auf dem Dach.

Weniger erfolgreich, aber nicht minder bemerkenswert war ein anderes Transportsystem der Zeit, der Bennie-Railplane. Der Ingenieur und Erfinder George Bennie baute bei Glasgow eine 400 Meter lange Versuchsstrecke für seinen »fliegenden Zug«. Es handelte sich um eine Einschienenbahn, bei der die Wagen als Gondeln an der auf Gitterstahlstützen stehenden Schiene hingen; für den Antrieb sorgten Flugzeugpropeller. Der Prototyp, den er am 8. Juli 1930 vorstellte, war prachtvoll ausgestattet. Die Vorführung lockte Besucher und Bahningenieure aus aller Welt an, und der Railplane wurde als »großartiges Produkt britischen Erfindergeistes« gepriesen. Leider fand Bennie für sein System keine Unterstützung in der Industrie und musste 1937 Konkurs anmelden.

Einige der schönsten Plakate aller Zeiten entstanden in dieser Dekade. 1931 kamen Tom Purvis' »East Coast Joys« heraus, eine Folge von Postern, die ein zusammenhängendes Bild ergaben, wenn man sie nebeneinander hängte. Jedes stellte ein Ferienvergnügen dar: Wandern, Sonnenbaden, Sandburgenbauen, Baden, Fischen und Segeln. Von Adolphe Mouron Cassandre stammt das bekannte Plakat, das in sechs Sprachen für den *Nord Express* wirbt. Das Bild brachte Tempo und Energie dieses berühmten Zuges aufs Schönste zum Ausdruck.

Doch dieses scheinbar endlose Jahrzehnt der Pracht, des Vergnügens und der schnellen Züge war mit Ausbruch des Zweiten Weltkriegs mit einem Schlag vorbei. Am 4. März 1938 berichtete die *Railway Gazette,* dass drei der größten chinesischen Eisenbahnbrücken entweder von chinesischen Truppen auf dem Rückzug oder von japanischen Bomben zerstört waren. Anfangs nahmen die Briten kaum Notiz davon und fühlten sich sicher auf ihrer Insel, aber im November 1939 beförderten die Bahnen schon Notvorräte an Nahrungsmitteln, transportierten Kriegsmaterial und stellten ihren Fahrplan auf Kriegsbetrieb um. Bei Kriegsausbruch wurden alle Reklametafeln demontiert, und überall in Europa stellten die Luxuszüge ihren Betrieb ein und machten Platz für die Kargheit des Krieges.

Not a man hiding under a large policeman's helmet but a railway workman carrying an engine dome at the locomotive works at Crewe, March 1936.

Kein Polizist mit einem zu großen Helm, sondern ein Arbeiter im Werk Crewe, der einen Lokomotivendom an seinen Platz bringt, März 1936.

Il ne s'agit pas d'un policeman ayant un casque trop grand mais d'un cheminot portant le dôme d'une locomotive dans les ateliers ferroviaires de Crewe, en mars 1936.

Les atrocités de la Première Guerre mondiale sont presque oubliées et la menace d'une nouvelle guerre, la montée du fascisme et les incertitudes de leurs effets sont assez largement occultées jusque dans années 1930. Chacun est bien résolu à se tourner vers l'avenir et à vivre pleinement sa vie. Les voyages en train connaissent leur apogée en termes de style, de vitesse et de diversité. La photographie d'ouverture de ce chapitre (pp. 224–225), prise par Hal Morey et qui montre la gare new-yorkaise de Grand Central en 1930, est le symbole même de cette décennie de l'histoire des chemins de fer : on y lit en effet tout l'optimisme, la fierté et la confiance du début des années 1930, l'ère des trains de luxe et des records.

En Amérique du Nord, l'un des services les plus rapides est assuré par l'*International Limited,* premier rapide du Canadian National, qui relie en dix-sept heures et demi Montréal à Chicago via Toronto, soit une distance de 1366 km. Ce train luxueux et du dernier cri offre à ses passagers une chambrette (un petit compartiment avec lit), une voiture-restaurant – avec menus spéciaux pour les enfants – et des voitures « coloniales » semblables aux troisième classe européennes, où il est possible de transformer les banquettes en couchettes et de faire ses repas sur un fourneau. Le *Continental Limited* circulait déjà entre Montréal et la côte Pacifique (Vancouver), tandis que le *Canadian National Maritime Express* reliait Halifax à la Nouvelle-Écosse et Montréal via Québec. Ils étaient tous deux remorqués par des locomotives de type Hudson ou 5700, disposant de trois essieux moteurs et capables de tracter jusqu'à 1000 tonnes, certaines disposant également d'un moteur « supplémentaire » à vapeur qui actionnait les roues de la bogie arrière, sous la cabine de la locomotive, et servait au démarrage. Le US Pennsylvania Railroad disposait du très chic *Broadway Limited,* concurrencé par le *Twentieth Century Limited* du New York Central Railroad. En 1935, la plus longue ligne électrifiée fut ouverte par le Chicago, Milwaukee, St Paul and Pacific Railroad. En mai de la même année, le Pioneer *Zephyr* du Burlington Railroad remportait le record du monde de vitesse avec 181 km/h. Ce train caréné de trois voitures en acier effectua également sans arrêt le trajet Denver–Chicago, soit 1633 km, à la vitesse moyenne de 124,9 km/h. Les gares ne sont plus seulement un centre de l'activité sociale mais deviennent également, en adoptant le nouveau style international, un symbole de modernité et l'expression architecturale de l'urbanisme. Le vaste hall de gare, construit à l'origine pour permettre une meilleure dispersion de la vapeur et de la fumée, se transforme et utilise désormais l'espace de manière plus rationnelle de sorte que la gare devient le nœud de communications de la plupart des grandes villes.

En Allemagne, le Zeppelin sur rails fut construit par Kruckenberg, de Hambourg. Un carénage réduit les frottements de l'air à leur minimum. Après la phase d'essais sur le Zeppelin, la Reichsbahn développa le *Fliegender Hamburger.* Celui-ci se compose d'une unique voiture-salon offrant des sièges pour une cinquantaine de voyageurs, avec un compartiment à bagages à l'avant et un bar au centre. En France, le PLM et les chemins de fer de l'État exploitent des autorails Bugatti en complément local des grands rapides que sont le *Nord Express,* un train transcontinental avec wagons-lits et voitures Pullman, et le *Sud Express,* mis en service sur la ligne Paris–Orléans–Midi entre Paris et la frontière espagnole. En Afrique du Sud, le *Blue Train,* mis en service en 1939 sur une ligne de 1540 km entre Le Cap et Pretoria, est considéré comme le train le plus luxueux du monde.

En Grande-Bretagne, les « Big Four » (les quatre grandes compagnies de chemin de fer) commencent également à baptiser leurs trains afin de stimuler les ventes. Appelé *Cheltenham Spa Express,* et bientôt mieux connu par son surnom, le « Cheltenham Flyer », l'express du GWR est annoncé en 1931 comme « le train le plus rapide du monde », même s'il n'effectue un trajet record que le 6 juin 1932. La locomotive qui remorque alors le convoi, composé de six voitures et pesant 196 tonnes, voyageurs et bagages compris, est la *Tregenna Castle,* une 230 à quatre cylindres de classe Castle portant le n°5006. En 1935, le *Cornish Riviera Express* du GWR circule deux fois par jour. De son côté, le SR, qui bénéficie de la première grande ligne électrifiée de Grande-Bretagne, met en service des trains de banlieue électriques, comme le *Brighton Belle,* composé de voitures Pullman. C'est cependant sur le service de la ligne Angleterre-Écosse que se manifeste la concurrence la plus forte entre compagnies britanniques, le LNER et le LMS. En 1937, leurs deux trains quittent simultanément, à 13h30, la gare centrale de Glasgow pour l'un et celle d'Euston à Londres pour l'autre, pour arriver à 20h00 à leur destination respective. Le *Coronation Scot* du LMS, roulant à la vitesse maximum de 183 km/h, fut le premier express caréné à effectuer le trajet entre les deux villes. Les cinq locomotives assurant la traction – les *Coronation, Queen Elizabeth, Princess Alice, Princess Alexandra* et *Queen Mary* –

avaient toutes été conçues par William Stanier et construites par le LMS dans ses ateliers de Crewe. Reliant la gare londonienne de King's Cross à Édimbourg, le *Coronation Express* de son rival le LNER était quant à lui remorqué par des locomotives Pacific de classe A4, dont la *Mallard*, construites par Nigel Gresley. Le *Coronation Scot* et le *Coronation Express*, qui se distinguaient par leurs locomotives et leurs voitures, étaient extrêmement populaires et se révélèrent bénéficiaires pour leurs compagnies. Le *Flying Scotsman*, dont la mise en service remontait à 1862, circulait toujours, tracté par une Pacific A4, son nom peint en lettres blanches sur le toit de la première voiture. Véritable hôtel mobile, il offrait à ses passagers eau chaude, salon de coiffure, salon pour dames et bar-cocktail ; la voiture-restaurant était décorée dans le style Louis XVI.

L'aérotrain de George Bennie, un ingénieur et un inventeur britannique, est un autre type de moyen de transport étudié à l'époque mais qui n'eut pas le succès escompté. Officiellement inaugurée le 8 juillet 1930, sa ligne d'aérotrain, installée sur 400 m dans les environs de Glasgow, était une sorte de monorail suspendu à des portiques en acier auquel était accrochée une unique voiture carénée, propulsée par deux hélices d'avion. Ce prototype attira des visiteurs et des ingénieurs des transports du monde entier, qui saluèrent cet aérotrain comme « une magnifique production de l'esprit britannique ». Malheureusement, George Bennie fut incapable de trouver le financement nécessaire à la réalisation à grande échelle de son projet et, après avoir dépensé tout son argent, fut déclaré en faillite en 1937.

C'est également au cours de cette décennie que furent créées certaines des plus mémorables publicités pour les chemins de fer. C'est en 1931 qu'apparut la célèbre série d'affiches de Tom Purvis – « East Coast Joys » (Les joies de la côte Est) – réalisées en à-plats de couleurs et formant un panorama une fois placées les unes à côté des autres. Elles représentaient les plaisirs de la villégiature, des promenades, des bains de soleil, de la construction des châteaux de sable, de la baignade, de la pêche et de la voile. Le Français Adolphe Mouron Cassandre réalisa quant à lui les célèbres affiches pour le *Nord Express*, marquées par un trait expressif et très art déco pour mieux symboliser la vitesse et la puissance du rapide.

Mais cette folle décennie de grandeur, d'élégance, de trains rapides et de plaisirs va connaître une fin brutale avec le déclenchement de la Seconde Guerre mondiale. Le 4 mars

1938, la *Railway Gazette* signale que trois des plus grands ponts de chemin de fer chinois ont été détruits, soit par les troupes chinoises en retraite soit lors d'un bombardement japonais. La Grande-Bretagne fit assez peu de cas de la nouvelle, se sentant protégée dans son île. Mais, en novembre 1939, les compagnies de chemin de fer commencèrent à transporter du ravitaillement et du matériel militaire tout en mettant en place un service de voyageurs de temps de guerre. Lors du déclenchement des hostilités, les publicités pour les chemins de fer avaient été enlevées et les trains de luxe cessèrent de circuler dans toute l'Europe. La guerre imposait désormais une période d'austérité.

Catering for the travellers' needs, June 1937, a portable milk bar operating at London Waterloo. It could be moved effortlessly from platform to platform and was the first of its kind in any station in Great Britain.

Stärkung am Wege, Juni 1937: eine fahrbare Milchbar auf dem Londoner Bahnhof Waterloo. Sie ließ sich leicht von einem Bahnsteig zum anderen schieben und war in Großbritannien die erste ihrer Art.

En juin 1937, ce bar à lait mobile – premier de son genre dans les gares britanniques – pouvait être facilement transporté de plate-forme en plate-forme et proposait aux voyageurs des rafraîchissements sur les quais de la gare de Waterloo.

Banff Springs Hotel, Banff

In 1888 workers on the Canadian Pacific Railway discovered
natural hot springs at the basin in Banff, Alberta. This opened
the way to the founding of the Banff National Park and
ultimately the luxurious Banff Springs Hotel (above); its
250 rooms made it the largest hotel in the world at the time.
The railways made it more easily accessible.

Banff Springs Hotel, Banff

Im Jahr 1888 entdeckten Arbeiter der Canadian Pacific Railway
im Becken von Banff, Alberta, heiße Quellen. Das war der
Anfang einer Entwicklung, die zum Banff-Nationalpark und
dem luxuriösen Banff Springs Hotel (oben) führte, mit 250 Zim-
mern seinerzeit das größte Hotel der Welt. Für eine bequeme
Anreise sorgte die Eisenbahn.

Hôtel de Banff Springs, à Banff

En 1888, des ouvriers de la Canadian Pacific Railway découvrent
des sources naturelles d'eau chaude dans le bassin de Banff, en
Alberta. Cela conduit à la création du parc national de Banff puis
à la construction du luxueux Banff Springs Hotel (ci-dessus),
dont les 250 chambres en font à l'époque le plus grand hôtel du
monde, rendu plus accessible grâce au chemin de fer.

North British Hotel, Edinburgh
The view from the west looking over the top of Waverley Market, Edinburgh, in the 1930s. Built by the North British Railway, with its main entrance on Princes Street and situated just below Carlton Hill, it was a monument to the Victorian hotel and travel industry. Completed in 1902, its huge clock tower, 185 feet from street level to its tip and visible for miles around, was nicknamed the Big Ben of Scotland.

North British Hotel, Edinburgh
Ein Blick von Westen über das Dach der Waverley-Markthalle in Edinburgh, dreißiger Jahre. Das von der North British Railway errichtete, 1902 fertig gestellte Hotel knapp unterhalb von Carlton Hill mit Haupteingang an der Princes Street war ein Inbegriff viktorianischer Reisekultur. Der gewaltige Uhrenturm, von Straßenhöhe bis zur Spitze 56 Meter hoch und meilenweit im Umkreis sichtbar, galt bald als »Big Ben von Schottland«.

L'hôtel du North British, à Édimbourg
Vu depuis l'ouest sur les toits du marché de Waverley, à Édimbourg, dans les années 1930. Cet hôtel, construit par le North British Railway juste au pied de Carlton Hill, était un monument à l'industrie hôtelière et touristique victorienne. Achevé en 1902, son haut beffroi de 56 mètres de hauteur, qui domine Princes Street et reste visible à des kilomètres à la ronde, fut surnommé le Big Ben d'Écosse.

As one driver to another...

At some stage in his childhood every boy wanted to be a train driver. Here a proud owner of a train set (the next best thing?) discusses his model engine with LNER drivers at King's Cross in 1933. His toy engine was probably made by Hornby or Bing table-top toy train manufacturers. The better-known Hornby Dublo did not start until just before the Second World War.

Lokomotivführer unter sich

Irgendwann in seiner Kindheit wollte jeder Junge Lokomotivführer werden. Hier fachsimpelt der Besitzer einer Modelleisenbahn (das Zweitbeste, wenn man keine große hatte) mit Kollegen von der LNER, King's Cross, 1933. Das Modell dürfte entweder von Hornby oder von Bing stammen, den größten britischen Herstellern. Die bekanntere Hornby-Dublo-Serie kam erst kurz vor dem Zweiten Weltkrieg heraus.

D'un chauffeur à l'autre ...

Pendant leur enfance, tous les garçons rêvaient de conduire une locomotive. Ici, en 1933, un fier détenteur d'un train miniature discute de sa machine à King's Cross avec des chauffeurs du LNER. Ce modèle réduit est de la marque Hornby ou Bing, les deux grands fabricants de chemins de fer de table. Hornby Dublo, demeurée la plus célèbre, commença ses activités juste avant le début de la Seconde Guerre mondiale.

School trip

In July 1934, 200 boys from a school in Westcliff-on-Sea, Essex, took their summer school trip to the LMS locomotive works in Derby, travelling on a special excursion train. Here they examine a pair of 6 foot 6 inch driving wheels.

Ein Schulausflug

Im Juli 1934 unternahmen 200 Schüler aus Westcliff-on-Sea in Essex ihren Sommer-Schulausflug per Sonderzug zu den Lokomotivenwerken der LMS in Derby. Hier bestaunen sie einen Satz Antriebsräder, Durchmesser 2 Meter.

Sortie d'école

En juillet 1934, 200 élèves d'une école de Westcliff-on-Sea (Essex), prirent un train d'excursion spécial pour se rendre en classe d'été à l'usine de locomotives du LMS à Derby. Ils examinent un essieu moteur à roues de 2 mètres de diamètre.

Trains and motor cars

Speed trials with the *Coronation Scot* and a racing car near King's Langley, Hertfordshire, in 1939. The *Coronation Scot* was the first streamlined Anglo-Scottish express to run between London Euston and Glasgow Central for the LMS. The speed record for the locomotive was 114mph, set in 1937, but the motor car was becoming a serious rival to rail travel.

Eisenbahn kontra Automobil

Ein Rennwagen fährt mit dem *Coronation Scot* um die Wette, aufgenommen 1939 in King's Langley, Hertfordshire. Der *Coronation Scot* war der erste Stromlinienzug auf der Schottlandstrecke der LMS von London Euston nach Glasgow Central. Die Lokomotive stellte 1937 einen Geschwindigkeitsrekord von 185 km/h auf – zu einer Zeit, in der der Motorwagen bereits ein ernsthafter Rivale für den Eisenbahnverkehr war.

Trains et voitures

Course de vitesse entre le *Coronation Scot* et une voiture de sport près de King's Langley (Hertfordshire), en 1939. Le *Coronation Scot* fut le premier express Londres–Écosse à assurer la liaison entre la gare d'Euston à Londres et la gare centrale de Glasgow pour le LMS. La locomotive établit en 1937 un record de vitesse à 185 km/h. Mais la voiture allait bientôt devenir un sérieux rival des transports ferroviaires.

Horse power

In 1825, when the Stockton & Darlington Railway, the first passenger railway, was opened, horses were used to pull the locomotive and to this day the distance between the rails in Britain and in most parts of the world remains at 4 foot 8 inches – the width required for a horse to walk between them. Here, however, a lady from Berkhamstead Riding School tries to keep up with the LMS locomotive *Princess Louise*.

Pferdestärke

Als 1825 die Strecke Stockton–Darlington eröffnet wurde, die erste Passagierlinie der Welt, sorgten noch Pferde für den Antrieb, und bis zum heutigen Tag beträgt die Spurbreite in Großbritannien und weiten Teilen der Welt 1424 mm – die Breite, die ein Pferd braucht, um zwischen den Schienen zu gehen. Die Dame von der Berkhamstead Riding School versucht, mit der LMS-Lokomotive *Princess Louise* mitzuhalten.

Chevaux-vapeur

En 1825, lorsque fut ouvert le Stockton & Darlington Railway, première ligne pour voyageurs, des chevaux participaient à la traction. C'est ce qui explique que l'écartement de la voie en Grande-Bretagne et dans d'autres parties du monde ait été de 1,42 m, soit la largeur nécessaire pour qu'un cheval puisse marcher entre les rails. Cette cavalière de l'école d'équitation de Berkhamstead a du mal à rester à la hauteur de la locomotive *Princess Louise* de la LMS.

Whatever the weather

Snowploughs were attached to the locomotive in winter weather
to clear the tracks. Occasionally trains were stranded but generally
services were maintained. (Above) A new type of snowplough in
front of an LMS locomotive taking on water at Garsdale, Yorkshire,
January 1936. Garsdale is on the famous Settle & Carlisle railway
line. (Below) A rotary snowplough clearing away drifts in Norway
between Bergen and Oslo, c. 1935.

Bei jedem Wetter

Im Winter wurde Lokomotiven ein Schneepflug anmontiert, der
die Strecke freiräumte. Manchmal blieb ein Zug stecken, doch
meistens lief der Betrieb auch bei Winterwetter weiter. (Oben) Ein
neues Schneepflug-Baumuster vor einer LMS-Lokomotive, die im
Januar 1936 in Garsdale, Yorkshire, Wasser fasst. Garsdale liegt
an der berühmten Strecke von Settle nach Carlisle. (Unten) Eine
norwegische Schneefräse räumt die Strecke von Bergen nach Oslo,
um 1935.

Quel que soit le temps

En hiver, il était possible de fixer un chasse-neige à l'avant de la
locomotive afin d'assurer la continuité du service, mais il arrivait
parfois que le temps soit si mauvais que les trains restent immobilisés. (En haut) Cette locomotive de la LMS, en train de faire de
l'eau à Garsdale (Yorkshire) en janvier 1936, est équipée d'un
nouveau type de chasse-neige. Garsdale se trouve sur la célèbre
ligne Settle & Carlisle. (En bas) Une locomotive à chasse-neige
rotatif dégage la voie entre Bergen et Oslo (Norvège), vers 1935.

Snow forecast

Permanent way workers brush snow off an LNER snowplough in preparation for its next job, c. 1930. At its height the LNER had twenty-four snowploughs of different designs housed all over the network. This one was built c. 1890 by the NER out of oak and pine; it was used mainly to assist in the delivery of goods in winter weather. Notice the second plough at the rear of the second engine in anticipation of a heavy storm.

Voraussage: Schnee

Streckenarbeiter der LNER fegen Schnee von einem Pflug und machen ihn bereit für seinen nächsten Einsatz, ein Bild von etwa 1930. In ihren besten Tagen verfügte die LNER über 24 Schneepflüge verschiedenster Bauart, auf Depots überall an der Strecke verteilt. Dieses Modell der NER, um 1890 aus Eichen- und Fichtenholz gebaut, kam vor allem auf Güterstrecken zum Einsatz. Mit einem zweiten Pflug vor der Lokomotive am anderen Ende ist das Kommando auch für schwerstes Wetter gerüstet.

Annonce de neige

Des cheminots balaient le chasse-neige d'une locomotive du LNER avant son départ, vers 1930. À son apogée, cette compagnie disposait de 24 modèles de chasse-neige sur l'ensemble de son réseau. Celui-ci, réalisé en pin et chêne vers 1890 par le NER, était généralement monté sur les trains de marchandises. Notez la présence d'un second chasse-neige en queue de convoi, en cas de forte tempête.

Hess the speech maker

Rudolf Hess, Hitler's deputy, addressing 5,000 German railway workers, c. 1935. The dissemination of the political ideas and doctrines of Nazi ideology was crucial in establishing support for the conquest of Europe and the support of the railway workers was essential.

Flammende Reden

Hitlers Stellvertreter Rudolf Heß hält eine Rede vor 5000 deutschen Bahnarbeitern, ca. 1935. Mit solchen Großveranstaltungen brachten die Nationalsozialisten ihre politischen Anschauungen unters Volk. Wenn die Eroberung ganz Europas gelingen sollte, war es entscheidend, dass sie die Eisenbahner auf ihrer Seite hatten.

Discours de Hess

Vers 1935, Rudolf Hess, l'un des principaux collaborateurs de Hitler, s'adresse à 5 000 cheminots et ouvriers des chemins de fer allemands, dont le soutien était essentiel dans la conquête de l'Europe.

Italian workers hail Hitler

To succeed in his aim of absolute domination in Europe, Hitler needed unquestioning loyalty throughout the ranks of soldiers and workers alike. There could be no criticism. Here, with one eye on the camera, Italian railway workers in a Rome station yard in February 1937, at the height of Mussolini's fascist power, salute Hitler with raised shovels. All good propaganda.

Heil Hitler!

Wenn er sein Ziel einer Herrschaft über ganz Europa erreichen wollte, brauchte Hitler die bedingungslose Loyalität nicht nur der Soldaten, sondern auch der Arbeiterschaft. Kritik war nicht geduldet. Auf einem römischen Güterbahnhof begrüßen Bahnarbeiter Hitler mit erhobenen Schaufeln, und werfen dabei ein Auge auf die Kamera – eine Propagandaaufnahme vom Februar 1937, als Mussolinis Faschisten auf dem Höhepunkt ihrer Macht waren.

Des ouvriers italiens saluent Hitler

Hitler avait besoin de la loyauté indéfectible de ses soldats comme de ses ouvriers pour parvenir à la domination absolue sur l'Europe, le régime ne souffrant aucune critique. En février 1937, à l'apogée du pouvoir fasciste de Mussolini, les cheminots italiens du dépôt de la gare de Rome saluent Hitler de la pelle, l'œil sur l'objectif. Le résultat d'une bonne propagande.

Beginning of the Holocaust

The fate of the Jews between 1933 and 1945 and the role of the railways was an irrevocable part of the history of railways. (Above and below) The Reichsbahn used the vast European network to transport some 3 million Jews to their deaths in the extermination camps. Grunewald Station, situated in an affluent Berlin suburb, served as the main deportation site for Jews in Berlin. The rolling stock played its part: the Jews were put into passenger trains in Germany and Western Europe and transferred to cattle and freight trucks for the final part of their journey through Eastern Europe.

Die Anfänge des Holocaust

Die Rolle, die die Eisenbahn bei der Vertreibung und Vernichtung der Juden zwischen 1933 und 1945 spielte, ist ein unauslöschlicher Teil ihrer Geschichte. (Oben und unten) Die Reichsbahn transportierte über das weitläufige europäische Streckennetz etwa 3 Millionen Juden in die Vernichtungslager und damit in den Tod. Die meisten Berliner Juden wurden vom Bahnhof im Villenvorort Grunewald aus deportiert. Die Wahl der Waggons sprach Bände: Aus Deutschland und Westeuropa kamen die Juden mit Personenzügen, doch den letzten Teil ihrer Reise durch Osteuropa legten sie in Vieh- und Güterwagen zurück.

Le début de l'Holocauste

Les chemins de fer jouèrent un rôle essentiel, et peu glorieux, dans le destin des Juifs entre 1933 et 1945. (En haut et en bas) La Reichsbahn utilisa le vaste réseau européen pour transporter près de trois millions de Juifs vers les camps d'extermination où ils trouvèrent la mort. La gare de Grunewald, située dans une banlieue aisée de Berlin, fut le principal camp de déportation des Juifs berlinois. Les Juifs étaient embarqués en Allemagne et en Europe de l'Ouest à bord de trains de passagers avant d'être transférés dans des wagons à bestiaux ou de marchandises pour effectuer leur dernier voyage à travers l'Europe de l'Est.

Hitler in Italy

When Italy entered the war the railways played an important role, not least in Mussolini's own propaganda machine. He claimed to have made the railways run on time and in so doing ensured the country greater prosperity. From 1935 he came even more firmly under the influence of Hitler. (Right) Bologna Station festooned with banners to welcome Hitler's train as the Führer passed through on the way to Rome to sign the Rome-Berlin pact with Mussolini on 25 October 1936. (Above) Hitler salutes from a window of the same train.

Hitler in Italien

Als Italien in den Krieg eintrat, waren die Eisenbahnen an prominenter Stelle dabei, nicht zuletzt in Mussolinis Propagandamaschine. Er rühmte sich, dass unter seiner Herrschaft die Züge pünktlich fuhren und damit den Wohlstand des Landes mehren halfen. Von 1935 an kam er mehr denn je unter Hitlers Einfluss. (Rechts) Der Bahnhof von Bologna, geschmückt für die Einfahrt von Hitlers Zug. Der Führer passierte den Bahnhof auf der Fahrt zur Unterzeichnung des Rom-Berlin-Pakts mit Mussolini am 25. Oktober 1936. (Oben) Hitler grüßt von einem Fenster dieses Zuges aus.

Hitler en Italie

Lorsque l'Italie entre en guerre, Mussolini fait des chemins de fer italiens un des pivots de sa propagande. Il proclame notamment que les trains arrivent et partent désormais à l'heure grâce à sa politique, assurant ainsi une plus grande prospérité du pays. (À droite) La gare de Bologne est entièrement pavoisée pour saluer le passage du train d'Hitler (ci-dessus), qui descend à Rome signer le pacte germano-italien avec Mussolini, le 25 octobre 1936.

Railway experiments

(Opposite, all photographs) The 'George Bennie Railplane' system of transport on a test run, 8 July 1930. It ran on an elevated track above an existing, unused railway at Burnbrae, Milngavie, near Glasgow, with a propeller-driven carriage suspended from a monorail. The engine was electric and Bennie claimed it would cost less than a conventional railway system. However, it was not a success and Bennie died bankrupt. The structure stayed up until 1956, when it was scrapped. (Right) A German experimental four-blade propeller-driven engine called the 'Railway Zeppelin', invented by Kruckenberg in 1931.

Bahnexperimente

(Gegenüberliegende Seite, alle Bilder) Der »George Bennie Railplane« auf einer Testfahrt, 8. Juli 1930. Die Probestrecke dieser Schwebebahn wurde über einer stillgelegten Strecke in Burnbrae, Milngavie, bei Glasgow eingerichtet. Die Kabinen wurden von elektrogetriebenen Propellern bewegt und waren laut Bennie billiger als jede konventionelle Eisenbahn. Doch das System setzte sich nicht durch, und sein Erfinder starb mittellos. Die Anlagen wurden erst 1956 verschrottet. (Rechts) Deutsche Experimente mit einem »Schienenzeppelin«, der von Kruckenberg 1931 erfunden wurde; getrieben wurde der Wagen von einem vierblättrigen Rotor.

Expériences du chemin de fer

(Ci-contre) C'est le 8 juillet 1930 qu'on procède aux essais du « George Bennie Railplane », un système de transport révolutionnaire dont son constructeur affirmait qu'il coûtait moins cher que le chemin de fer traditionnel. Ce véhicule circulait accroché au rail d'un portique, édifié au-dessus d'une voie désaffectée proche de Burnbrae Dye Works, près de Milngavie, dans la région de Glasgow. La propulsion était assurée par deux hélices d'avion mues par un moteur électrique. L'invention n'eut pas de succès et la structure fut détruite en 1956. Bennie mourut ruiné et oublié quelques années plus tard. (À droite) Inventée par Kruckenberg en 1931, cette motrice allemande expérimentale propulsée par une hélice à quatre pales fut surnommée le « Zeppelin du rail ».

Streamlined locomotives – test run

A display of streamlined locomotives at the London King's Cross shed on 30 November 1937. These hugely successful locomotives were designed by the LNER's chief mechanical engineer, Sir Nigel Gresley, and built at Doncaster works from 1936. (Above, from the left) the *Dominion of New Zealand*, *Golden Shuttle*, *Empire of India*, *Golden Eagle* and *No. 10,000*.

Stromlinienlokomotiven im Test

Eine Versammlung von Stromlinienloks vor dem Londoner Lokomotivenschuppen King's Cross, 30. November 1937. Diese ausgesprochen erfolgreichen Maschinen waren eine Konstruktion des LNER-Chefingenieurs Sir Nigel Gresley und wurden seit 1936 im Lokomotivenwerk in Doncaster gebaut. (Oben, von links) *Dominion of New Zealand*, *Golden Shuttle*, *Empire of India*, *Golden Eagle* und *No. 10 000*.

Des locomotives carénées ...

Ces locomotives carénées, alignées au dépôt de la gare londonienne de King's Cross, le 30 novembre 1937, furent conçues par sir Nigel Gresley, ingénieur en chef du LNER, et construites dans les ateliers de Doncaster à partir de 1936. (Ci-dessus, à partir de la gauche) La *Dominion of New Zealand*, la *Golden Shuttle*, l'*Empire of India*, la *Golden Eagle* et la *N° 10 000*.

And finishing touches

A close-up view of the *Dominion of New Zealand* (left) and *Empire of India*. Their nameplates have just been attached. It was claimed that they could travel at 130mph but the fastest speed recorded was by the *Mallard*, at nearly 126mph on the East Coast main line on 3 July 1938. The *Mallard* is still known as the fastest steam locomotive in the world.

Der letzte Schliff

Ein näherer Blick auf *Dominion of New Zealand* (links) und *Empire of India*. Eben haben die Mechaniker die Namens-schilder montiert. Die Loks sollten ein Tempo von 209 km/h erreichen, doch die schnellste gemessene Zeit waren knapp 203 km/h, die am 3. Juli 1938 die *Mallard* auf der Hauptstrecke entlang der Ostküste erreichte. Die *Mallard* gilt bis heute als schnellste Dampflokomotive der Welt.

... et leur entretien

Gros plan sur la *Dominion of New Zealand* (à gauche) et l'*Empire of India*, dont les plaques de nom viennent d'être fixées. Elles auraient été capables de rouler à 209 km/h mais seule la *Mallard* atteignit la vitesse record de 203 km/h sur la ligne principale de la côte Est, le 3 juillet 1938. La *Mallard* reste la locomotive à vapeur la plus rapide du monde.

Rival streamlined trains

(Above left) The LMS train the *Coronation Scot* at speed at Watford, c. 1938. The first streamlined train to run from London to Scotland in 1937, it was hauled by one of five locomotives: the *Queen Elizabeth*, *Queen Mary*, *Princess Alice*, *Princess Alexandra* and *Coronation*. (Above right) The LNER train the *Silver Jubilee* ran between London King's Cross and Newcastle. Here it is being hauled by the *Silver Link* locomotive.

Stromlinienrivalen

(Oben links) Der *Coronation Scot* der LMS in voller Fahrt bei Watford, aufgenommen etwa 1938. Der Zug fuhr seit 1937 und bot die erste Stromlinienverbindung von London nach Schottland; fünf Lokomotiven waren im Einsatz: *Queen Elizabeth*, *Queen Mary*, *Princess Alice*, *Princess Alexandra* und *Coronation*. (Oben rechts) Der *Silver Jubilee* der LNER verkehrte von London King's Cross nach Newcastle, hier gezogen von der Lokomotive *Silver Link*.

La concurrence entre trains carénés

(En haut à gauche) Le *Coronation Scot* du LMS, ici photographié à pleine vitesse à Watford, vers 1938, fut le premier train caréné britannique à assurer la liaison Londres-Écosse en 1937. Il était tracté par l'une des cinq locomotives suivantes : *Coronation*, *Queen Elizabeth*, *Queen Mary*, *Princess Alice* et *Princess Alexandra*. (En haut à droite) Le *Silver Jubilee* du LNER, ici tracté par la *Silver Link*, circulait entre King's Cross (Londres) et Newcastle.

In close-up

The LMS locomotive *Coronation*, No. 6220, which was used to pull the *Coronation Scot*, being admired at Euston, 23 June 1937. The stripes, which emphasised the streamlined look, can be seen in detail. The *Coronation* reached a speed of 114mph on a demonstration run from London Euston to Crewe in 1937. It was designed by William Stanier and built at Crewe locomotive works.

Aus nächster Nähe

LMS-Nr. 6220 *Coronation*, die Lokomotive des *Coronation Scot*, steht am 23. Juni 1937 auf dem Bahnhof Euston im Mittelpunkt der Aufmerksamkeit. Die Streifenlackierung, mit der die Stromlinienform unterstrichen wurde, ist hier im Detail zu sehen. Die *Coronation* erreichte 1937 auf einer Probefahrt von London Euston nach Crewe eine Höchstgeschwindigkeit von 183 km/h. Konstrukteur war William Stanier, gebaut wurde sie in den Lokomotivenwerken in Crewe.

De près

Des jeunes femmes admirent la *Coronation* n° 6220 de la LMS, à Euston le 23 juin 1937. Dessinée par William Stanier et construite aux ateliers ferroviaires de Crewe, cette locomotive au carénage élégamment souligné par des filets, tractait le *Coronation Scot*. En 1937, elle atteignit la vitesse de 183 km/h sur un parcours d'essai entre la gare londonienne d'Euston et Crewe.

Streamlined locomotives

Streamlined locomotives and rail coaches came in various guises. (Above) An oil-driven rail coach arriving in England from France on 18 February 1935. It had rubber-tyred wheels and could go forwards and backwards at 95mph. (Right) A 1935 French streamlined Atlantic locomotive. This locomotive ran on the PLM (Paris, Lyon & Mediterranean) railway and reflects the style and sophistication of the French Riviera. (Opposite) The first GWR diesel-mechanical bullet railcars were introduced in 1934. They were all withdrawn in 1939 at the outbreak of war and reintroduced in peacetime.

Triumph der Stromlinie

Stromlinienlokomotiven und -triebwagen gab es in jeder erdenklichen Gestalt. (Oben) Ein Dieseltriebwagen, der am 18. Februar 1935 in England aus Frankreich ankommt. Er hatte gummibelegte Reifen und erreichte vor- wie rückwärts über 150 km/h. (Rechts) Eine französische Stromlinienlok vom Typ Atlantic, gebaut 1935. Sie war bei der PLM (Paris, Lyon & Méditerranée) im Einsatz und brachte Stil und Raffinesse der Côte d'Azur, an die sie fuhr, aufs Schönste zum Ausdruck. (Gegenüberliegende Seite) Diese Dieseltriebwagen der GWR nahmen 1934 ihren Betrieb auf. 1939 wurden sie eingemottet und fuhren erst nach Kriegsende wieder.

Locomotives profilées

Il existait des locomotives et des voitures profilées de modèles très différents. (Ci-dessus) Une automotrice diesel arrive de France en Angleterre le 18 février 1935. Elle était équipée de pneumatiques et pouvait rouler à 152 km/h en marche avant ou arrière. (À droite) Cette Atlantic carénée, qui circulait sur le chemin de fer du PLM (Paris Lyon Méditerranée), symbolisait l'élégance et la sophistication de la Riviera française. (Ci-contre) Les premiers trains à grande vitesse diesel du GWR furent introduits en 1934 avant d'être remisés à la déclaration de guerre en 1939, puis remis en service la paix revenue.

In and out of fashion – the *Crusader*
A Reading Railroad locomotive 4–6–2 No. 118, built by the company at Reading workshops in July 1918 and rebuilt with the streamlining and named *Crusader* in 1937. It was stripped of the streamlining in August 1952.

Der *Crusader* – immer mit der Mode
Die 2 C 1 Lokomotive Nr. 118 der Reading Railroad, gebaut im Juli 1918 im Lokomotivenwerk Reading. 1937 erhielt sie eine Stromlinienverkleidung und den Namen *Crusader*, im August 1952 wurde die Verkleidung wieder abgenommen.

À la mode et démodé – le *Crusader*
Cette Pacific 251 n°118 du Reading Railroad, construite par la compagnie dans ses ateliers de Reading en juillet 1918, fut pourvue d'un carénage en 1937 et baptisée *Crusader*. Ce carrossage lui fut retiré en août 1952.

American streamliner – Hudson 4–6–4, 1937
These locomotives, designed by Henry Dreyfuss and built by the American Locomotive Company, were said to be the ultimate in American streamlining. They ran on the New York Central Railroad and pulled the famous *Twentieth Century Limited* train between New York and Chicago.

Stromlinie in Amerika – Hudson 2 C 2, 1937
Diese Lokomotiven, entworfen von Henry Dreyfuss und gebaut von der American Locomotive Company, galten als Nonplus- ultra des amerikanischen Stromlinienbaus. Sie waren bei der New York Central Railroad im Einsatz und zogen den berühm- ten *Twentieth Century Limited* zwischen New York und Chicago.

Aérodynamique américaine – la Hudson 232 de 1937
On disait que les locomotives américaines dessinées par Henry Dreyfuss et construites par l'American Locomotive Company étaient du dernier cri en matière d'aérodynamisme. Elles circu- laient sur le New York Central Railroad et remorquaient le célèbre *Twentieth Century Limited* entre New York et Chicago.

North American streamliners

(Left) The diesel-powered Pioneer *Zephyr* (on the left) was a radically new idea in motive power with a lightweight stainless steel car. Launched in America during the Depression, it symbolised the Chicago, Burlington & Quincey Railroad's determination to create new business. (Opposite) A Canadian National Railways locomotive No. 6401, built in Montreal locomotive works in 1936. This 4–8–6 class locomotive was famous for four things: steam generation, steam utilisation and moving both passenger and goods trains.

Amerikanische Avantgarde

(Links) Der dieselgetriebene Pioneer *Zephyr* (der linke Zug) mit seinen leichten Edelstahlwagen war ein radikal neuer Ansatz. Die Chicago, Burlington & Quincey Railroad brachte ihn mitten in der Wirtschaftskrise heraus, als ein sichtbares Zeichen, dass sie den Kampf um neue Kundschaft nicht aufgab. (Gegenüberliegende Seite) Die Nr. 6401 der Canadian National Railways, gebaut 1936 in den Lokomotivenwerken Montreal. Diese Maschine der 2 D 3 Klasse war für vier Dinge berühmt: Dampfaufbau, Dampfökonomie, Transport von Personen und Güterverkehr.

Trains carénés américains

(À gauche) Lancée aux États-Unis pendant la Dépression, la Pioneer *Zephyr* diesel (à gauche), une voiture légère construite en acier, concrétisait une idée radicalement novatrice et symbolisait la détermination de la Chicago, Burlington & Quincey Railroad de s'ouvrir de nouveaux marchés. (Ci-contre) Cette locomotive n° 6401 type 243, construite dans les ateliers de Montréal en 1936 pour les Canadian National Railways, avait quatre atouts : son mode de génération et de circulation de vapeur, ainsi que sa pluridisciplinarité – voyageurs et marchandises.

Meals on wheels

By the 1930s railway catering was well established: passengers were served in style all over the world. (Above) Chinese diners enjoy Western food, 1936. (Below) Christmas fare on the LMS, 23 December 1938. (Opposite, clockwise from top left) A new Southern Railway buffet car, on show at Waterloo Station, 1938; a new GWR buffet car, 1934; an American club lounge car on the *Golden State Limited* train, Chicago, Rock Island & Pacific Railways; Christmas party time on the GWR, 28 December 1934 (note the mistletoe).

Essen auf Rädern

In den dreißiger Jahren hatten die Bahngesellschaften bei der Bewirtung an Bord ihrer Züge weltweit einen hohen Standard erreicht. (Oben) Reisende in China lassen sich eine westliche Mahlzeit schmecken, 1936. (Unten) Weihnachtsessen bei der LMS, 23. Dezember 1938. (Gegenüberliegende Seite, im Uhrzeigersinn von oben links) Ein neuer Speisewagen der Southern Railway, vorgestellt auf dem Bahnhof Waterloo, 1938; ein neuer GWR-Buffetwagen, 1934; ein amerikanischer Clubwagen, der mit dem *Golden State Limited* der Chicago, Rock Island & Pacific Railways fuhr. Zeit für Weihnachtspartys bei der GWR (das Mistelzweig-Dekor verrät es), aufgenommen am 28. Dezember 1934.

Des repas en roulant

La restauration ferroviaire est déjà bien ancrée dans les habitudes des voyageurs des années 1930, qui bénéficient d'un service stylé dans le monde entier. (En haut) En 1936, des dîneurs chinois goûtent à la nourriture occidentale. (En bas) Voyage de Noël sur le LMS, le 23 décembre 1938. (Ci-contre, en haut à gauche) Une nouvelle voiture-restaurant du Southern Railway est présentée en gare de Waterloo, en 1938 ; (en haut à droite) une nouvelle voiture-restaurant du GWR, en 1934 ; (en bas à droite) voiture-salon du *Golden State Limited* des Chicago, Rock Island & Pacific Railways ; (en bas à gauche) dîner de Noël sur le GWR, le 28 décembre 1934 (remarquez le gui).

Using modern materials

The railways were keen to use modern man-made materials, especially for first class passenger travel. (Left) America's first streamlined train, the *Zephyr*, seen here somewhere in Nebraska in 1934, boasted that it used stainless-steel exterior casing. Being relatively light, this had the advantage of allowing increased speed. (Above right) The Illinois Railroad's *Green Diamond* passenger car, 1936; it made use of stainless steel and other alloys. The new paints in bright colours were also more durable and practical. (Below right) The Solarium end of New York Central's *Twentieth Century Limited* state-of-the-art, streamlined train.

Mit modernen Materialien

Die Bahngesellschaften waren modernen synthetischen Materialien gegenüber sehr aufgeschlossen, gerade für den Personenverkehr der ersten Klasse. (Links) Der erste amerikanische Stromlinienzug, der *Zephyr* – hier bei einer Vorführung in Nebraska, 1934 –, konnte mit einer Karosserie aus Edelstahl aufwarten. Das eingesparte Gewicht kam dem Tempo zugute. (Rechts oben) Der *Green Diamond* der Illinois Railroad, 1936, hier ein Salonwagen, machte sich Edelstahl und andere leichte Materialien zunutze. Hellere, haltbarere Farben kamen hinzu. (Rechts unten) *Twentieth Century Limited* – der Aussichtswagen des Stromlinienzugs der New York Central war auf der Höhe der Zeit.

L'emploi de matériaux modernes

Les chemins de fer tenaient beaucoup à utiliser des matériaux synthétiques modernes, notamment pour les voitures de première classe. (À gauche) Son carrossage en acier faisait la fierté du *Zephyr*, premier train caréné américain, que l'on voit ici quelque part dans le Nebraska en 1934. Sa relative légèreté lui permettait d'atteindre des vitesses moyennes plus élevées. (En haut à droite) La *Green Diamond*, de l'Illinois Railroad, en 1936, était une voiture construite en acier et autres alliages dont les vives couleurs étaient plus durables et plus pratiques. (En bas à droite) Le solarium de la voiture-salon du *Twentieth Century Limited*, le train caréné et tout dernier cri du New York Central.

Period architecture

Moving with the times meant new art deco-style stations and trains. Both America and Europe embraced the idea with great panache. (Left) A New York Central Railroad station, c. 1940, somewhere outside the city. The NYCR ran from New York to Chicago via Buffalo. (Above) Helsinki Railway Station, Finland. The architect was Eliel Saarinen who was thirty-one at the time of the competition to build the station in 1904. The station was not inaugurated until fifteen years later, in 1919. The architecture, it has been said, reflects the character of the Finns: 'the direct and unadorned use of materials with a fundamentally classic sense of composition.'

Neue Architektur

Wer modern sein wollte, brauchte Züge und Bahnhöfe im Art-déco-Stil, und beiderseits des Atlantiks wurde das neue Ideal überzeugend umgesetzt. (Links) Ein Vorstadtbahnhof der New York Central Railroad, etwa 1940. Die NYCR verkehrte von New York über Buffalo nach Chicago. (Oben) Der Bahnhof von Helsinki, Finnland. Der Architekt Eliel Saarinen war 31 Jahre alt, als er am Wettbewerb zum Bau des Bahnhofs 1904 teilnahm. Er wurde erst 15 Jahre später, 1919, eröffnet. Diese Architektur, so sagte man, bringt den Charakter der Finnen zum Ausdruck: »die unmittelbare, schmucklose Verwendung der Materialien mit einem zutiefst klassischen Sinn für Proportionen.«

Architecture d'époque

Appliquant le slogan « se déplacer avec son temps », les compagnies de chemin de fer, américaines et européennes notamment, adoptèrent le nouveau style art déco alors à la mode pour leurs gares et leurs trains. (À gauche) Une des gares de banlieue du New York Central Railroad, vers 1940. Le NYCR assurait la liaison New York–Chicago via Buffalo. (Ci-dessus) La gare de Helsinki (Finlande). Eliel Saarinen, qui, en 1904 remporta le concours à l'âge de 31 ans, en est l'architecte. La gare fut seulement inaugurée 15 ans plus tard, en 1919. Son architecture, a-t-on dit, reflète le caractère des Finlandais : « l'emploi direct et sans artifice des matériaux dans une composition d'ordre fondamentalement classique. »

Roof construction

Stazione Centrale, Milan, and its roof construction were considered to be amongst the most modern and up to date in the world in 1930. This suited Milan for it was, and still is, the industrial and commercial capital of Italy. The station was built as a temple to the Italian fascist movement.

Gewölbebau

Die Mailänder Stazione Centrale und ihre Dachkonstruktion zählten 1930 zu den modernsten der Welt. Das passte zu Mailand, denn es war – und ist bis heute – die Wirtschafts- und Handelsmetropole Italiens. Erbaut wurde der Bahnhof als ein Tempel des italienischen Faschismus.

Construction de toiture

La gare centrale de Milan, magnifiée par sa toiture, fut considérée comme l'un des bâtiments les plus modernes des années 1930 et un temple au mouvement fasciste italien. Cette architecture correspondait parfaitement au statut de Milan, qui était, et demeure, la capitale industrielle et commerciale de l'Italie.

Overhead metalwork

Paddington Station, 1933, the Gateway to the West for the tired commuter and the holiday-maker. Paddington was built by Isambard Kingdom Brunel and Matthew Digby Wyatt in 1854 and included these impressive wrought-iron arabesques. The station was remodelled in 1933; oddly, its main concourse is known as 'the Lawn' which is also the site of a statue of Brunel.

Triumph der Schmiedekunst

Paddington Station, 1933, für Pendler am Ende eines langen Arbeitstages und für erholungsuchende Londoner das Tor zum englischen Westen. Isambard Kingdom Brunel und Matthew Digby Wyatt erbauten den Bahnhof 1854 und schmückten ihn mit drei großen schmiedeeisernen Arabesken; 1933 wurde er neu gestaltet. Die Bahnhofs-halle von Paddington, wo heute auch ein Brunel-Denkmal steht, hört auf den kuriosen Namen »the Lawn« (der Rasen).

Ferronnerie en toiture

Remaniée en 1933, la gare de Paddington était alors la Porte de l'Ouest pour les banlieusards fatigués et les vacanciers. Ses impressionnantes arabesques en fer forgé datent de la construction de cette gare, dessinée par Isambard Kingdom Brunel et Matthew Digby Wyatt en 1854. Son hall principal, où se dresse une statue de l'archi-tecte, est étrangement appelé « the Lawn » (la Pelouse).

New style information board

The Arrival, or 'Tote', Indicator board used the principle of the totalizator and was used for the first time on the GWR at Paddington on 27 March 1934. Instead of having to find an information desk or passimeter (passenger/ticket office) clerk, a traveller could instantly see the time of arrival of his train and the platform.

Alles auf einen Blick

Die GWR nahm ihre neue, elektrisch gesteuerte Fahrplananzeige auf dem Bahnhof Paddington am 27. März 1934 in Betrieb. Statt an den Auskunftsschalter zu gehen oder einen Schaffner zu fragen, konnte der Reisende sich nun auf einen Blick über Ankunfts- und Abfahrtszeiten und die Bahnsteige der Züge informieren.

Nouveau style de panneau indicateur

Le tableau indicateur des Arrivées, ou « Tote », utilisait le principe du totalisateur et fut employé pour la première fois à Paddington le 27 mars 1934 pour les trains du GWR. Le voyageur n'avait ainsi plus besoin de demander l'heure et le quai d'arrivée de son train à un employé ou au guichet.

Railway clocks

With timekeeping of the utmost importance on the railways, enormous care and attention was paid to making, resetting and overhauling railway timepieces. (Above) An LNER worker cleans the face of a clock at London King's Cross in 1931. (Below) The GWR station and signal box clocks being cleaned and overhauled at their workshops in Reading in the 1930s.

Bahnhofsuhren

Die exakte Zeit war für die Eisenbahnen von größter Bedeutung, und so wurde auf Herstellung und Instandhaltung der Uhren entsprechende Sorgfalt verwendet. (Oben) Ein Arbeiter der LNER putzt das Zifferblatt einer Uhr im Londoner Bahnhof King's Cross, 1931. (Unten) In einer eigenen Werkstatt in Reading wurden, wie diese Aufnahme aus den dreißiger Jahren zeigt, die Bahnhofs- und Stellwerkuhren der GWR gereinigt und überholt.

Horloges de chemins de fer

L'exactitude devant être l'une des qualités majeures des chemins de fer, chaque compagnie apportait une attention et un soin tout particuliers à la fabrication, à la mise à l'heure et à l'entretien des horloges. (En haut) Un ouvrier du LNER nettoie le cadran d'une horloge de la gare londonienne de King's Cross, en 1931. (En bas) Le nettoyage et la révision des horloges des gares et des postes d'aiguillage du GWR à ses ateliers de Reading, dans les années 1930.

From eggs to elephants…

In the 1930s the railways were still the only practical way of transporting goods and mail. In Britain, until 1962, railway companies were required by law to carry any load offered to them. And they did: from the mundane to the unusual. (Above) A record number of Christmas parcels waiting at London Bridge Station to be distributed by the mail train, 22 December 1936. (Below) More than 150 tons of luggage at St Pancras belonging to Canadians travelling back from a pilgrimage to Vimy, northern France, in July 1936. The luggage was afterwards taken to various hotels in London.

Vom Ei bis zum Elefanten …

Auch in den dreißiger Jahren blieben die Eisenbahnen das einzig zuverlässige Transportmittel für Güter und Post. In Großbritannien gab es bis 1962 ein Gesetz, das die Bahnen verpflichtete, alles zu befördern, was ihnen anvertraut wurde. Und das taten sie: von kleinsten Alltagsdingen bis zum ausgefallensten Stück. (Oben) Bahnhof London Bridge, 22. Dezember 1936 – mehr Weihnachtspäckchen als je zuvor warten auf den Postzug. (Unten) Über 150 Tonnen Gepäck auf dem Bahnhof St. Pancras, Juli 1936. Die Koffer und Kisten gehörten Kanadiern, die von einer Pilgerreise nach Vimy in Nordfrankreich zurückkehrten, und wurden vom Bahnhof an die verschiedenen Londoner Hotels weitergeleitet.

Des œufs aux éléphants…

Dans les années 1930, le chemin de fer restait le moyen de transport le plus pratique pour les marchandises et le courrier. Les compagnies de chemin de fer britanniques étaient obligées par la loi, ce jusqu'en 1962, de transporter toute marchandise qui leur était confiée, de la plus ordinaire à la plus insolite. (En haut) Un nombre record de colis de Noël attend à la gare de London Bridge d'être distribué par les trains postaux, le 22 décembre 1936. (En bas) En juillet 1936, plus de 150 tonnes de bagages appartenant à des Canadiens revenant d'un pèlerinage sur le champ de bataille de Vimy, dans le nord de la France, durent être triés par les employés de la gare de St Pancras avant d'être ensuite livrés dans différents hôtels de Londres.

Goods porters: unsung heroes

An evocative photograph that could have been taken on any city station in the 1930s. The porters hold a conversation, leaning on their loaded trolleys. Goods handling was an essential and prosperous part of the work of the railways. Unlike passengers, goods had to be brought to the goods depot, sorted, recorded, loaded, transported and then delivered from another goods depot at the destination.

Transportarbeiter: die heimlichen Helden

Dieses stimmungsvolle Bild könnte in den dreißiger Jahren auf jedem Großstadtbahnhof entstanden sein. Die Gepäckträger halten ein Schwätzchen, auf ihre beladenen Karren gelehnt. Der Güterverkehr war ein wichtiger und einträglicher Zweig der Eisenbahn. Waren wurden zum Güterbahnhof gebracht, sortiert, registriert, verladen, zum Bestimmungsort gebracht und vom dortigen Güterbahnhof wieder ausgeliefert.

Les porteurs : des héros oubliés

Cette photographie à l'atmosphère évocatrice pourrait avoir été prise dans n'importe quelle gare des années 1930. Le transport des marchandises était l'une des activités essentielles, et rentables, des chemins de fer mais qui nécessitait un gros travail de manutention : les marchandises devaient d'abord être entreposées dans les dépôts, puis triées, enregistrées, chargées et transportées en train avant d'être livrées à leur destination finale.

Customer care

After the British Railway grouping of 1923, railway companies in
Great Britain became aware that they were in competition and had to
treat ticket buyers and passengers with due respect and consideration.
(Above) An SR company station announcer at work in his tower above
Brighton Station concourse in 1933. (Right) In the same year the SR
introduced a number of platform enquiry offices on the concourse of
Waterloo Station to give out immediate travel information.

Kundendienst

Nach der Konsolidierung der britischen Eisenbahnen im Jahr 1923 war
den Gesellschaften klar, dass sie im Wettbewerb miteinander standen
und dass man Fahrgäste umwerben und zuvorkommend behandeln
musste. (Oben) Ein Ansager der SR an seinem Arbeitsplatz, einem
Turm hoch über den Gleisen des Brightoner Bahnhofs, 1933. (Rechts)
Ebenfalls 1933 stellte die SR auf dem Bahnhof Waterloo eine Reihe von
Kiosken auf, an denen die Fahrgäste direkt auf dem Bahnsteig Auskünfte
erhalten konnten.

Le soin du client

Après leur fusion en quatre groupes en 1923, les compagnies de chemin de
fer britanniques prirent conscience qu'elles se trouvaient en concurrence
et devaient traiter les acheteurs de billets et les voyageurs avec un respect
et une considération accrus. (Ci-dessus) Un annonceur du SR en plein
travail à son poste dominant le hall de la gare de Brighton, en 1933.
(À droite) Cette même année, le SR mit en place plusieurs guichets
d'informations dans le hall de la gare de Waterloo afin de renseigner les
voyageurs en partance.

'Your comfort is our delight'

Passengers' comfort and interests were foremost in the railway companies' minds. (Above left) The sleeping car attendant for the LMS at Euston Station places hot water bottles in sleeping compartments on the Inverness (Scotland) express in January 1935. (Above centre) An attendant for the SR at Waterloo Station, 1933, overburdened with lost luggage. (Above right) Mrs Tyrell, an LNER cleaner, about to start work at King's Cross, 1938.

»Wir sind erst zufrieden, wenn Sie es sind«

Die Bahngesellschaften taten alles für die Bequemlichkeit der Reisenden. (Oben links) Ein Schlafwagenschaffner der LMS versorgt im Januar 1935 auf dem Bahnhof Euston die Schlafabteile des Zugs nach Inverness, Schottland, mit Wärmflaschen. (Oben Mitte) Ein schwer beladener Angestellter der SR im Fundbüro des Bahnhofs Waterloo, 1933. (Oben rechts) Mrs Tyrell, Putzfrau bei der LNER, geht in King's Cross an die Arbeit, 1938.

« Votre confort est notre plaisir »

Le confort et l'intérêt de leurs voyageurs étaient essentiels dans l'esprit des compagnies de chemin de fer. (Ci-dessus à gauche) En gare d'Euston, un contrôleur des wagons-lits du LMS distribue des bouillottes dans les compartiments à couchettes de l'express d'Inverness (Écosse), en janvier 1935. (Ci-dessus, au centre) Un préposé du SR en gare de Waterloo montre les objets trouvés en 1933. (Ci-dessus à droite) Mrs Tyrell, femme de ménage au LNER, s'apprête à prendre son service à la gare de King's Cross, en 1938.

Running repairs

Maintaining the infrastructure: (clockwise, from top left) LNER workers cleaning and painting along a stretch of glass roof at York Station, 1934; GWR workers taking a break on the roof at Paddington, 1930; SR construction workers dismantling the old signal gantry at Waterloo Station, 1958; SR workers painting and cleaning at Cannon Street Station, 1936. (Opposite) LNER workers carrying out track maintenance at King's Cross, 1931.

Instandhaltung

Einrichtungen müssen gepflegt werden: (Im Uhrzeigersinn von oben links) Arbeiter der LNER säubern und streichen das Glasdach des Bahnhofs von York, 1934; eine Putzkolonne der GWR macht Pause auf dem Dach von Paddington Station, 1930; Bauarbeiter der SR montieren die alte Signalbrücke der Waterloo Station ab, 1958; Reinigungs- und Ausbesserungsarbeiten am SR-Bahnhof Cannon Street, 1936. (Gegenüberliegende Seite) Gleisarbeiter der LNER in King's Cross, 1931.

Les réparations

L'entretien des infrastructures : (en haut à gauche) des ouvriers du LNER repeignent les verrières de la gare de York, en 1934; (en haut à droite) des ouvriers du GWR sur le toit de la gare de Paddington, en 1930; (en bas à droite) des ouvriers du SR démontent l'ancien portique de signalisation de la gare de Waterloo, en 1958; (en bas à gauche) des ouvriers du SR s'apprêtent à repeindre la toiture de la gare de Cannon Street, en 1936. (Ci-contre) Des ouvriers du LNER à la gare de King's Cross, en 1931.

Locomotive maintenance

Railway workshops not only built the locomotives but also had to repair and maintain them so that everything ran safely and smoothly. (Above left) This steel wheel has to be removed from the locomotive after 300,000 miles by means of a ring-shaped gas burner. (Above right) A welder puts the finishing touches to a set of driving wheels. (Opposite) Thousands of wheels at the LMS works, Derby, 1935.

In der Lokomotivenwerkstatt

Die Werkstätten der Bahngesellschaften bauten die Lokomotiven nicht nur, sie reparierten und warteten sie auch, damit ein reibungsloser Betrieb gewährleistet war. (Oben links) Dieser stählerne Radreifen muss nach 300 000 Meilen ausgewechselt werden; zum Abnehmen wird er mit einem ringförmigen Gasbrenner erhitzt. (Oben rechts) Ein Schweißer legt letzte Hand an ein Paar Antriebsräder. (Gegenüberliegende Seite) Tausende von Rädern bei den LMS-Werken in Derby, 1935.

L'entretien des locomotives

Les ateliers des compagnies ferroviaires doivent non seulement construire les locomotives et le matériel roulant mais aussi les réparer et les entretenir en s'assurant qu'ils fonctionnent en toute sécurité. (Ci-dessus à gauche) Cette roue en acier de locomotive est détachée à l'aide d'un brûleur à gaz circulaire après 480 000 kilomètres. (Ci-dessus à droite) Un soudeur au travail sur l'une des roues d'un essieu moteur. (Ci-contre) Des milliers de roues en attente de montage dans les ateliers du LMS à Derby, en 1935.

Odd jobs

Some jobs on the railways were less appealing than others, but someone had
to do them. (Left) The sleeper creosoting works of the GWR at Hayes, Middlesex.
The works dealt with half a million sleepers annually. The photograph shows the
cylinders in which the sleepers were impregnated with creosote, 1936.
(Above) Two ratcatchers with tools of the trade and their kill.

Kuriose Arbeiten

Manche Arbeiten bei der Eisenbahn waren weniger schön als andere, aber auch
sie mussten getan werden. (Links) Die Schwellenimprägnieranlage der GWR in
Hayes, Middlesex, die Jahr für Jahr eine halbe Million Schwellen präparierte.
Das Bild aus dem Jahr 1936 zeigt die Kessel, in denen das Holz mit Kreosot getränkt
wurde. (Oben) Zwei Rattenfänger mit Ausrüstung und Beute.

Métiers étranges

Certains métiers des chemins de fer étaient moins attrayants que d'autres.
(À gauche) L'atelier de créosotage du GWR à Hayes (Middlesex) traitait près d'un
million de traverses par an. Cette photographie de 1936 montre la chaudière de
créosotage dans laquelle les traverses étaient imprégnées de créosote (un liquide
huileux assurant une meilleure conservation du bois). (Ci-dessus) Deux chasseurs
de rats avec leurs instruments de travail et une de leurs proies.

The *Royal Scot* in North America

The first *Royal Scot* express train left London for Scotland
on 1 June 1862. By 1933 it was on tour in Canada and America.
It was the first time that an entire train had been sent across
the Atlantic and she was rapturously received. US regulations
nonetheless had to be complied with, hence the lamp and bell
on the front of the locomotive.

Der *Royal Scot* in Amerika

Am 1. Juni 1862 verließ der erste *Royal Scot*-Express London in
Richtung Schottland. 1933 unternahm er eine Tournee durch
Kanada und die Vereinigten Staaten. Es war das erste Mal, dass
ein ganzer Zug über den Atlantik geschickt wurde, und der
Empfang war begeistert. Allerdings musste er nach US-Regeln
ausgerüstet sein, und die Lokomotive bekam Scheinwerfer und
Glocke anmontiert.

Le *Royal Scot* aux États-Unis

Le premier *Royal Scot,* un train express, quitta Londres pour
l'Écosse le 1ᵉʳ juin 1862. Il fut envoyé en 1933 au Canada et aux
États-Unis pour démontrer ses capacités et y reçut un accueil
chaleureux. C'était la première fois qu'un train complet était
expédié de l'autre côté de l'Atlantique. La lampe et la cloche à
l'avant de la locomotive furent ajoutées afin de satisfaire à la
réglementation américaine.

The Royal Scot comes home

The Royal Scot left Tilbury docks on 11 April 1933. The first tour began on 1 May and she arrived back in Britain in 1934, on a typically cold and misty winter's day. To celebrate her home-coming, the locomotive's name was recast in a larger size to give her the recognition she deserved. She still runs daily from Euston at 10 a.m. to travel across the Midlands, through the Lake District and over the Scottish border.

Der *Royal Scot* kehrt zurück

Der *Royal Scot* verließ die Docks von Tilbury am 11. April 1933, und die Tournee begann am 1. Mai. An einem typisch kalten und nebligen Wintertag des Jahres 1934 kehrte er auf britischen Boden zurück. Zur Feier der Wiederkehr bekam die Lokomo-tive ein neues, größeres Namensschild, das ihrem besonderen Rang entsprach. Noch heute bricht der *Royal Scot* täglich um zehn Uhr morgens am Bahnhof Euston auf und fährt durch die Midlands und den Lake District hinauf nach Schottland.

Le retour du *Royal Scot*

Le *Royal Scot* quitta les entrepôts de Tilbury le 11 avril 1933 pour commencer sa tournée aux États-Unis le 1er mai. Il revint en Grande-Bretagne en 1934 par une froide et brumeuse jour-née d'hiver. La locomotive reçut une plaque aux lettres plus grosses pour saluer son retour et lui montrer la reconnaissance qu'elle méritait. Ce train continue de circuler quotidiennement, partant de Euston à 10 heures du matin jusqu'en Écosse à travers les Midlands et le Lake District.

Adventure and anticipation

Travelling by train for the commuter, the schoolchild or the shopper could be mundane but some journeys led to greater things. (Left) Tourists gaze from their carriage windows in an Argentine station somewhere on the Transandine Railway over the Andes. The Transandine crossed the Andes at Uspallata Pass. (Above) London Victoria Station, where passengers embark for the boat train to Southampton, thence to take a liner to America.

Spannung und Abenteuer

Die Fahrt zur Arbeit, zur Schule oder zum Einkaufen war längst alltäglich, aber manchmal war eine Bahnfahrt auch der Auftakt zu Größerem. (Links) Reisende schauen auf einem argentinischen Bahnhof aus den Fenstern der Trans-andenbahn. Die Linie überquerte die Anden am Uspallata-Pass. (Oben) Victoria Station in London – Ausgangspunkt des Anschlusszuges nach Southampton, der die Reisenden zu den Ozeandampfern nach Amerika brachte.

Aventure et anticipation

S'il peut paraître banal aux banlieusards, aux écoliers ou aux passagers ordinaires de prendre le train, certains voyages conduisent à des choses plus grandes. (À gauche) Des touristes profitent d'un arrêt du Transandin dans une gare d'Argentine, quelque part dans les montagnes, pour se dégourdir les jambes. Le Transandin franchissait la Cordillère au col d'Uspallata. (Ci-dessus) C'est à la gare Victoria à Londres que les passagers prenaient le train pour Southampton en correspondance avec un paquebot vers les États-Unis.

Trains as image makers 1. The film star

In 1931 Marlene Dietrich appeared in the role of Shanghai Lily in the film *Shanghai Express* (left). Railway scenes enriched hundreds of American films of the Thirties; few were accurate although the atmosphere they provided could be thrilling. In *Shanghai Express*, the Chinese railways are obviously American and, from the size of the carriage interiors, the railway must have been a 10-foot gauge!

Züge machen Bilder: 1. Der Filmstar

1931 spielte Marlene Dietrich die Shanghai-Lily in dem Film *Shanghai Express* (links). Eisenbahnszenen belebten Hunderte von amerikanischen Filmen der Dreißiger; nur wenige waren realistisch, auch wenn die Atmosphäre oft spannend genug war. Die chinesischen Züge in *Shanghai Express* sind offensichtlich amerikanisch, und der Größe der Abteile nach zu urteilen muss die Spurweite ungefähr drei Meter betragen haben!

Les trains comme décor de cinéma I. La star

En 1931, Marlene Dietrich incarne Shanghai Lily dans le film *Shanghai Express* (à gauche). Si des centaines de films américains des années 1930 utilisent le chemin de fer pour corser l'atmosphère, c'est malheureusement trop souvent au détriment du réalisme ou de la fidélité historique. Ainsi, les trains chinois de *Shanghai Express* sont-ils à l'évidence américains et, si l'on en juge aux dimensions intérieures des voitures, les voies auraient dû avoir un écartement de trois mètres !

Trains as image makers 2. The politician

The glamour of the railways also appealed to politicians, who used the railways as a tool and a useful mobile billboard. (Above) A Chinese propaganda train complete with portrait of the candidate and ideograms, 1931. (Below) Democratic presidential candidate Franklin D. Roosevelt with two wranglers on an electioneering train in Laramie, Wyoming, 1932.

Züge machen Bilder: 2. Der Politiker

Den Glanz der Eisenbahnen machten sich auch Politiker gern zunutze, die für sie nicht nur Transportmittel, sondern auch mobile Reklametafeln waren. (Oben) Ein chinesischer Propagandazug mit Schriftzeichen und einem Bild des Kandidaten, 1931. (Unten) Franklin D. Roosevelt als demokratischer Präsidentschaftskandidat mit zwei Cowboys vor einem Wahlkampfzug in Laramie, Wyoming, 1932.

Les trains comme décor de cinéma II. Le politique

La fascination des chemins de fer touche également les hommes politiques, qui utilisent alors les trains comme support d'affichage ambulant. (En haut) En 1931, ce train chinois, tout entier consacré à la propagande, est décoré d'un portrait du candidat et d'idéogrammes. (En bas) Franklin D. Roosevelt, candidat démocrate à la présidence des États-Unis en 1932, a invité deux cow-boys de Laramie (Wyoming) à bord de son train électoral.

Moving the railways

Two unusual ways of manoeuvring trains. (Above) An LNER locomotive, *No. 10,000*, being hand-turned on a turntable whilst a cameraman (foreground) captures the operation at King's Cross. (Opposite) One of four sleeping coaches being lifted by crane on to the SS *Belpemela* at Newport docks in South Wales prior to being shipped to China, 26 December 1935.

Bahntransport

Nicht immer fuhren Bahnen aus eigener Kraft. (Oben) Die LNER-Lokomotive *No. 10 000* wird in King's Cross für den Kameramann (im Vordergrund) von Hand auf einer Drehscheibe gedreht. (Gegenüberliegende Seite) Einer von vier Schlafwagen, die am 26. Dezember 1935 in den Docks von Newport, Südwales, per Kran auf die SS *Belpemela* verladen wurden. Die Wagen gingen nach China.

Grandes manœuvres

Voici deux moyens insolites de déplacer des trains. (Ci-dessus) Des cheminots manœuvrent à la main la *N° 10 000* du LNER, immobilisée sur la plaque tournante de King's Cross, sous l'objectif d'un cameraman (au premier plan). (Ci-contre) Le 26 décembre 1935, quatre wagons-lits destinés à la Chine sont chargés à bord du SS *Belpemela* dans les docks de Newport (Galles du Sud).

Still flying

(Left) The *Flying Scotsman* at King's Cross Station, right, about to set off for the Easter holidays, 12 April 1933. (Right) En route from King's Cross to Edinburgh, 20 May 1932. Flying above the train was the forty-two-seater Imperial Airways airliner *Hercules*. A Marconi wireless was fitted in both train and plane and messages exchanged between passengers. To help the pilot identify the train, its name was painted on the roof of one of the carriages.

Flugs wie eh und je

(Links) Der *Flying Scotsman* läuft aus dem Bahnhof King's Cross zur Fahrt in die Osterferien aus, 12. April 1933. (Rechts) Von King's Cross nach Edinburgh, 20. Mai 1932. Das 42. Passagierflugzeug *Hercules* der Imperial Airways flog dieselbe Route. Zug und Flugzeug waren mit Marconi-Funkgeräten ausgestattet, sodass Fahr- und Fluggäste Nachrichten austauschen konnten. Zur Orientierung des Piloten schrieb man den Namen des Zuges auf das Dach eines Waggons.

Toujours actif

(À gauche) Le *Flying Scotsman* est prêt à prendre le départ de la gare de King's Cross lors des vacances de Pâques, le 12 avril 1933. (À droite) Le 20 mai 1932, un *Hercules* de 42 places, des Imperial Airways, survola le train sur la ligne Londres–Écosse. Les passagers du train et de l'avion purent échanger des messages grâce à une liaison Marconi sans fil. Le nom du train avait été peint sur le toit de l'une de ses voitures afin que le pilote puisse identifier plus facilement le convoi.

Camping coaches

In the 1930s, the LNER put old coaches in holiday sites and called them 'camping coaches', forerunners of today's caravan sites. For a fee a group or family could spend a week in a well-equipped coach. It offered a solid alternative to sleeping under canvas. (Above) Happy campers going to fetch water from their coach at Southminster, near Burnham, Essex. (Right) LMS workers at Derby put bedding into coaches in readiness for the holiday season, 1937.

Campingwagen

In den dreißiger Jahren stellte die LNER ausgemusterte Waggons in Feriengebieten auf und nannte sie »Campingwagen« – die Vorläufer der heutigen Caravanparks. Gruppen oder Familien konnten die gut ausgerüsteten Wagen wochenweise mieten, eine gute Alternative zum Zelt. (Oben) Glückliche Camperinnen in Southminster bei Burnham in Essex gehen Wasser holen. (Rechts) Arbeiter im LMS-Betriebswerk in Derby richten Schlafwagen für die Feriensaison 1937 her.

Des voitures de camping

Dans les années 1930, le LNER abandonna des voitures de réforme sur différents lieux de vacances, précurseurs des camps de caravanes actuels. Ces « camping coaches » (voitures de camping), bien équipées et louées pour quelques livres, permettaient à une famille ou un groupe d'amis de passer des vacances confortables et éviter de coucher sous la tente. (Ci-dessus) L'heure de la corvée d'eau pour ces joyeuses occupantes d'un wagon de camping de Southminster, près de Burnham (Essex). (À droite) En 1937, des employés de la gare LMS de Derby installent les matelas des voitures-lits en prévision des vacances.

A long, steep haul
A Princess Pacific locomotive negotiating Camden bank out of London Euston. When the London & Birmingham Railway began in 1837 they had to build winding engines at Camden to help locomotives up this bank; these were dispensed with by 1844, since then locomotives could work up the bank under their own steam.

Ein steiler Anstieg
Eine Princess-Pacific-Lokomotive bewältigt die Steigung von Camden an der Ausfahrt des Londoner Bahnhofs Euston. Als die London & Birmingham Railway 1837 ihren Betrieb aufnahm, waren in Camden noch Winden installiert, die den Lokomotiven den Berg hinaufhalfen; 1844 waren sie schon nicht mehr nötig: Die Maschinen waren nun stark genug, die Steigung aus eigener Kraft zu bewältigen.

Un long voyage en montée
Une Pacific de la série Princess négocie la montée de Camden, à la sortie de la gare londonienne de Euston. Dès sa création en 1837, le London & Birmingham Railway dut installer à Camden des machines de halage pour aider les convois à franchir cette rampe ; elles furent supprimées en 1844, les locomotives en service étant désormais assez puissantes pour monter seules la pente.

Across the river
Steam in an industrial landscape as a Prussian freight locomotive crosses the River Ruhr at dusk. The Friedrich Wilhelm Iron Foundry can be seen in the background, framed by the bridge.

Überqueren des Flusses
Dampf und Industrielandschaft: Eine preußische Güterzug-lokomotive überquert im Morgengrauen die Ruhr. Im Hinter-grund die Friedrich-Wilhelm-Eisengießerei, eingerahmt von der Brücke.

La traversée du fleuve
La locomotive d'un train de marchandises prussien franchit la Ruhr au crépuscule. On reconnaît la fonderie Friedrich Wilhelm, encadrée par le pont à l'arrière-plan de ce paysage industriel enfumé.

Classics of their kind

Certain photographs epitomise the railways of the 1930s. (Left) The final batch
of the new 'King' locomotives leaves the
GWR shed at Swindon in July 1930.
They were designed by C.B. Collet in
1927 to haul the heaviest passenger
expresses between Paddington and the
west of England. Thirty were built, all
of them completed by 1930. (Above)
Wheels in motion – an LNER locomotive,
17 March 1931.

Lokomotivenklassiker

Zwei Aufnahmen, die geradezu Sinnbilder
der Eisenbahn in den dreißiger Jahren
sind. (Links) Die letzte Serie neuer
»King«-Lokomotiven verlässt den Lokschuppen der GWR in Swindon, Juli 1930.
C. B. Collet hatte sie 1927 für die schwers-
ten Personen-Expresszüge zwischen
Paddington und dem englischen Westen
konstruiert. 30 Exemplare entstanden,
die letzten davon 1930. (Oben) Räder in
Bewegung – eine Lokomotive der LNER,
17. März 1931.

Classiques à leur manière

Certaines photographies illustrent parfaitement les chemins de fer des années 1930.
(À gauche) En juillet 1930, les dernières
locomotives de classe King, dessinées par
Collet en 1927, quittent le dépôt de Swindon du GWR. Elles remorquent les trains
rapides de voyageurs les plus lourds entre
la gare de Paddington et l'ouest de l'Angleterre. Les 30 unités construites furent
livrées vers 1930. (Ci-dessus) Les roues
motrices en pleine action d'une locomotive du LNER, le 17 mars 1931.

Worlds apart

(Left) A hobo rests beside a freight train in the Yakima Valley, Washington, 1939, photographed by Dorothea Lange. Between 1865 and 1939, hoboes – itinerants – crisscrossed the country in their thousands. (Opposite) These rails in England would have been made in sections and joined with two bars, known as fish plates, to allow for heat expansion. This has now been replaced with flat-bottomed, continuously welded track.

Eine andere Welt

(Links) Ein Hobo macht Pause neben einem Güterzug, aufgenommen 1939 von Dorothea Lange im Yakima Valley, Washington. Zwischen 1865 und 1939 waren solche Eisenbahn-Landstreicher in den Vereinigten Staaten zu Tausenden unterwegs. (Gegenüberliegende Seite) Diese Schienen wurden in England in Einzelteilen verlegt und mit so genannten Fußlaschen zusammengefügt, sodass sie sich bei Erwärmung ausdehnen konnten. Inzwischen sind in einem Stück geschmiedete Schienen an ihre Stelle getreten.

Un autre monde

(À gauche) Un hobo se repose près d'un train de marchandises, photographié en 1939 par Dorothea Lange dans la Yakima Valley (Washington). Les hobos – ces vagabonds itinérants parcoururent par milliers les États-Unis entre 1865 et 1939. (Ci-contre) Les voies anglaises sont constituées de sections de rails reliées entre elles par deux plaques d'acier, appelées éclisses, permettant leur dilatation longitudinale. Ce système a été depuis remplacé en Grande-Bretagne par des rails à base plane, soudés en continu.

—— 5 ——
All Change

After the Second World War many different kinds of trains and tracks were developed, all providing newer and quicker ways to travel. The upheaval of the War made the world see itself and its future in a new way. The old ways of doing things in all aspects of life were questioned and revised. Nowhere was this more apparent than on railway transportation.

Exhausted and starved of investment after the enormous strains and demands of war, railways across Europe were rebuilt and reorganised. 1948 was one of the most important years in British railway history. The 'Big Four' railway companies were nationalised and 19,414 miles of railway were split into six operative regions – Eastern, London Midland (the largest), North Eastern, Scottish, Southern, and Western. Not only were the main line railways nationalised but also London Transport, road freight and bus operatives. These were called the British Transport Commission and the branch that ran the railways was called the Railway Executive. By the mid-1950s a modernisation plan was proposed which would completely revolutionise the railway system. The proposals included the abolition of steam power altogether in favour of diesel and electric power, which would allow higher speeds and an extension of colour light signals, track circuiting and automatic warning systems along with a total modernisation of rolling stock and updating and refurbishment of stations.

A memorable phenomenon of this decade was that good old standby, the British weather, which was at its harshest in the winter of 1947. While the crisis officially lasted for three weeks between 10 February and 5 March, its actual duration was much longer. It snowed every day between 22 January and 17 March; the temperature seldom rose above freezing and snowdrifts blocked roads and railways, sometimes cutting people off for days. During the first three months of the year, Britain had to deal with the collapse of fuel and power supplies. Factories were closed and three million people were made unemployed. Rail traffic was badly affected. Lines were blocked by drifting snow and photographs of stranded trains being laboriously dug out of drifts by gangs of men with shovels became a commonplace in the popular press. There were some bizarre accidents. In one of them, on 29 January, the fireman on the 6.23 am from Huddersfield to Bradford was knocked out by an enormous icicle hanging from a bridge. However, although the snowploughs were brought out and the lines quickly opened after blizzards, there was also much disruption in the form of delays, cancellations, frozen points and short-circuiting electrics. After seven years of being asked, 'Is your journey really necessary?', the British were accustomed to railway disruption and bore the inconvenience with a degree of stoicism. Troops were again called in to drop supplies to isolated villages and farms. Once the snow thawed, rivers burst their banks and whole valleys were flooded. On 5 March it took twenty-six hours for the 1.50 pm to travel from Wolverhampton to London.

The wheels turned around the world. In 1947 India became independent. It also inherited a shattered railway system which was further depleted by the subsequent partitioning of the country which led to a division of assets and manpower. There were changes too in the United States. The latest commercially built locomotive by Lima and Baldwin left the plant in 1949. The diesels were coming... The first diesel engine had been built by Dr Rudolf Diesel in 1897 and it was perfected in 1956 with the prototype Deltic locomotive. It was the most powerful diesel electric single unit in the world and was to replace the A4 Pacific type of locomotive. It did this first on the British east coast main line between London and Edinburgh. In the 1950s the British Railways board announced a massive new locomotive building scheme. The first gas turbine locomotive arrived from Switzerland and the first east coast main line electrics were built as well as some BR standard locomotives. The first was No. 70004 *Britannia* from Crewe. One of the new trains, *William Shakespeare*, was exhibited at the Festival of Britain in 1951 and went on to operate on BR (SR) as one of the locomotives pulling the *Golden Arrow* service.

In the United States the advantages of diesel electric transmission and high horse power were also taken on board. The greater speed, efficiency and improved breaking power meant that freight trains could be longer and assigned to a single crew; this had its advantages, one of which was greater profit for the railroad companies. By 1958 only a handful of US steam locomotives remained and by 1960 the country's 40,000 steam locomotives had been replaced altogether by some 27,000 diesel units. However, this economic and commercial gain was not without social cost. The end of steam in America affected many communities in Canada as well as the USA. Altoona in Pennsylvania, a town whose social and economic fabric was founded on the steam locomotive industry, was turned upside down: 75 per cent of its workforce lost their jobs. Indeed, this happened all over the world in this period but on such a huge continent dependent on freight traffic it affected America the most drastically. The devastating and poignant effects were summarised by a resident of Altoona: 'When Pennsylvania gave up steam, something in this town died too. Trains used to be the way you went, sent and received all your goods. The railways employed you, your father and your friends – but all that changed.' In 1968 the Pennsylvania Railroad and New York Central Railroad merged to become the Penn Central, only to declare itself bankrupt in 1970. Similarly, the National Railroad Corporation in Canada took over the Canadian National Railways and Canadian Pacific Railway in 1977–1978.

In 1960 the Blue Pullman services were introduced to the Midland main line in Britain. They sported a special blue livery and were pulled by 1,000hp diesel electric-powered cars. They ran on fast, limited-stop schedules with air conditioning and waitress service at every seat. Also in 1960 the very last steam locomotive was built – No. 92220 – at Swindon works. It was called, appropriately, the *Evening Star*. The new railway shed built in the same year at Neville Hill in Leeds was designed to handle diesel engines only.

Although this book is concerned with the story of the railways from the early days to the 1950s, a brief look beyond at some of the events and developments will put those early days into perspective. In 1963 Dr Beeching revealed his proposals for the reshaping of the BR network. His draconian measures introduced and accelerated line closure and many classes of locomotives completely disappeared. Ironically, this was also the year of the Great Train Robbery when, on 8 August, a gang of sixteen held up the Glasgow to London Royal Mail train and escaped into folklore with £2.6 million after brutally injuring the guard. Many would say that both events were as scandalous as each other. In 1966 the 'Intercity' brand name was introduced as a symbol of fast, sophisticated rail travel. Intercity claimed to be 'the best, most civilised way to travel at speed from centre to centre'. It became Europe's only main line railway to operate without a subsidy. 1968 saw the rebuilding of Euston Station after the tragic demolition of the old London & Birmingham's Euston Arch, built by Philip Hardwick in 1838. The Intercity 125 power cars were first introduced in 1973 and the 150th anniversary of the opening of the very first passenger railway, the Stockton and Darlington, was celebrated in 1975. In 1976 high speed trains were introduced on to the London Paddington to Bristol line.

The Italians went on to develop tilting high speed trains to avoid the cost of building new tracks. Special electric rapid transit systems were developed in major industrial cities to improve the links between road, rail and air transport systems. An example of this is the Maglev, which works using magnetic levitation. Instead of travelling on wheels the car hovers above a metal track and is pulled along by magnets. It has the advantages of having no moving parts to wear out, little maintenance demands and is almost silent. Other modern innovations include the driverless trains which are used on light rail systems, such as the Docklands Light Railway in London.

Other notable more recent developments were in the new high speed passenger trains. The first of these was the 'Bullet train', or electric *Shinkansen*, built in 1964 to run between Tokyo and Osaka. This was a new generation of high speed railways built exclusively for intercity passenger travel. It travelled at an average speed of 101mph and at a maximum speed of 130mph. The French TGV – Trains à Grande Vitesse – were introduced in 1981 between Paris and Lyon and the new German electric high speed intercity express – ICE – introduced in 1991. For a short period it set the world speed record during its tests, reaching 252mph.

While the period from the sixties to the end of the century saw the end of the golden age of travel – the care lavished on the *Limited*s, for example, was never to return and many branch lines were to close – there is a new permanent way ahead. Many preserved railways now operate and trains still fascinate children and adults alike and will, no doubt, continue to do so in the future. There is another glimmer of hope for those interested in railways. The World Heritage Convention of 1976 allowed UNESCO to designate places of cultural significance around the world and some of these are railway sites. This recognises the ways in which railways have contributed to the social, economic, political, cultural and technical evolution of almost every country in the world; it ensures too that the achievements of the past are both recognised and appreciated. Among the sites designated are the Ironbridge Gorge in England, the Semmering Pass in Austria and the Darjeeling Himalayan Railway in India.

When the railways were nationalised, sign painters had to obliterate the old company lettering on thousands of locomotives. Here the familiar GWR sign is overpainted at Paddington coach works, January 1948.

Nach der Verstaatlichung mussten Lackierer auf Tausenden von Lokomotiven die alten Firmenzeichen tilgen. Hier, im Januar 1948 im Betriebswerk Paddington, verschwindet das altvertraute GWR-Signet.

Des peintres durent effacer les anciennes inscriptions sur des milliers de locomotives lors de la nationalisation des chemins de fer britanniques. Ici, le sigle familier du GWR est recouvert de peinture dans les ateliers ferroviaires de Paddington, en janvier 1948.

Als der Zweite Weltkrieg vorüber war, experimentierte man mit verschiedensten Bahntypen , und alles sollte schöner und schneller werden. Überall gab es nach dem Krieg einen Neuanfang, doch in wenigen Bereichen so radikal wie bei der Eisenbahn.

Kapitalschwach und durch die enormen Belastungen des Krieges verbraucht, wurden die Bahnen überall in Europa neu aufgebaut und organisiert. In Großbritannien stellte man 1948 die Weichen gründlich neu. Die »Großen Vier« wurden verstaatlicht und die 31 237 Kilometer Streckennetz auf sechs Regionen aufgeteilt: Eastern, London Midland (die größte), North Eastern, Scottish, Southern und Western. Nicht nur die großen Bahnlinien gingen in öffentliches Eigentum über, auch die Londoner Verkehrsbetriebe, die Speditionen und die Busunternehmen. Gemeinsam unterstanden sie von nun an der British Transport Commission. Der für die Eisenbahnen zuständige Zweig, die Railway Executive, arbeitete Mitte der fünfziger Jahre ein umfassendes Modernisierungskonzept aus. Es sah vor, dass die Dampfkraft ganz zugunsten von Diesel- und Elektroantrieb aufgegeben wurde, was nicht nur höhere Geschwindigkeiten, sondern auch eine vollständige Neuausstattung des Schienennetzes möglich machte, mit elektrischen Signalen, Schalt- und Kontrollanlagen; außerdem sollten der gesamte Wagenpark und die Bahnhöfe generalüberholt werden.

Dass die erste Zeit nach dem Krieg spannend wurde, dafür sorgte auch das britische Wetter. Der Winter von 1947 war hart wie selten zuvor; offiziell herrschte Notstand nur zwischen dem 10. Februar und dem 3. März, aber in Wirklichkeit dauerte die Krise weitaus länger. Zwischen dem 22. Januar und dem 17. März schneite es tagtäglich, die Temperaturen stiegen nur selten über den Gefrierpunkt, und Schneeverwehungen blockierten Straße und Schiene; manche Landstriche waren tagelang von der Umwelt abgeschnitten. Während der ersten drei Monate des Jahres brach die Brennstoff- und Stromversorgung zusammen. Fabriken wurden geschlossen, drei Millionen Menschen verloren ihre Arbeit. Der Bahnverkehr war schwer beeinträchtigt und Bilder von festsitzenden Zügen, die mühsam mit der Schaufel ausgegraben wurden, erschienen in jeder Ausgabe der Regenbogenpresse. Es gab bizarre Unfälle – bei einem wurde der Heizer des 6.23-Uhr-Zuges von Huddersfield nach Bradford am 29. Januar von einem riesigen Eiszapfen niedergestreckt, der von einer Brücke herabhing. Auch wenn die Schneepflüge im Einsatz waren und nach jedem Schneegestöber die Strecken räumten, gab es unzählige Verspätungen und Ausfälle, eingefrorene Weichen und Kurzschlüsse in der Elektrik. Sieben Jahre lang waren die Briten bei jeder Fahrt gefragt worden: »Ist sie wirklich notwendig?«, sie waren Störungen des Betriebes gewohnt und hielten sich stoisch. Wieder kam das Militär zum Einsatz und warf über isolierten Dörfern und Bauernhöfen Lebensmittel ab. Als der Schnee schließlich taute, traten die Flüsse über ihre Ufer, und ganze Täler waren überflutet. Am 5. März brauchte der 1.50-Uhr-Zug von Wolverhampton 26 Stunden nach London.

Weltweit setzten sich die Räder in Bewegung. 1947 erlangte Indien seine Unabhängigkeit und erbte ein heruntergekommenes Eisenbahnnetz, das noch untüchtiger wurde, als mit der Abspaltung Pakistans Material und Belegschaft geteilt wurden. Auch in den USA bahnten sich Veränderungen an. Der Lokomotivenbauer Lima and Baldwin stellte 1949 seine neueste Konstruktion vor – der Siegeszug der Dieseltraktion begann … Der vorläufige Höhepunkt der Entwicklung, die mit Rudolf Diesels erstem Motor von 1897 begonnen hatte, war 1956 der Prototyp der Deltic-Lokomotive. Als kraftvollste dieselelektrische Lokomotive der Welt sollte sie die Nachfolge der A4-Pacific antreten und kam zuerst auf der Strecke London–Edinburgh zum Einsatz. In den fünfziger Jahren kündigte das British Railways Board ein umfassendes Lokomotiven-Neubauprogramm an; eine Gasturbinenlok bezog man aus der Schweiz, die erste elektrische nahm auf der Ostküstenstrecke ihren Betrieb auf, und neue BR-Standardloks entstanden. Die erste kam aus Crewe, Nr. 70004 *Britannia*. Ein Exemplar dieser Baureihe, *William Shakespeare*, war 1951 beim Festival of Britain zu sehen und ging dann an BR (SR) als Zugmaschine für den *Golden Arrow*.

Auch in den USA setzten sich dieselelektrischer Antrieb und leistungsstarke Motoren durch. Höheres Tempo, größere Leistung und mehr Bremskraft machten es möglich, dass eine Mannschaft weitaus längere Güterzüge betreute als zuvor, nicht zuletzt zum größeren Profit der Bahngesellschaften. 1958 war nur noch eine Hand voll von ehemals 40 000 amerikanischen Dampflokomotiven übrig, und 1960 hatten etwa 27 000 Dieselloks sie vollständig ersetzt. Dieser ökonomische und kommerzielle Gewinn hatte jedoch durchaus seine sozialen Schattenseiten. Das Ende des amerikanischen Dampfzeitalters machte mancher Gemeinde in Kanada und den USA schwer zu schaffen. Eine Stadt wie Altoona in Pennsylvania, die ganz von der Dampflok gelebt hatte, war völlig entwurzelt: 75% der Beschäftigten verloren ihre Arbeit. Solche tief greifenden Veränderungen waren rund um die Welt keine Seltenheit, aber

A new Belgian diesel electric locomotive (No. 202017) arrives in Cologne after a 2 hour 50 minute test run from Brussels, 1948.

Eine neue belgische Dieselelektrolok (Nr. 202017) trifft auf einer Probefahrt in Köln ein, 1948. Die Fahrt von Brüssel dauerte 2 Stunden und 50 Minuten.

Une nouvelle locomotive diesel électrique belge (la n° 202017) arrive à Cologne après un parcours d'essai de 2 h 50 au départ de Bruxelles, en 1948.

nirgendwo waren sie deutlicher zu spüren als auf dem riesigen Kontinent, der ganz auf den Güterverkehr angewiesen war. Ein Einheimischer beschreibt, wie den Menschen in Altoona zumute war: »Als Pennsylvania den Dampf aufgab, ist auch bei uns in der Stadt etwas gestorben. Wenn man verreiste, wenn man etwas geliefert bekam, wenn man etwas schickte – alles ging mit dem Zug. Man arbeitete bei der Eisenbahn, der Vater und die Freunde arbeiteten bei der Eisenbahn – aber das ist alles vorbei.« 1968 schlossen sich Pennsylvania Railroad und New York Central Railroad zur Penn Central zusammen, die jedoch 1970 Konkurs anmelden musste. In Kanada übernahm die National Railroad Corporation 1977–1978 die Canadian National Railways und die Canadian Pacific Railway.

In Großbritannien wurde 1960 auf der Midland-Hauptstrecke der »Blue Pullman«-Service eingeführt, mit Zügen in einer eigenen blauen Lackierung und 1000-PS-Dieselloks. Es waren Schnellzüge, die nur an ausgesuchten Bahnhöfen hielten, mit Klimaanlage und Bedienung am Platz. Ebenfalls 1960 entstand in Swindon die allerletzte Dampflok – Nr. 92220 –, und der Name *Evening Star* war nur angemessen. Der neue Lokomotivenschuppen, der im selben Jahr in Neville Hill, Leeds, gebaut wurde, war nur noch für Diesellokomotiven eingerichtet.

Unser Buch erzählt die Geschichte der Eisenbahn von den Anfängen bis in die Fünfziger, aber ein kurzer Blick auf die spätere Entwicklung eröffnet interessante Perspektiven. 1963 legte Dr. Beeching sein Konzept zur Sanierung der britischen Bahn vor. Zu seinen drakonischen Maßnahmen zählten zahlreiche Streckenstilllegungen, und ganze Klassen von Lokomotiven verschwanden. Ironischerweise war dies auch das Jahr des großen Eisenbahnraubs, bei dem am 8. August eine sechzehnköpfige Bande den Postzug Edinburgh–London stoppte, brutal einen Schaffner niederschlug und sich mit 2,6 Millionen Pfund Beute ins Reich der Folklore davonmachte. Welches von beiden der größere Skandal war, darüber könnte man streiten. 1966 wurde der Begriff »Intercity« eingeführt, der für schnellen und zeitgemäßen Bahnverkehr stehen sollte; die Werbung sprach von der »besten, kultiviertesten Art, zügig von Stadt zu Stadt zu kommen«. Die britischen Intercity-Strecken waren damals die einzigen Hauptstrecken in Europa, die kostendeckend fuhren. 1968 war der neue Bahnhof Euston fertig gestellt; der 1838 von Philip Hardwick für die alte London & Birmingham erbaute Torbogen wurde bei den Umbauten trotz großer Proteste abgerissen. 1973 kamen die ersten Intercity-125-Schnelltriebwagen, und 1975 beging man den 150. Jahrestag

der Eröffnung der Strecke Stockton–Darlington, der ersten Personenbahn der Welt. 1976 kamen Hochgeschwindigkeitszüge auf die Strecke von London-Paddington nach Bristol.

Die Italiener entwickelten Schnellzüge mit Neigetechnik, um die Kosten des Gleisausbaus zu sparen. In den Großstädten entstanden neue elektrische Schnellbahnen zur besseren Verbindung von Straßen-, Schienen- und Luftverkehr. Ein Beispiel dafür ist die Magnetschwebebahn Maglev, die ohne bewegliche Teile, die verschleißen könnten, auskommt, nur ein Minimum an Wartung braucht und fast lautlos fährt. Eine andere Entwicklung der neuesten Zeit sind die fahrerlosen Züge, wie sie in London als Docklands Light Railway verkehren.

Hochgeschwindigkeitszüge gehörten zu den neuen bemerkenswerten Entwicklungen. Pionier war der elektrische *Shinkansen*, der 1964 auf der Strecke Tokio–Osaka fuhr. Er war der erste Vertreter einer neuen Generation von Zügen, die ausschließlich für den Personenverkehr zwischen den Großstädten bestimmt waren. Die Höchstgeschwindigkeit betrug 209, die Durchschnittsgeschwindigkeit 163 km/h. Der erste französische TGV – Train à Grande Vitesse – verkehrte 1981 von Paris nach Lyon, in Deutschland kam 1991 der neue Intercity-Express (ICE) und hielt mit den auf einer Testfahrt erreichten 405 km/h für kurze Zeit den Geschwindigkeitsweltrekord.

Seit den Sechzigern bis zum Ende des Jahrhunderts ging die goldene Zeit der Eisenbahnreise zu Ende – den Komfort der amerikanischen *Limited*-Züge, hat es nie wieder gegeben, und viele kleinere Linien bestehen nicht mehr; doch heute sehen wir wieder Licht am Ende des Tunnels. Eine ganze Reihe klassischer Strecken lebt als Museumsbahnen fort, nach wie vor faszinieren Eisenbahnen Jung und Alt und werden es gewiss auch in Zukunft weiter tun. Einen weiteren Hoffnungsschimmer gibt es für alle, denen die Bahn am Herzen liegt. Die Konvention zum Schutz des Weltkulturerbes von 1976 schuf für die UNESCO die Möglichkeit, weltweit kulturhistorisch bedeutsame Stätten unter Schutz zu stellen, und bei einigen unter ihnen handelt es sich um Denkmäler der Eisenbahngeschichte. Damit wird dem wichtigen Beitrag Rechnung getragen, den die Eisenbahnen zur sozialen, ökonomischen, politischen, kulturellen und technischen Entwicklung in fast jedem Land der Erde geleistet haben, und ein Anfang ist gemacht, dass die Meisterwerke vergangener Generationen erkannt und gewürdigt werden. Zu den ausgewählten Stätten gehören das Tal von Ironbridge in England, die österreichische Semmeringbahn und die Himalaya-Gebirgsbahn nach Darjeeling in Indien.

A family and their dog wait for the last *Nord Express* to leave Berlin Zoological Garden station on 27 April 1948. The Soviet government banned rail travel from West to East thereafter. The last train was packed with French government officials.

27. April 1948: Eine Familie mit Hund wartet auf den letzten *Nord Express*, der den Berliner Bahnhof Zoologischer Garten verlässt. Vom folgenden Tag an hatte die sowjetische Verwaltung sämtlichen Ost-West-Verkehr untersagt. Der letzte Zug war vollbesetzt mit französischen Regierungsangestellten.

Une famille et leur chien attendent que le dernier *Nord Express* quitte la gare du Zoo de Berlin, le 27 avril 1948. Le gouvernement soviétique interdit ensuite les voyages en train entre l'Est et l'Ouest. Le dernier convoi était presque entièrement peuplé par des fonctionnaires de l'administration d'occupation du gouvernement français.

La période après la Seconde Guerre mondiale voit naître différentes sortes de trains et de lignes, qui offrent des moyens de transport nouveaux et plus rapides. La Guerre et les transformations qu'elle a engendrées font que le monde désormais se voit et envisage son avenir différemment, remettant en question les habitudes anciennes. Ces bouleversements en profondeur ne sont nulle part plus évidents que dans les transports ferroviaires.

Comme après la Première Guerre mondiale, les chemins de fer européens ont beaucoup souffert du conflit et, privés d'investissements pendant toutes ces années, doivent être de nouveau entièrement réorganisés. L'année 1948 est sans doute l'une des plus importantes de l'histoire des chemins de fer britanniques. En effet, les « Big Four » sont alors nationalisées et le réseau de 31 237 km de voies réparti entre six régions – Eastern, London Midland (la plus grande), North Eastern, Scottish, Southern et Western. Outre les principales compagnies de chemin de fer, sont également nationalisés le London Transport (les transports en commun londoniens, les transports routiers et les compagnies d'autobus, tous regroupés sous la tutelle de la British Transport Commission, les chemins de fer étant gérés par le Railway Executive). Le plan de modernisation proposé au milieu des années 1950 va révolutionner le réseau ferroviaire. Il s'agit pas moins d'abandonner la vapeur en faveur des tractions diesel et électrique, qui permettent d'atteindre des vitesses plus élevées, d'étendre à tout le réseau le système automatique de signalisation, de contrôle et de sécurité des voies, ainsi que de moderniser entièrement le matériel roulant et les gares.

Aux difficultés nées de la guerre viennent s'ajouter d'épouvantables conditions météorologiques lors de l'hiver 1947. Si le mauvais temps ne dure officiellement en Grande-Bretagne que trois semaines, du 10 février au 3 mars, sa durée véritable est beaucoup plus longue. Il neige en effet tous les jours du 22 janvier au 17 mars et la température s'élève rarement au-dessus de 0 °C. Des congères bloquent les routes et les voies ferrées, coupant du monde les habitants des régions les plus touchées. Pendant ces trois premiers mois de l'année, la Grande-Bretagne connaît d'énormes difficultés d'approvisionnement en fuel et en électricité. Les usines doivent fermer et trois millions d'habitants sont alors contraints au chômage technique. Le trafic ferroviaire est gravement touché et les photographies de trains immobilisés sous la neige que dégagent difficilement des équipes de cheminots armés de pelles deviennent récurrentes à la une de la presse populaire. Le froid produisit quelques

étranges accidents, comme celui où, le 29 janvier, le chauffeur du 6 h 25 de Huddersfield à Bradford se fait assommer par un énorme stalactite tombé d'un pont. Bien que les chasse-neige soient sortis rapidement et que les lignes aient rapidement réouvert, le trafic est fortement perturbé à cause de retards, d'annulations, du gel ou de courts-circuits. Après sept ans passés à répondre à la question « Votre déplacement est-il vraiment nécessaire ? », les Britanniques sont désormais habitués aux interruptions du trafic ferroviaire et en supportent les inconvénients avec un certain stoïcisme. Le 5 mars, il fallut 26 heures au 13 h 50 pour se rendre de Wolverhampton à Londres.

Les bogies des locomotives tournent autour du monde. En 1947, l'Inde devient indépendante et hérite un réseau ferroviaire en ruines, bientôt morcelé à cause de la partition du pays. Les chemins de fer des États-Unis aussi entrent dans une nouvelle ère. La dernière locomotive construite par Lima & Baldwin quitte l'usine en 1949. Les diesel arrivent … Le moteur diesel inventé à l'origine par Rudolf Diesel en 1897 est perfectionné en 1956 et conduit à la construction de la Deltic, la locomotive diesel-électrique la plus puissante du monde, qui ne va pas tarder à remplacer les Pacific de classe A4 et effectue son premier voyage sur la ligne principale de la côte est britannique, entre Londres et Édimbourg. Dans les années 1950, la direction des British Railways annonce un nouveau plan de construction de locomotives. Si la première locomotive à turbine à gaz fut importée de Suisse, on construisit des locomotives aux normes standard de la BR ainsi que des locomotives électriques destinées à la ligne de l'Est, dont la première fut la *Britannia* n° 70004, provenant des ateliers de Crewe. La *William Shakespeare*, exposée au Festival of Britain en 1951, va être mise en service pour tracter les *Golden Arrow* sur la ligne des BR (SR).

Aux États-Unis, on prend également bonne note des avantages que procure la transmission diesel électrique : puissance motrice et au freinage, vitesse et efficacité permettent d'allonger les trains de marchandises et de ne leur affecter qu'une seule équipe de conduite … ce qui est tout bénéfice pour les compagnies de chemins de fer. En 1958, il ne reste plus qu'une poignée de locomotives à vapeur et, dès 1960, les 40 000 locomotives à vapeur des États-Unis sont déjà toutes remplacées par 27 000 locomotives diesel. Mais ce progrès économique et financier n'est pas sans conséquences sociales. La fin de la vapeur en Amérique du Nord affecte de nombreuses villes du Canada et des États-Unis. Près de 75 % des travailleurs d'Altoona, une cité dont le tissu social et économique s'appuie sur l'industrie des

In September 1946 French customs officials went on strike for five days and thousands of pounds of goods were smuggled across various borders by rail. Customs officials blatantly ignored all such movements; some blithely played cards, as here.

Im September 1946 streikten fünf Tage lang die französischen Zollbeamten, und zentnerweise Güter wurden per Bahn über die Grenzen geschmuggelt. Die Zöllner ignorierten es mit Absicht – manche spielten genüsslich Karten.

Lorsque les douaniers français firent grève pendant cinq jours en septembre 1946, des centaines de tonnes de marchandises passèrent en fraude les frontières, dans l'indifférence la plus totale de ces fonctionnaires, dont certains jouaient aux cartes sur les quais mêmes.

locomotives à vapeur, perdent leur emploi. Certes, le phénomène se reproduit presque à l'identique dans le monde entier mais le coup est ressenti particulièrement durement sur un continent aussi vaste et qui dépend autant des transports ferroviaires. La situation, dévastatrice et poignante, fut ainsi résumée par un habitant d'Altoona : « Lorsque la Pennsylvanie a abandonné la vapeur, quelque chose est mort dans cette ville. C'est en train qu'on se déplaçait, et qu'on expédiait ou recevait des marchandises. Les chemins de fer employaient tout le monde, de votre père à vos amis – et tout a été chamboulé ». En 1968, le Pennsylvania Railroad et le New York Central Railroad fusionnent pour devenir le Penn Central. De même au Canada, où la National Railroad Corporation reprend le Canadian National Railways et le Canadian Pacific Railway en 1977–1978.

C'est en 1960 que sont introduits les services du Blue Pullman sur la ligne principale de la Midland en Grande-Bretagne. Ces trains présentaient une livrée bleue spéciale et étaient remorqués par des voitures diesel électriques de 1 000 ch. Ils circulaient avec des horaires rapides à arrêts limités avec air conditionné et service à la place. C'est également en 1960 que fut construite la toute dernière locomotive à vapeur – la n° 92220 – aux ateliers de Swindon. Elle fut baptisée l'*Evening Star*. Le nouveau dépôt ferroviaire construit la même année à Neville Hill à Leeds fut conçu pour l'entretien exclusif des diesel.

Bien que ce livre soit concerné par l'histoire des chemins de fer depuis ses débuts jusqu'aux années 1950, un bref regard au-delà sur les événements et les développements permet de mettre ses premières années en perspective. En 1963, le D' Beeching révéla ses propositions pour le réaménagement du réseau des BR. Ses mesures draconiennes introduisirent et accélérèrent la fermeture des lignes et nombre de classes de locomotives disparurent. Ironiquement, ce fut également l'année de l'attaque du train postal, au cours de laquelle, le 8 août, une bande de 16 voleurs attaquèrent le train Glasgow–Londres de la poste royale et s'échappèrent dans la nature avec 2,6 millions de livres après avoir grièvement blessé le garde. En 1966, la marque « Intercity » fut introduite comme un symbole de voyage en train rapide et sophistiqué. Intercity prétendait être « le moyen le plus civilisé de voyager rapidement de centre à centre ». Il devint la seule ligne de chemin de fer à fonctionner sans subvention. L'année 1968 vit la reconstruction de la gare d'Euston après la tragique démolition de l'ancienne Euston Arch du London & Birmingham, construite par Philip Hardwick en 1838. Les voitures puissantes Intercity 125 furent d'abord introduites en

1973 et le 150ᵉ anniversaire de l'ouverture du premier chemin de fer de voyageurs, le Stockton and Darlington, fut célébré en 1975. En 1976, des trains à grande vitesse furent introduits sur la ligne Londres Paddington–Bristol.

Les Italiens se mirent à développer des trains à grande vitesse pendulaires. Des systèmes de transit rapide électrique furent développés dans les villes industrielles pour améliorer les liaisons entre les réseaux routiers, ferroviaires et aériens. Le meilleur exemple est le Maglev, qui, dépourvu de roues, utilise la force magnétique pour circuler au-dessus d'une voie métallique. Cela permet d'éviter toute usure des parties mobiles et d'être pratiquement silencieux. Il y eut aussi d'autres innovations pour la desserte sur de courtes distances. C'est le cas notamment du Docklands Light Railway à Londres.

Les trains de voyageurs à grande vitesse sont d'évolution plus récente. Le premier d'entre eux fut le « train obus » japonais, le *Shinkansen*, construit en 1964 pour circuler entre Tokyo et Osaka. Il s'agissait alors de la toute nouvelle génération de trains électriques à grande vitesse construits exclusivement pour les relations interurbaines, capables de circuler à la vitesse moyenne de 163 km/h avec des pointes à 209 km/h. En France, le TGV fut mis en circulation en 1981 entre Paris et Lyon tandis que le nouvel express interurbain électrique à grande vitesse allemand – l'ICE – ne circula qu'à partir de 1991. Ce dernier s'est arrogé brièvement le record du monde de vitesse au cours de ses essais en atteignant 405 km/h.

Si la période allant des années soixante à la fin du XXᵉ siècle marque la fin de l'âge d'or des voyages – en Grande-Bretagne, les *Limiteds* vont être progressivement négligés et nombre de lignes secondaires seront fermées – les trains d'antan connaissent une vie nouvelle sinon prolongée. Il subsiste nombre de chemins de fer anciens qui fonctionnent toujours aujourd'hui et continueront, pour longtemps encore sans doute, de fasciner enfants comme adultes. L'étincelle d'espoir, pour tous ceux que passionnent les chemins de fer, est venue déjà de la World Heritage Convention de 1976, qui autorisait l'UNESCO à classer dans le patrimoine de l'humanité des sites d'importance culturelle ; on compte parmi ceux-là quelques lignes ferroviaires. On reconnaît ainsi non seulement la valeur des réalisations du passé mais surtout la contribution qu'ont apportées les chemins de fer à l'évolution sociale, économique, politique, culturelle et technique des pays du monde. Parmi ces sites « protégés » figurent l'Ironbridge Gorge en Angleterre, le col de Semmering en Autriche, et le Darjeeling Himalayan Railway en Inde.

Two women relax in a British railway bar in the Fifties while the waiter prepares cocktails. How times had changed: Britain, the originator of the steam engine, now borrowed the newest thing from America – the cocktail – as well as the pseudo-American decor in the bar.

In den fünfziger Jahren entspannen sich zwei Frauen in der Bar einer britischen Bahn, und der Kellner mixt ihnen Cocktails. Wie hatten sich die Zeiten geändert: Großbritannien, Ursprungsland der Dampfmaschine, machte nun die neueste amerikanische Mode – die Cocktails – nach, und auch das Dekor der Bar ist ganz im amerikanischen Stil gehalten.

Dans les années 1950, deux femmes se détendent au bar d'un train britannique tandis que le garçon leur prépare des cocktails. Les temps ont alors bien changé : la Grande-Bretagne, patrie de la machine à vapeur, emprunte désormais aux États-Unis sa plus récente invention – le cocktail – et adopte un décor pseudo-américain.

Off to war – again

Going to war could be as painful for those left behind as it was for those going away. Railway stations were the scenes of many a sad farewell. (Opposite) British troops in the spring of 1939 at Victoria Station, London, off to the war in Europe. (Right) A sad farewell to departing soldiers at Paddington Station during the middle years of the war, May 1942.

Und wieder in den Krieg

Wieder rückten die Soldaten ein, und die Beklemmung derer, die zurückblieben, war ebenso groß wie die der Männer, die ins Feld zogen. Bahnhöfe sahen manch schmerzlichen Abschied. (Gegenüberliegende Seite) Britische Truppen im Frühjahr 1939 auf der Londoner Victoria Station, bereit zur Fahrt auf den Kontinent. (Rechts) Unter Tränen werden Soldaten auf dem Bahnhof Paddington auf den Weg gebracht, Mai 1942, gegen Mitte des Krieges.

De nouveau la guerre

Le départ à la guerre est souvent aussi douloureux pour ceux qui restent que pour ceux qui s'en vont, et les gares furent le théâtre de nombreux adieux déchirants. (Ci-contre) Au printemps 1939, les troupes britanniques se rassemblent à la gare Victoria, à Londres, avant leur départ pour le front en Europe. (À droite) Un triste adieu aux soldats en gare de Paddington, en mai 1942.

A time of constant movement

All across Europe trains had their passengers – both soldiers and civilians. (Opposite, clockwise from top left) Italian soldiers wave swastikas on arrival at Berlin Station, c. 1940; British troops return from Dunkirk, 1940; German soldiers at Aarhus, Denmark, c. 1940; Canadian soldiers at a station 'somewhere in England', 1940. (Above) Children leaving Ealing Broadway Station in 1939, the first stage in their evacuation.

Alles ist in Bewegung

In ganz Europa waren Soldaten wie Zivilisten unterwegs. (Gegenüberliegende Seite, im Uhrzeigersinn von oben links) Italienische Soldaten schwenken Hakenkreuzfähnchen bei der Ankunft in Berlin, ca. 1940; britische Männer kehren aus Dünkirchen zurück, 1940; deutsche Soldaten im dänischen Aarhus, um 1940; kanadische Soldaten auf einem Bahnhof »irgendwo in England«, 1940. (Oben) Evakuierung englischer Kinder, Ealing Broadway Station, 1939.

Une époque de mouvements perpétuels

Tous les trains d'Europe transportaient des voyageurs, civils comme militaires : (ci-contre, en haut à gauche) soldats italiens agitant des fanions frappés de la swastika à Berlin, vers 1940 ; (en haut à droite) soldats britanniques à leur retour de Dunkerque, en 1940 ; (en bas à droite) soldats allemands à Aarhus (Danemark), vers 1940 ; (en bas à gauche) soldats canadiens dans une gare en Angleterre, en 1940 ; (ci-dessus) enfants quittant la gare de Ealing Broadway en 1939.

Wartime destruction of the railways

Bombs being dropped on a railway yard at Vénissieux, south of Lyon, in 1940 by Allied B17 Flying Fortresses. The yard was crucial to the rail network between France and Italy. Strategic rail centres such as this were frequent targets for bombers in the years of attrition.

Bombardierung der Bahnstrecken

B-17-Bomber (»Fliegende Festungen«) der Alliierten bombardieren den Güterbahnhof Vénissieux südlich von Lyon, einen wichtigen Umschlagplatz im Bahnverkehr zwischen Frankreich und Italien. Solche Eisenbahnknotenpunkte kamen in den Kriegsjahren immer wieder ins Visier.

Destruction des chemins de fer

En 1940, le dépôt et la gare de triage de Vénissieux, au sud de Lyon, furent bombardés par les Forteresses Volantes B17 alliés. Les centres ferroviaires stratégiques comme celui-ci, essentiel au trafic entre la France et l'Italie, furent fréquemment la cible des bombardiers.

London suffers

St Pancras Station was targeted by German bombers during the war, as were many London stations. It was hit on 26 August 1942 but little lasting damage was done; once the censors had released this photograph it was announced that the famous single-span roof had survived almost undamaged.

Angriffsziel London

Deutsche Bomber flogen Angriffe auf viele Londoner Bahnhöfe, darunter auch St. Pancras. Aber der Treffer vom 26. August 1942 richtete keine irreparablen Schäden an; als die Zensoren diese Aufnahme freigaben, wurde dazu vermeldet, dass das berühmte einspännige Dach fast unversehrt geblieben war.

Londres souffre

De nombreuses gares londoniennes furent fréquemment visées par les bombardiers allemands. La gare de St Pancras fut touchée le 26 août 1942 mais ne subit pas de dommages trop importants. La légende accompagnant la publication de la photographie, après accord de la censure, indiquait que la célèbre verrière – d'une seule travée – était restée pratiquement intacte.

The railways carry on

London Transport permanent way men repairing the track
after bomb damage to railway tracks in west London, February
1942. They are wearing decontamination suits and gas masks.
Such work was both urgent and essential to the continuation
of rail transport during the war.

Der Betrieb geht weiter

In Schutzanzug und Gasmaske setzen Streckenarbeiter
von London Transport im Februar 1942 eine durch Bomben
zerstörte Linie wieder instand. Mit solchen Notmaßnahmen
konnte der Bahnbetrieb auch in Kriegszeiten aufrechterhalten
werden.

Les chemins de fer continuent

Les cheminots du London Transport, vêtus de vêtements de
protection et de masques à gaz, réparent les voies de chemin
de fer de l'ouest de Londres après leur bombardement en
février 1942. Leur action rapide était essentielle pour éviter
l'interruption des transports ferroviaires pendant la guerre.

Women behind the Allied forces

In America, women were also contributing to the war effort. When the men joined up, the women left behind – as these in New York – took on essential railway work. Behind them is a Long Island Railroad 4–6–0 locomotive built by the Pennsylvania Railroad, c. 1928.

Alliierte Frauen

Auch in Amerika leisteten die Frauen ihren Beitrag zum Kriegsdienst. Als die Männer einrückten, übernahmen sie – wie hier in New York – deren Arbeit bei der Bahn. Hinter ihnen eine 2 C Lokomotive der Long Island Railroad, etwa 1928 von der Pennsylvania Railroad gebaut.

Les femmes soutiennent les forces alliées

Aux États-Unis, les femmes contribuèrent également à l'effort de guerre. Une fois les hommes partis, les femmes restées au pays durent prendre la place des cheminots, comme celles-ci à New York, posant devant une locomotive 230 du Long Island Railroad, construite par la Pennsylvania Railroad vers 1928.

Eastern and Western Fronts
(Above left) A German First World War rail-mounted artillery piece being prepared for action by soldiers, c. 1940. (Above right) A refugee train carrying Chinese civilians away from the Eastern Front.

Fronten in Ost und West
(Oben links) Ein deutsches Eisenbahngeschütz, noch aus dem Ersten Weltkrieg, wird in Stellung gebracht, um 1940. (Oben rechts) Ein Flüchtlingszug bringt chinesische Zivilisten hinter die Linien der Ostfront.

Fronts de l'Est et de l'Ouest
(Ci-dessus à gauche) Des soldats allemands mettent en batterie une pièce d'artillerie mobile de la Première Guerre mondiale, vers 1940. (Ci-dessus à droite) Un train de réfugiés emmène des civils chinois loin du front.

All clear for the guns

By 1941, Britain's railways were in crisis. They were required to carry goods that had previously travelled by sea, more passengers than ever before (as a result of petrol rationing), and weapons of war, such as the Cruise Mk IV tanks, from northern factories to southern ports.

Freie Fahrt für Kanonen

1941 hatten die britischen Eisenbahnen die Grenzen ihrer Leistungsfähigkeit erreicht. Sie mussten Güter transportieren, die zuvor den Seeweg genommen hatten, sie beförderten (weil das Benzin rationiert war) mehr Fahrgäste denn je, und auch schweres Kriegsgerät wie dieser Panzer des Typs Cruise Mk IV kam per Bahn von den Fabriken im Norden zu den Häfen im Süden des Landes.

Toute la place aux canons

Les chemins de fer britanniques connurent une activité parti-culièrement soutenue vers 1941. En effet, ils devaient désormais prendre en charge des marchandises qui voyageaient autrefois par bateau, accueillir plus de passagers qu'auparavant en rai-son du rationnement de l'essence, et transporter du matériel de guerre – comme ces chars Cruise Mk IV – depuis les usines du nord de la Grande-Bretagne jusqu'aux ports de la côte sud.

Aftermath – railway relief

At the end of the war the railways were witness to the movement of millions: the homeless, the displaced, returning soldiers, all looking for a new life or the old one they once had. (Opposite) Civilians and soldiers mass at a dilapidated platform in Berlin, October 1945. (Above) Polish ex-prisoners at Weimar Station, Germany, receiving food and blankets after being freed from concentration camps.

Die Bahn bringt Hilfe

Nach Kriegsende transportierten die Eisenbahnen Millionen Menschen: Zwangsverschleppte und -vertriebene, heim-kehrende Soldaten, die alle auf einen neuen Anfang oder auf Rückkehr in den Alltag hofften. (Gegenüberliegende Seite) Soldaten und Zivilisten drängen sich in den Überresten eines Berliner Bahnhofs, Oktober 1945. (Oben) In Weimar werden auf dem Bahnhof Decken und Lebensmittel an befreite polni-sche Häftlinge verteilt.

L'après-guerre – l'aide du rail

À la fin de la guerre, les chemins de fer transportèrent des millions de gens – sans-abri, personnes déplacées, soldats rapatriés – qui aspiraient à une nouvelle vie ou à reprendre celle qu'ils avaient eue auparavant. (Ci-contre) Civils et soldats se massent sur le quai d'une gare de Berlin, en octobre 1945. (Ci-dessus) Des prisonniers de guerre polonais, libérés des camps de concentration, dans la gare de Weimar (Allemagne), reçoivent une aide alimentaire et des couvertures.

Return of the *Golden Arrow*

In October 1947 the *Golden Arrow*, or *Flèche d'Or* (opposite and above), service was resumed. Although the railways were doing their best to return to the pre-war golden era of luxury travel, there was little enthusiasm, or money, amongst the travelling public for such things. On the day these photographs were taken, the train left Victoria Station half empty.

Der *Golden Arrow* kehrt zurück

Im Oktober 1947 nahm der *Golden Arrow* oder *Flèche d'Or* seinen Betrieb wieder auf (gegenüberliegende Seite und oben). Die Bahnen gaben sich alle Mühe, an die goldene Vorkriegszeit der Luxusreisen anzuknüpfen, doch das Publikum zeigte nur wenig Interesse oder hatte nicht das Geld dafür. Am Tag, an dem diese Aufnahmen auf dem Bahnhof Victoria entstanden, war der Zug nur halb besetzt.

Le retour du *Golden Arrow*

Le *Golden Arrow* ou la *Flèche d'Or* reprend du service en octobre 1947 (ci-contre et ci-dessus). Bien que les chemins de fer aient fait de leur mieux pour revenir à l'âge d'or des luxueux voyages d'avant-guerre, les voyageurs ne montraient désormais plus autant d'enthousiasme – ou avaient moins d'argent pour se l'offrir. Le jour où ces photographies furent prises, le train a quitté la gare de Victoria à moitié vide.

The electrics are coming

By the late 1940s, mainline diesel electric trains were being developed. (Opposite) The first diesel electric locomotive to run on a main line from London St Pancras to Derby and Manchester travelled on its test run on 15 January 1948. Climbing aboard is the locomotive's designer, H.A. Watt. (Above) The new American Diesel Electric on the Santa Fe Railroad, 7 October 1946.

Die Elektrischen kommen

Ende der vierziger Jahre tauchten auch auf den Hauptstrecken dieselelektrische Lokomotiven auf. (Gegenüberliegende Seite) Die erste britische Strecke, die von einer solchen Lok bedient wurde, lief von London St. Pancras über Derby nach Manchester. Die Aufnahme stammt von der Probefahrt am 15. Januar 1948; der Konstrukteur H. A. Watt klettert soeben in den Führerstand. (Oben) Die neue amerikanische Dieselelektrolok auf der Santa Fe Railroad, aufgenommen am 7. Oktober 1946.

Les locomotives électriques arrivent

La mise en service des trains diesel s'accéléra à partir de la fin des années 1940. (Ci-contre) La première locomotive diesel affectée à une grande ligne, de Londres St Pancras à Derby et Manchester, fit son voyage inaugural le 15 janvier 1948. Le concepteur de cette locomotive, H. A. Watt, monte à bord de la motrice. (Ci-dessus) La nouvelle motrice diesel électrique sur la Santa Fe Railroad, le 7 octobre 1946.

All-weather railways

In Britain, the railways were justifiably proud of their perseverance in all weathers. (Above) An LMS train steams out of Nottingham Station on 20 March 1947. Not for the first time, the River Trent had burst its banks. (Below) This frozen train took twenty hours to reach London from Wolverhampton in the winter of 1947. (Opposite) Shunting in a British Railways (Southern Region) yard on a winter's night, February 1948.

Alle Wetter: die Bahn

Die britischen Eisenbahnen waren zu Recht stolz darauf, dass sie bei jedem Wetter fuhren. (Oben) Ein Zug der LMS dampft am 20. März 1947 aus dem Bahnhof von Nottingham. Es war nicht das erste Mal, dass der Trent über die Ufer getreten war. (Unten) Dieser vereiste Zug brauchte im Winter 1947 20 Stunden, um sich von Wolverhampton nach London durchzukämpfen. (Gegenüberliegende Seite) Eine Rangierlok der British Railways (Southern Region), aufgenommen an einem Februarabend 1948.

Des trains tous temps

En Grande-Bretagne, les chemins de fer étaient à juste titre fiers de pouvoir circuler par tous les temps. (En haut) Un train du LMS quitte la gare de Nottingham, le 20 mars 1947, lors d'une nouvelle inondation de la Trent. (En bas) Ce train couvert de gel a mis 20 heures pour relier Wolverhampton à Londres, au cours de l'hiver 1947. (Ci-contre) Manœuvres d'aiguillage dans un dépôt des British Railways (Région sud) par une nuit de février 1948.

LONDON (EUSTON) - BIRMINGHAM - WOLVERHAMPTON

Well met by moonlight
Shunting by night at a British Railways (Southern Region) freight yard in February 1948, just after nationalisation. To enable a quicker turnaround and greater safety, a 150-foot steel tower was hung with powerful lamps at Hither Green, south London. The new lamps were nicknamed 'double moonlight'.

Begegnung im Mondschein
Nächtlicher Rangierbetrieb auf einem Güterbahnhof der British Railways (Southern Region) im Februar 1948, kurz nach der Verstaatlichung. In Hither Green, Südlondon, stattete man einen 45 Meter hohen Stahlturm mit kräftigen Lampen aus, die für schnelleren Betrieb und mehr Sicherheit sorgten. Die Beleuchtung war bald als »zweites Mondlicht« bekannt.

Activités au clair de lune
Manœuvres d'aiguillage nocturnes dans un dépôt de marchandises des British Railways (Région sud) en février 1948, juste après la nationalisation des chemins de fer. Une tour en acier de 45 m de hauteur supportant des lampes puissantes, surnommées « double moonlight », fut construite à Hither Green, dans le sud de Londres, pour faciliter les manœuvres et améliorer la sécurité des cheminots.

Indian Independence

With independence in India in August 1947 came the inevitable and large-scale movement of millions of people between India and Pakistan. (Left) A special train leaves Delhi Station, one of thirty to take the staff of the Pakistani government to Karachi. (Above) Travellers say goodbye to friends before departure. Note the tall taps for supplying water to carriages on the opposite platform.

Indien wird unabhängig

Als Indien im August 1947 unabhängig wurde, zogen Millionen von Menschen von Indien nach Pakistan oder von dort nach Indien. (Links) Ein Sonderzug verlässt den Bahnhof von Delhi, einer von 30, mit denen pakistanische Regierungsangestellte nach Karatschi zogen. (Oben) Reisende verabschieden sich von ihren Freunden. Auf dem Bahnsteig gegenüber fallen die Hähne auf, aus denen die Wagen mit Wasser versorgt wurden.

L'indépendance de l'Inde

La déclaration d'indépendance de l'Inde, en août 1947, provoque le déplacement inévitable et gigantesque de millions d'habitants entre l'Inde et le Pakistan. (À gauche) Un train spécial, l'un des 30 convois qui emmèneront le personnel du gouvernement pakistanais à Karachi, quitte la gare de Delhi. (Ci-dessus) Les voyageurs disent au revoir à leurs amis avant le départ. Remarquez les robinets en hauteur permettant l'alimentation en eau des voitures de l'autre quai.

Fifties innovations

In the Fifties, diesels stole the show. (Above) A powerful German 'Krauss Maffei'-built diesel hydraulic locomotive pulling a heavy goods train in the Rockies, where the gradient rises from sea level to 3,100 metre. (Left) The *Canadian* running on the Canadian Pacific. In 1955 a new 'gyralite' headlight was introduced which bounced light of low-lying clouds along the train's path.

Neuerungen der Fünfziger

In den fünfziger Jahren waren Diesellokomotiven die Stars der Schiene. (Oben) Eine mächtige dieselhydraulische Lok, gebaut bei Krauss-Maffei in Deutschland, zieht einen schweren Güterzug durch die Rockies, wo die Strecke von Meereshöhe auf 3100 Meter ansteigt. (Links) Die *Canadian* der Canadian Pacific. 1955 wurde der gyralite-Scheinwerfer eingeführt; er strahlte tief hängende Wolken an, die das Licht dann auf die Strecke reflektierten.

Innovations des années 1950

Les diesels tiennent la vedette dans les années 1950. (Ci-dessus) Une puissante locomotive diesel à transmission hydraulique, construite par la firme allemande Krauss-Maffei, remorque un lourd convoi de marchandises dans les Rocheuses, où la pente s'élève à l'altitude de 3100 m du niveau de la mer. (À gauche) En 1955, un nouveau phare « gyralite » fut installé sur la motrice du rapide *Canadian*, du Canadian Pacific.

More new locomotives

(Above) A diesel Deltic engine locomotive hauling an express train from Lime Street Station, Liverpool, to London in 1958. The diesel Deltic engine was first built by English Electric in 1955. The cylinders are arranged in a triangular unit which resembles the Greek Δ. (Right) The first British-built gas turbine locomotive. These were originally developed in America as an alternative to the diesel engine.

Innovative Triebwerke

(Oben) Der Expresszug nach London, gezogen von einer Diesel-Deltic-Lokomotive, Lime Street Station, Liverpool, 1958. Der seit 1955 bei English Electric gebaute Deltic-Motor trug seinen Namen nach der Anordnung der Zylinder in Form des griechischen Δ. (Rechts) Die erste britische Gasturbinen-Lokomotive. Das Konzept stammte aus den Vereinigten Staaten, wo die Turbine als Alternative zum Dieselmotor entwickelt wurde.

D'autres nouvelles locomotives

(Ci-dessus) Une locomotive à moteur diesel Deltic tracte un train express de la gare de Lime Street, à Liverpool, vers Londres, en 1958. Le moteur diesel de la Deltic fut construit en 1955 par la English Electric et doit son nom – de Δ grec – à la disposition en triangle de ses cylindres. (À droite) La première locomotive à turbine à gaz construite en Grande-Bretagne fut développée à l'origine aux États-Unis pour servir d'alternative à la locomotive diesel.

Spanish electric locomotives

(Opposite) An inspection by Spanish government representatives and engineers at the Vulcan locomotive works, Newton le Willows, in England, as the most powerful electrical locomotive ever built leaves the sheds on 29 April 1952. It was destined for RENFE in northern Spain for extensive main line electrification projects around Madrid and Barcelona. (Above) A Spanish diesel locomotive in the late 1950s.

Strom für Spanien

(Gegenüberliegende Seite) Spanische Regierungsvertreter und Ingenieure bei den Vulcan-Lokomotivenwerken im englischen Newton le Willows, wo die stärkste je gebaute Elektrolok am 29. April 1952 die Werkshallen verlässt. Sie war für die nordspanische RENFE bestimmt, die ihre Hauptstrecken rund um Madrid und Barcelona im großen Stil elektrifizierte. (Oben) Eine spanische Diesellokomotive der späten fünfziger Jahre.

Locomotives électriques espagnoles

(Ci-contre) Une visite de représentants du gouvernement espagnol et d'ingénieurs aux ateliers de locomotives Vulcan, à Newton le Willows, dont sort le 29 avril 1952 la locomotive électrique la plus puissante jamais construite. Elle était destinée à la RENFE pour la desserte du nord de l'Espagne, où était entrepris un projet d'électrification des grandes lignes autour de Madrid et Barcelone. (Ci-dessus) Une locomotive diesel espagnole de la fin des années 1950.

Summer holidays (previous pages)
Victoria Station, 26 July 1958 and a
crowded concourse. Victoria was the
departure point for many holiday
trains to the south coast. Scenes like
this would become less familiar as
the motor car became a more popular
and accessible means of travelling to
millions.

Sommerferien (vorherige Doppelseite)
Eine belebte Bahnhofshalle, Victoria
Station, 26. Juli 1958. Von Victoria gingen
viele Züge zu den Ferienorten an der
Südküste ab. Bald sollten solche Bilder
der Vergangenheit angehören, denn das
Automobil löste die Bahn zusehends als
Transportmittel für die Massen ab.

Vacances d'été (pages précédentes)
Ce 26 juillet 1958, la foule se presse dans
le hall de la gare Victoria, à Londres,
point de départ de nombreux trains en
direction de la côte sud de l'Angleterre.
Des scènes comme celle-ci devinrent
progressivement moins fréquentes à
mesure que la voiture devenait un
moyen de transport plus populaire et
plus accessible à des millions de gens.

Dinner in the diner
(Above) The exterior view of the
prototype cafeteria car, Victoria Station,
1951. (Below) An observation buffet
lounge in the Pennsylvania Railway's
'Trail Blazer' dining coach, 1955.

Speisen mit Stil
(Oben) Der Prototyp eines Cafeteria-
Wagens, Victoria Station 1951. (Unten)
Gepflegte Gastlichkeit im Aussichts-
wagen des »Trail Blazer«, Pennsylvania
Railway, 1955.

Dîner au restaurant
(Ci-dessus) L'extérieur du wagon-
cafétéria prototype en gare de Victoria,
en 1951. (Ci-dessous) Un salon-buffet
panoramique de la voiture-restaurant
du « Trail Blazer », un train du
Pennsylvania Railway, en 1955.

First fast food

The early 1950s saw the introduction of self-service catering in both Britain and America. (Above left) In May 1952 new 'help yourself meals' were being advertised at economical prices in prototype cafeteria cars at Victoria Station. (Above right) Experimental food vending machines – a bank of five coin-operated machines on a train running between New York and Washington, DC, on the Pennsylvania Railroad, September 1951.

Fastfood an Bord

Anfang der fünfziger Jahre kamen in Großbritannien und Amerika die Self-Service-Cafeterien auf. (Oben links) Im Mai 1952 werden Prototypen der preiswerteren Selbstbedienungs-wagen auf dem Bahnhof Victoria vorgestellt. (Oben rechts) Experimente mit Automatenrestaurants – fünf Münzautomaten in einem Zug der Pennsylvania Railroad zwischen New York und Washington, D.C., September 1951.

Premier fast-food

Le début des années 1950 voit l'avènement de la restauration en self-service en Grande-Bretagne et aux États-Unis. (Ci-dessus à gauche) En mai 1952, de nouveaux « plats en libre service » furent proposés en gare de Victoria à bord de voitures-cafétéria prototypes. (Ci-dessus à droite) En septembre 1951, 5 distributeurs automatiques de nourriture sont placés dans le train du Pennsylvania Railroad assurant la liaison entre New York et Washington.

Railway disasters

(Above) The aftermath of a crash at Louvain, Belgium, on 2 December 1954. One of the trains was carrying German football fans returning from England. (Opposite) Casualties being removed from a triple train crash at Harrow, Middlesex, on 8 October 1952. The *Night Scot* from Perth hit a local train which piled across onto the adjoining line, causing the north-bound Euston to Liverpool express to collide with both.

Der Tod fährt mit

(Oben) Bergungsarbeiten nach einem Unglück im belgischen Löwen, 2. Dezember 1954. Einer der beiden Züge war mit deutschen Fußballfans auf der Rückkehr aus England besetzt. (Gegenüberliegende Seite) Die Opfer des Zugunglücks von Harrow, Middlesex, werden geborgen. Dort war am 8. Oktober 1952 der aus Perth kommende *Night Scot* auf einen Vorortzug aufgefahren, den er aufs Gegengleis schob, und der Euston-Liverpool-Express raste in beide.

Catastrophes ferroviaires

(Ci-dessus) Le 2 décembre 1954, un train transportant des spectateurs allemands d'un match de football revenant d'Angleterre déraille à Louvain (Belgique). (Ci-contre) On évacue les blessés d'un triple accident de train survenu à Harrow (Middlesex), le 8 octobre 1952. L'express de Euston à Liverpool entre en collision avec un train de desserte locale et le *Night Scot*, venant de Perth, qui vient de le faire dérailler.

Pure nostalgia

Such evocative photographs illustrate how railway enthusiasts like to remember the age of British Railways travel. (Opposite) Lime Street Station, Liverpool, where, in 1954, *Picture Post* photographer Bert Hardy spent a few days recording events at the station. (Right) Two American soldiers photographed at Liverpool Street Station, London. The photographer, Ron Case, took it on 9 April 1951; he called it 'In the Sunlight'. It mirrors the earlier, famous photograph shot in Penn Station, New York, by Hal Morey.

Schiere Nostalgie

In solchen stimmungsvollen Bildern behalten Eisenbahnfreunde das Reisen mit British Railways gern im Gedächtnis. (Gegenüberliegende Seite) Lime Street Station, Liverpool. Bert Hardy, der Fotograf der *Picture Post,* verbrachte 1954 einige Tage dort und hielt das Leben auf dem Bahnhof fest. (Rechts) Zwei amerikanische Soldaten, aufgenommen in der Liverpool Street Station, London. Der Fotograf Ron Case nannte dieses Bild vom 9. April 1951 »Im Sonnenlicht«; es erinnert an Hal Moreys frühere berühmte Aufnahme aus der New Yorker Penn Station.

Pure nostalgie

De telles photographies illustrent le romantisme qui anime les ferrovipathes lorsqu'ils évoquent les voyages avec les British Railways. (Ci-contre) La gare de Lime Street, à Liverpool, où le photographe Bert Hardy passa quelques jours en 1954 à photographier ce qui s'y passait pour le *Picture Post.* (À droite) Deux soldats américains dans la gare de Liverpool Street, à Londres. Le photographe, Ron Case, prit ce cliché le 9 avril 1951 et le baptisa « Sous les projecteurs ». Il rappelle une vieille et célèbre photographie prise par Hal Morey à la gare de Pennsylvania, à New York.

The British abroad

The British always saw themselves as the consummate travellers abroad but this was under threat in 1954. (Opposite) This photograph of the night ferry at Victoria Station was published to reflect the country's apprehension over travel restrictions. The caption read 'The spirit of discovery is stifled'. (Right) The Queen's messenger, Walter Kirkwood, boards the *Orient Express* to Belgrade and Istanbul, c. 1950. This was one of the few overland routes (as opposed to aerial) left to travellers by the early Fifties.

Engländer auf Reisen

Die Briten waren von jeher begeisterte Reisende, doch 1954 waren solche Reisen nicht mehr so leicht wie früher. (Gegenüberliegende Seite) Diese Aufnahme vom Bahnhof Victoria, wo der Zug zur Nachtfähre auf den Kontinent bereitsteht, soll den Unmut zum Ausdruck bringen, mit dem Reisebeschränkungen aufgenommen wurden. Die Bildunterschrift lautete: »Der Entdeckergeist wird erstickt.« (Rechts) Der Botschafter der Queen, Walter Kirkwood, besteigt den *Orient-Express* nach Belgrad und Istanbul, um 1950. Dieser Zug war eine der wenigen Landrouten (im Gegensatz zum Flugverkehr), die den Reisenden Anfang der fünfziger Jahre noch offen standen.

Les Britanniques à l'étranger

Les Britanniques se sont toujours considérés comme de grands voyageurs mais, en 1954, leurs certitudes sont menacées. (Ci-contre) Cette photographie du train de nuit en gare de Victoria fut publiée pour illustrer les préventions du pays à l'égard des restrictions de circulation, accompagnée de cette légende : « L'esprit d'aventure est étouffé ». (À droite) Le messager de la Reine, Walter Kirkwood, monte à bord de l'*Orient Express* pour se rendre à Belgrade et Istanbul, vers 1950. C'était l'une des rares lignes terrestres (par opposition aux lignes aériennes) dont pouvaient disposer les voyageurs britanniques au début des années 1950.

Farewell to a king

On 15 February 1952 the funeral train of the late King George VI left Paddington for Windsor. By now the railway that carried the monarch to his final resting place was called British Railways (Western Region). Pipers play a sad farewell.

Abschied von einem König

Am 15. Februar 1952 fuhr der Trauerzug für König Georg VI. von Paddington nach Windsor. Zu diesem Zeitpunkt hörte die Bahn, die den Monarchen zur letzten Ruhe brachte, schon auf den Namen British Railways (Western Region). Dudelsackpfeifer spielten einen melancholischen Gruß.

L'adieu au roi

Le 15 février 1952, le train funéraire – transportant la dépouille du roi George VI – quitte la gare de Paddington pour Windsor au son déchirant des cornemuses. Le convoi était organisé par les British Railways (Région ouest), récemment créés.

Farewell to a tyrant

Josef Stalin died on 3 March 1953. Four million spectators gathered in Red Square, Moscow, for his funeral. Here railway work at Jarosavsko, near Moscow, has ground to a halt as workers pay their respects to 'Uncle Joe'. The locomotives in the background are class SU 2–6–2's (the 'U' stands for *usilenny*, meaning 'strengthened') built at Kolomna works in 1926.

Abschied von einem Tyrannen

Josef Stalin starb am 3. März 1953. Vier Millionen Menschen versammelten sich auf dem Roten Platz in Moskau zu seinem Begräbnis. Hier ruhen die Arbeiten auf dem Betriebshof Jarosavsko bei Moskau, als die Belegschaft dem »Stählernen« ihren Tribut zollt. Die Lokomotiven im Hintergrund sind SU 1 C 1, 1926 in den Kolomna-Werken gebaut (das U steht für usilenny, »verstärkt«).

L'adieu au tyran

Joseph Staline mourut le 3 mars 1953. Quatre millions de fidèles se réunirent à Moscou sur la place Rouge lors de ses funérailles. Les ouvriers des chemins de fer rendent hommage au « Petit Père des Peuples » lors d'une halte du convoi dans les ateliers ferroviaires de Jarosavsko, près de la capitale soviétique. Les locomotives à l'arrière-plan sont des 131 classe SU (le u signifiant usilenny, c'est-à-dire « renforcé »), construites dans les ateliers de Kolomna en 1926.

Kitchen and crew quarters
Cabin crew assembled outside a Pennsylvania Railroad twin unit dining car, c. 1950. The *Limited*, a kind of Pullman, ran from New York to Chicago through Pittsburgh as a rival route to that taken by the *Twentieth Century Limited* of the New York Central. The twin unit of the dormitory car (above, in 1950) for the staff was first built in 1958.

Küche und Kajüte
Die Belegschaft ist vor einem zweiteiligen Speisewagen der Pennsylvania Railroad angetreten. Der Pullmanzug *Limited* fuhr als Konkurrenz zum *Twentieth Century Limited* der New York Central von New York über Pittsburgh nach Chicago. Zweiteilige Schlafwagen mit Unterkünften für das Personal (oben, aufgenommen 1950) waren seit 1958 im Dienst.

Cuisines et quartiers du personnel
Le personnel de cabine pose à l'extérieur d'un wagon-restaurant jumelé du Pennsylvania Railroad, vers 1950. Le *Limited*, une sorte de rapide Pullman, assurait la liaison New York–Chicago via Pittsburgh en concurrence avec le *Twentieth Century Limited* du New York Central. La voiture-couchettes jumelée (ci-dessus en 1950) destinée au personnel fut construite en 1958.

Index

gettyimages

This book was created by Getty Images, 21-31 Woodfield Road, London W9 2BA

Over 70 million images and 30,000 hours of film footage are held by the various collections owned by Getty Images.
These cover a vast number of subjects from the earliest photojournalism to current press photography, sports, social history
and geography. Getty Images' conceptual imagery is renowned amongst creative end users.
www.gettyimages.com

Über 70 Millionen Bilder und 30 000 Stunden Film befinden sich in den verschiedenen Archiven von Getty Images.
Sie decken ein breites Spektrum an Themen ab – von den ersten Tagen des Fotojournalismus bis hin zu aktueller
Pressefotografie, Sport, Sozialgeschichte und Geographie. Bei kreativen Anwendern ist das Material von Getty Images
für seine ausdrucksstarke Bildsprache bekannt.
www.gettyimages.com

Plus de 70 millions d'images et 30 000 heures de films sont détenus par les différentes collections dont Getty Images
est le propriétaire. Cela couvre un nombre considérable de sujets – des débuts du photojournalisme aux photographies actuelles de
presse, de sport, d'histoire sociale et de géographie. Le concept photographique de Getty Images est reconnu des créatifs.
www.gettyimages.com

Pictures in this book have been taken exclusively from Getty Images.
Additional acknowledgements: page 148-9 National Railway Museum/Science &
Society Picture Library, page 200 SVT Bild/DAS FOTOARCHIV